DESIGN AND ANALYSIS OF DISTRIBUTED EMBEDDED SYSTEMS

IFIP - The International Federation for Information Processing

IFIP was founded in 1960 under the auspices of UNESCO, following the First World Computer Congress held in Paris the previous year. An umbrella organization for societies working in information processing, IFIP's aim is two-fold: to support information processing within its member countries and to encourage technology transfer to developing nations. As its mission statement clearly states,

IFIP's mission is to be the leading, truly international, apolitical organization which encourages and assists in the development, exploitation and application of information technology for the benefit of all people.

IFIP is a non-profitmaking organization, run almost solely by 2500 volunteers. It operates through a number of technical committees, which organize events and publications. IFIP's events range from an international congress to local seminars, but the most important are:

- The IFIP World Computer Congress, held every second year;
- open conferences;
- working conferences.

The flagship event is the IFIP World Computer Congress, at which both invited and contributed papers are presented. Contributed papers are rigorously refereed and the rejection rate is high.

As with the Congress, participation in the open conferences is open to all and papers may be invited or submitted. Again, submitted papers are stringently refereed.

The working conferences are structured differently. They are usually run by a working group and attendance is small and by invitation only. Their purpose is to create an atmosphere conducive to innovation and development. Refereeing is less rigorous and papers are subjected to extensive group discussion.

Publications arising from IFIP events vary. The papers presented at the IFIP World Computer Congress and at open conferences are published as conference proceedings, while the results of the working conferences are often published as collections of selected and edited papers.

Any national society whose primary activity is in information may apply to become a full member of IFIP, although full membership is restricted to one society per country. Full members are entitled to vote at the annual General Assembly, National societies preferring a less committed involvement may apply for associate or corresponding membership. Associate members enjoy the same benefits as full members, but without voting rights. Corresponding members are not represented in IFIP bodies. Affiliated membership is open to non-national societies, and individual and honorary membership schemes are also offered.

DESIGN AND ANALYSIS OF DISTRIBUTED EMBEDDED SYSTEMS

IFIP 17th World Computer Congress —
TC10 Stream on Distributed and Parallel Embedded Systems
(DIPES 2002)
August 25-29, 2002, Montréal, Québec, Canada

Edited by

Bernd Kleinjohann
University of Paderborn / C-LAB
Germany

K.H. (Kane) Kim
University of California, Irvine (UCI)
USA

Lisa Kleinjohann
University of Paderborn / C-LAB
Germany

Achim Rettberg
University of Paderborn / C-LAB
Germany

KLUWER ACADEMIC PUBLISHERS
BOSTON / DORDRECHT / LONDON

Distributors for North, Central and South America:
Kluwer Academic Publishers
101 Philip Drive
Assinippi Park
Norwell, Massachusetts 02061 USA
Telephone (781) 871-6600
Fax (781) 681-9045
E-Mail <kluwer@wkap.com>

Distributors for all other countries:
Kluwer Academic Publishers Group
Post Office Box 322
3300 AH Dordrecht, THE NETHERLANDS
Telephone 31 786 576 000
Fax 31 786 576 474
E-Mail <services@wkap.nl>

 Electronic Services <http://www.wkap.nl>

Library of Congress Cataloging-in-Publication Data

A C.I.P. Catalogue record for this book is available from the Library of Congress.

Design and Analysis of Distributed Embedded Systems
Edited by Bernd Kleinjohann, K.H. (Kane) Kim, Lisa Kleinjohann, Achim Rettberg
ISBN 1-4020-7156-6

Contents

Session 9: Design Methods and Frameworks

Preface

New intelligent features in technical systems are often based on embedded software. One reason for this is that software features can be realized without a major increase of production costs for the target system. Nevertheless, customers tend to pay higher prices for such intelligent systems. Examples can be found in different application domains such as automotive and household appliances as well as in industrial products. In most cases these intelligent features have the same security and real-time requirements as those imposed on the entire embedded systems.

Once a customer gets used to these intelligent features she or he expects their availability also in future product lines. Hence, they have to be easily adaptable to different platforms. Consequently, the development cycle for embedded systems has to cover design, maintenance, and reuse and adaptation of functionality for new product generations. Toward fulfilling these requirements two complementary developments can be observed. New specification paradigms and languages such as UML support higher levels of abstraction as entry points into a better automated design cycle. This eases the adoption of new features into the next generation of a product line. Furthermore, middleware architectures for various application domains are realized to ease the reuse of standard services needed in these domains.

However, the verification of system correctness during the entire design cycle, the consideration of real-time support and other resource restrictions, and dependability techniques must still be integrated into the emerging development approaches. Since these non-functional requirements play a key role in designing distributed embedded systems, they are the focus of this book.

This book documents recent approaches and results presented at the TC 10 Stream on Distributed and Parallel Embedded Systems (DIPES 2002), which was held as part of the International Federation for Information Processing (IFIP) World Computer Congress. This TC 10 Stream was organized by the IFIP WG 10.5 Special Interest Group on Embedded Systems (SIG-ES) in co-operation with WG 10.3 and WG 10.4 and took place during August 25-29, 2002 in Montreal, Canada.

This book is organized following the structure of the conference. Chapters 1 and 2 deal with specification methods and their analysis while Chapter 6 concentrates on timing and performance analysis. Chapter 3 describes approaches to system verification at different levels of abstraction.

Chapter 4 deals with fault tolerance and detection. Middleware and software reuse aspects are treated in Chapter 5. Chapters 7 and 8 concentrate on the distribution related topics such as partitioning, scheduling, and communication. The book closes with a chapter on design methods and frameworks.

In addition to the papers presented in this book the following two invited talks were given during DIPES 2002.

- Bran Selic, Rational Inc., Canada, gave a talk entitled "The Engineering of Software Systems: Beyond Mere Logic".
- Nikil Dutt, University of California, Irvine, CA, USA presented "New Compiler Trends in Embedded Systems".

Bernd Kleinjohann, K.H. (Kane) Kim,
Lisa Kleinjohann and Achim Rettberg

IFIP World Computer Congress 2002 - TC 10 Stream on Distributed and Parallel Embedded Systems (DIPES 2002)

General Chair
Bernd Kleinjohann

Co-Chair
K. H. (Kane) Kim

Sponsoring Institution
IFIP TC 10

Program Committee
Bernd Kleinjohann (Chair, Germany)
K. H. (Kane) Kim (Co-Chair, USA)
Arndt Bode (Germany)
Nikil Dutt (USA)
Guang R. Gao (USA)
Ahmed A. Jerraya (France)
Lisa Kleinjohann (Germany)
Jean-Claude Laprie (France)
Erik Maehle (Germany)
Carlos E. Pereira (Brazil))
Franz J. Rammig (Germany)
Achim Rettberg (Germany)
Bernd-Heinrich Schmidtfranz (Germany)
Ralf Stolpe (Germany)
Dieter Wuttke (Germany)

Invited Speakers
Nikil Dutt (USA)
Bran Selic (Canada)

Acknowledgements
We thank the organizing committee of the IFIP World Computer Congress for their support and especially for the local arrangements in Montreal.

Can UML be a System-Level Language for Embedded Software? *

João M. Fernandes, Ricardo J. Machado
Dep. Informática & Dep. Sistemas de Informação
Universidade do Minho, Braga, Portugal

Abstract: The main purpose of this paper is to discuss if the Unified Modeling Language (UML) can be used as a system-level language (SLL) for specifying embedded systems, in co-design environments. The requirements that a language has to fulfil to be considered as an SLL are presented and the advantages and disadvantages of using UML as an SLL are also indicated. The contribution of this paper consists on the explicit discussion of the key issues that must be taken into account when deciding if UML is to be used in a project as an SLL for embedded software.

1. INTRODUCTION

The discussion on the "best" system-level language is a key topic on the area of embedded software development. Among the alternatives, the following are generally identified: C++, Java, domain-specific languages and pure semantics. This last choice is not a language, in the proper sense, but is typically introduced taking into consideration that the language (i.e. its syntax) is not an issue, and what really matters is its semantics.

Although the designers have several alternatives to choose from, a vast majority of people still use C/C++ as the languages for solving their co-design problems and find them good SLLs. C/C++ are indeed suitable solutions for implementing embedded systems, but those languages are not adequate for system-level modelling. Although C++ is an object-oriented extension of C, both present the same basic characteristics. This implies that

* Research funded by FCT and FEDER under project *METHODES* (POSI/37334/CHS/2001).

C/C++ are languages near the hardware, which is a good characteristic for achieving strong predictability on execution time (a fundamental issue for real-time systems), but also that they lack some of the characteristics that an SLL should present, which, are hierarchy, concurrency, programming constructs, abstract communication, synchronization mechanisms, exception handling, structural representation and state-based constructs [13].

The analysis presented in this paper is especially oriented for heterogeneous environments, where the hardware and the software components are equally treated, during the analysis phase, namely in what concerns the modelling and specification of behavioural and non-functional requirements. This does not mean, however, that the ideas presented here are limited to that specific field. Several concepts and arguments presented here can also be applied to systems that can be classified as being complex and with strong non-functional constraints. Typical hardware-based solutions, where systems-on-a-chip are the most constringent instances, are not being considered. Instead, software-based systems with strong constrictions, such as real-time, fault-tolerance and explicit concurrency, are the main kind of systems to consider. The paper does not address how to technically use UML for the specification of embedded systems, since that topic is well covered in the literature. For example, in [12] a UML profile called "Embedded UML" is presented and several other groups have made proposals for developing embedded systems with UML [3, 7, 16]. The opinions expressed in this paper about the system-level capabilities of UML are based on the experience gained with its application in real industrial projects [5, 6].

2.   EMBEDDED SYSTEMS DESIGN

Until recently, researchers have largely ignored embedded systems development since, as a scientific problem, it was small and not interesting. This reality has changed for many different factors, and now computer scientists are beginning to pay more attention to the embedded arena [9].

Typically, embedded systems have specialized functionality, incorporate microprocessors and have a limited capacity of memory. To meet size and performance requirements, designers usually use a real-time operating system (RTOS) and proprietary development tools, well-tuned for meeting the devices' memory limitations.

In the past, embedded systems were developed in assembly languages. Later, due to more complex functionality, some companies turned to higher-level languages (HLLs) like C and C++. HLLs make it easier to develop the systems, but they still present problems, due to their inherent complexity, which implies long schedules and high non-recurring engineering costs.

To exacerbate these problems, there were a greater number of target operating systems and processors, sometimes even within the same product families. Manufacturers faced enormous competitive pressures, and were asked to develop their products in a shorter time.

Nowadays, embedded systems are networked and distributed and, more importantly, consumers demand more complex functionality, which greatly increases software complexity. As a consequence, these systems can no longer be designed as was done traditionally, and new approaches and new languages are required. This implies that describing and modelling a modern embedded system requires an SLL.

UML is one possible solution to this problem, since it promotes a more open, standard-based pre-implementation development environment, which would lower costs and speed development.

3.   SYSTEM-LEVEL IN EMBEDDED DESIGN

The system-level is generally described as the abstraction level where the differences between hardware and software are minimal. At this level, the entire system is looked at as a set of cooperating subsystems [15]. This represents a big advantage for real-time embedded systems development, because it allows the system to be specified with a unified (homogeneous) representation, and makes co-design an effective approach for developing heterogeneous implementations.

Since it is quite obvious that traditional languages, especially procedural HLLs and HDLs (Hardware Description Languages), are not able to cope with the ever increasing complexity of embedded systems, a race for defining "the" SLL for co-design of embedded systems is emerging. Among the several alternatives for winning that race, the following ones seem strong and firm candidates: ANSI C/C++, SystemC, Java, Superlog, and Rosetta.

It is not uncommon to mix concepts of using a language for specification (what to design) and using it for implementation (how to design). When referring to SLLs, it should be highlighted that its main usage, within the design flow, is based on a specification-oriented approach, however, it must also allow the introduction of design decisions, by syntactic inscription of refinement tags, to semantically support the (semi-)automatic implementation of the system.

Although there are a variety of different opinions, visions and (commercial and scientific) motivations, with respect to SLLs, as the previous enumeration suggests, it is possible to describe a generic set of requirements that the co-design community accepts more or less consensually for an SLL [1]:

- **Modelling:** An SLL must allow the software and the hardware components of a system to be collectively developed (i.e. co-specified and functionally co-refined), in such a way that the system as a whole can be easily perceived by the project members. Ideally, an SLL should be able to treat all the design space, supporting the semantical specification of the non-functional requirements, which may be provided by different technological areas.
- **Implementation:** An SLL must give an effective support to the system's implementation, based on automatic (or at least, semi-automatic) refinements, to feed synthesizable HDLs and HLLs, in order to justify a co-design approach at the system-level. As a consequence, the complexity can be coped, but, more importantly, the development time is reduced and a guarantee can be given with respect to the implementation of the user's requirements (models' continuity).
- **Simulation:** An SLL must be able to support (and be supported by) powerful simulation environments, where the designed system may be analysed and experimented in relation not only to its functional behaviour but also to its expected performance. The executability of an SLL is a vital characteristic to facilitate the requirements' capture and validation.

In addition to the 3 previous points, there are many others that may be considered. Thus, an SLL should: (i) allow the explicit (or implicit) description of concurrency; (ii) possess a well-defined semantic; (iii) be sufficiently appealing and advantageous to be naturally adopted by designers; (iv) be supported by user-friendly tools; and (v) ensure a reduced learning curve. Nevertheless, they still need a mature decision, since some are pure intentions and others are not at all possible to be satisfied at the moment.

It is not expected that the migration to the system-level with relation to language issues will be fulfilled by SLLs. It is admissible, at least during a transitory phase, to use other languages that may be helpful to describe functionalities not within the scope of the SLLs available at a precise moment. Apart from defining efficient SLLs, it is important to conceive development methodologies to support the design at the system-level. This implies the selection of the various languages to be used, the definition of the development phases, and the relation amongst languages and phases.

Thus, the main question is how to obtain a system-level co-design environment to support the modelling of embedded systems and to assist their semi-automatic implementation. This must be made in such a way that:
-    the models may be iteratively reified until the final implementation is obtained, without the need to manually perform macro-refinements, with the transparent reuse of pre-designed hardware target architectures and software modules;

– the activities of the different project members that are involved in complex projects are properly integrated.

4.   UML FOR SYSTEM-LEVEL

UML is a general-purpose modelling language for specifying and visualizing the artefacts of computer-based systems, as well as for business modelling and other non-software systems [2]. UML is a standard language for defining and designing software systems, and is being progressively accepted as a language in industrial environments. UML is meant to be used universally for the modelling of systems, including automatic control applications with both hardware and software components, so it seems an adequate choice for embedded systems.

Although UML does not guarantee project success, it may improve many related topics. For example, it substantially decreases the cost of training, when there is the need to make changes in projects or organizations. It also provides the opportunity for new integration among tools, processes and domains. Finally, UML enables designers to focus on delivering business value and provides them the tools and techniques to accomplish this.

4.1   Advantages of using UML

4.1.1   Standard

UML is a multiple-view and graphical notation that presents a variety of diagrams for different modelling purposes. Although the novice UML user can get confused with all these possibilities, it is possible and desirable to choose the important diagrams for a specific application field. One of the main advantages of using UML is that it is a standard. UML is an OMG standard and is expected to become an ISO standard very soon [8]. Being a standard implies that in the near future it is likely that every TI professional will understand it, so it will be widely accepted. This also implies that several computer tools will be produced for simplifying the tasks of drawing the diagrams and for automatically obtaining implementation code.

4.1.2   Communication with the customer

UML is inherently a graphical language. Graphical languages are quite important for promoting the communication between the system's designers and customers. If the communication is not established in a proper way, the designers are not sure that they are building the right system, even if they know how to build the systems right.

Usually, customers have some special interest in the application, but they are not supposed to, although they can, be aware of the technical problems associated with the system. Additionally, designers are expected to be competent in technical matters, but usually it is unlikely that they are experts in every field of application. Thus, to be effective communication between designers and customers must use a notation that is useful for both of them.

If specifications are intended to serve as a communication medium among customers and designers, using graphical notations is essential, as long as they are clear and intuitive (to be created, modified, and inspected by both customers and designers), and also precise and rigorous (to be validated, simulated or analysed by computers).

UML is a valid alternative for this purpose, since it is graphical and not too complicated, but, at the same time, precise. Dialoguing with the customers in C is not possible, at least generally speaking, and communicating in a natural language, although extremely easy, is also not a proper solution, since it introduces too many ambiguities.

4.1.3   Object-oriented modelling

UML is perfectly suited for specifying object-oriented (OO) systems, since it includes several diagrams for that modelling paradigm. Although many embedded systems are still implemented with non-OO languages, the great majority is already developed with OO techniques and in the future it is expected that an even greater majority will use OO principles and languages.

A methodology to system development based on the operational approach is essential to guarantee that complex systems can be addressed. The main idea of this approach is based on an executable specification that evolves through transformational refinements to obtain the final implementation. Object-oriented models are expected to fully address the above requirement, since they allow the easy refinement of application-domain objects during the whole process.

4.1.4   Platform independence

Specifying a system in UML can be absolutely platform-independent, since the specification can be reused for different target architectures, different technologies, different environments, and other non-functional requirements. This is possible because, during the analysis and design phases, UML supports views that can be reified without early introducing undesired implementation decisions, allowing the specification to preserve its system-level nature, until the final implementation synthesis steps.

4.1.5   Automatic code generation

Being an OO notation, the structural and behavioural views of UML can be "easily" transformed into code. UML has the potential to be automatically transformed into any language, being it OO or not. There are some tools that give support to this automatic code generation task, which imply that we are near to reach the point where the specification is the implementation.

In contrast to the situation where the designers specify the system in the final implementation language, using UML and automatic code generation tools allows the system to be converted into different languages. This may be a strong advantage, allowing the same specification to give origin to different implementations for different purposes or for different architectures. The existence of code generators is a key issue to allow different hardware-software partitions to be obtained from the same unbiased specification. In the authors' co-design approach [10], the code generation allows the usage of the software parts with different pre-designed hardware target architectures. The main point is to generate implementation code only for the software parts and not for the hardware target architectures being used. Thus, for this possibility to be real, it is absolutely necessary to model both parts at the system-level.

Generating code from UML may result in problems, if some points are forgotten. Generally, UML is missing implementation details, so it is not easy to perform implementation specific optimisations (for size or speed) from a given UML specification. If the generated code is not good for the purpose in hand, the designer has to write code for implementation. To do this, generated code must be easy to read in order to improve it manually.

4.1.6   Extensions

UML can be extended, since it was elaborated with that particular purpose. This means that UML is not restricted to its original aims (specification and visualization), but that it can be used to other purposes, if the extension mechanism is properly used. Extensions in UML are achieved through stereotypes, that augment the semantics of the meta-model.

There are several proposals to extend UML to support the modelling of embedded systems. *Real-Time UML* [3] is one of the most popular, since it treats all the development phases (analysis, design and implementation) in a simple way. It is worth mentioning that Real-Time UML presents code in C++ that was obtained after modelling the systems in UML.

4.2   Disadvantages of using UML

4.2.1   Number of diagrams

UML is a multiple-view syntactic meta-model, which means that it defines many different diagrams, each one covering a particular modelling perspective of the system. By one hand, this is an advantage, since it allows the designers to specify the aspects they find important for a specific purpose, without imposing a particular development process model. By another hand, this may be a disadvantage, since the diagrams are interrelated, although not formally, which means that inconsistencies can be introduced in the system specification.

Another related problem lies on the fact that there are different diagrams for similar purposes. For example, use case, collaboration, sequence, statecharts and activity diagrams are all used for describing behavioural perspectives of a given system. Although these five diagrams handle different behavioural aspects, this may be confusing for some designers.

4.2.2   Not precise semantics

UML is not a formal notation, i.e., it has not a well-defined semantics. UML is a semi-formal language, because it has a formal syntax, but its semantics is not formal. This fact may impose different interpretations on the semantics, which implies that a diagram may not be equally interpreted by two different designers. Some authors have proposed formal (or at least, precise or rigorous) semantics for the UML diagrams, but these proposals have not been yet incorporated in the UML standard meta-model [4].

The OMG's UML 2.0 OCL RfP process is not finished, which implies that the OCL definition has not come yet with a final proposal for a precise object-oriented meta-modelling approach within the UML views [14]. Nevertheless, in their industrial projects, the authors are using UML with OCL 1.0 for dealing with non-functional requirements. Sequence diagrams with time inscriptions have been used for the specification of the canonical latency and duration constraints, which are viewed as composites for more accurate categories of timed requirements (for performance and safety constraints specification).

4.2.3   New layer in the project

Modelling the different system's views in UML and later transforming the multiple-view model into an implementation language imposes a new layer in the development process if compared with a situation where the systems are directly coded in the implementation language. This may be understood as a disadvantage because it implies that the designers must know one more language. A more optimistic perspective is however possible. If automatic code generation tools are available the final implementation language may be transparent to the designer, which means that he/she specifies the systems in UML, simulate their behaviour with the specifications, and pushes a button to obtain the system's implementation.

4.2.4   State Orientation

State models can be specified for the system's components that possess a complex or interesting dynamic behaviour. UML has two different meta-models for this purpose: statecharts and activity diagrams. Although these two meta-models present many important characteristics for reactive systems, namely concurrency and hierarchy, they do not allow an elegant treatment of the data path/plant resources management and the specification of dynamic parallelism. These are two crucial topics for complex, distributed and parallel embedded systems, since different parts of the system may require the simultaneous access to the same resource.

For embedded systems, the application of Petri nets (PNs) to the specification of the behavioural view is a proper alternative. PNs constitute a formal meta-model that can be simulated, formally analysed, and for which several implementation techniques are possible. In this context, for replacing UML's statecharts and activity diagrams, it is suggested the adoption of the shobi-PN, an extended object-oriented PN meta-model, to specify the reactive and dynamic behaviour of the system's software components, with the OCL 1.0 syntax to specify the non-functional requirements [11].

5.   CONCLUSIONS

Based on the identified set of requirements for SLLs, this paper has discussed if UML can be used as an SLL for modelling the different views of embedded software systems. The answer to the question posed in the title is definitively positive. Some arguments were presented in what concerns the usage of UML as a solution to the problems faced by engineers when dealing with complex embedded software, namely in what concerns the user's requirements capture. For the system's requirements, UML lacks some adequate solutions, since the "statecharts+activity diagrams" approach is not satisfactory for describing the detailed behaviour in the presence of asynchronism, hierarchical level violations and dynamic concurrency.

A description of UML's main features for modelling embedded software is presented and its main advantages (standard, communication with the customer, object-oriented nature, platform independence, automatic code generation, extensions mechanism) and disadvantages (number of diagrams, not precise semantics, new project's layer, state orientation) are discussed within this field of software engineering.

6.   REFERENCES

1. C. Ajluni. System-Level Languages Fight to Take Over as the Next Design Solution. *Electronic Design*, 48(2):68-78+110, Jan-2000.
2. G. Booch, J. Rumbaugh, I. Jacobson. *The Unified Modeling Language User Guide*. Addison-Wesley, 1999.
3. B.P. Douglass. *Real-Time UML: Developing Efficient Objects for Embedded Systems*. Addison-Wesley, 1998.
4. A. Evans, J.-M. Bruel, R. France, K. Lano, B. Rumpe. Making UML Precise. *13th Conf. on Object-Oriented Programming, Languages and Applications (OOPSLA'98)*, 1998.
5. J.M. Fernandes, R.J. Machado, H.D. Santos. Modeling Industrial Embedded Systems with UML. *8th Int. Workshop on Hardware/Software Codesign (CODES 2000)*, pp. 18-22, 2000. ACM Press.
6. J.M. Fernandes, R.J. Machado. System-Level Object-Orientation in the Specification and Validation of Embedded Systems. *14th Symp. on Integrated Circuits and System Design (SBCCI'01)*, 2001. IEEE CS Press.
7. R. Jigorea, S. Manolache, P. Eles, Z. Peng. Modeling of Real-Time Embedded Systems in an Object-Oriented Design Environment with UML. *3rd Int. Symp. on Object-Oriented Real-Time, Distributed Computing (ISORC 2000)*, pp. 210-213, 2000.
8. C. Kobryn. UML 2001: A Standardization Odyssey. *Communications of the ACM*, 42(10):29-37, Oct-1999.
9. E.A. Lee. What's Ahead for Embedded Software? *IEEE Computer*, 33(9):18-26, Sep-2000.
10. R.J. Machado, J.M. Fernandes, H.D. Santos. A Methodology for Complex Embedded Systems Design: Petri Nets within a UML Approach. *Architecture and Design of Distributed Embedded Systems*, B. Kleinjohann (ed.), chapter 1, pp. 1-10, 2001. Kluwer.
11. R.J. Machado, J.M. Fernandes. A Petri Net Meta-Model to Develop Software Components for Embedded Systems. *2nd Int. Conf. on Application of Concurrency to System Design (ICACSD'01)*, pp. 113-22, 2001, IEEE CS Press.
12. G. Martin, L. Lavagno, J. Louis-Guerin. Embedded UML: a merger of real-time UML and co-design. *9th Int. Symp. on Hardware/Software Codesign (CODES'01)*, pp. 23-28, 2001. ACM Press.
13. S. Narayan, D.D. Gajski. Features Supporting System-Level Specification in HDLs. *2nd European Design Automation Conference (EuroDAC - EuroVHDL'92)*, Sep-1992.
14. OMG. *Response to the UML 2.0 OCL RfP (ad/2000-09-03)*. OMG Document ad/2001-08-01, v. 1.0, Aug-2001.
15. F.J. Rammig. Approaching System-Level Design. *VHDL for Simulation, Synthesis and Formal Proofs of Hardware*, J. Mermet (Ed.), pp. 259-278, Kluwer, 1992.
16. W. Wolf. *Computers as Components: Principles of Embedded Computing System Design*. Morgan Kaufmann, 2001.

PEARL for Distributed Embedded Systems
"Object Oriented Perspective"

Roman Gumzej   &   Wolfgang A. Halang
University of Maribor   *FernUniversität Hagen*
Faculty of Electrical Engineering   *Faculty of Electrical Engineering*
and Computer Science   *58084 Hagen*
Smetanova 17, SI-2000 Maribor   *Germany*
Slovenia   *wolfgang.halang@fernuni-hagen.de*
roman.gumzej@uni-mb.si

Abstract: This article is meant to highlight Specification PEARL in an object-oriented perspective. Specification PEARL is a specification and description language, which originates from Multiprocessor PEARL (DIN 66253, Part 3), also named PEARL for distributed systems. It extends the standard by allowing the description of asymmetrical distributed architectures as well as by additional parameters for the parameterisation of the RTOS and later feasibility analysis.

PEARL itself in its latest implementation still is a procedural language although it supports features like tasking and synchronisation, being supported only by some object oriented languages. Due to the nature of its applications, transferring PEARL into an object-oriented language was not an easy nor straightforward process; hence, there are several implementations of object-oriented PEARL. For Multiprocessor PEARL there was no attempt in this direction so far. In Specification PEARL HW/SW co-design methodology we are striving to use the Specification PEARL language as a specification language with the current release of PEARL (PEARL90).

The aim of this article is to give Specification PEARL and its components an object oriented perspective - to structure them in a way, which would lead to natural generalisation-specialisation and whole-part relationships and define their interfaces. It will also show why it would be convenient for Specification PEARL to support classes of objects.

Key words: real-time systems, co-design, object-orientation, PEARL.

1.   INTRODUCTION

Since the complexity of most automation and real-time processing applications requires the programming of distributed, fault-tolerant multiprocessor systems, PEARL has been extended with constructs for the programming of multiprocessors. In PEARL for distributed systems [6] the language is enhanced with constructs, which enable the abstract description of hardware and software. These enable the real-time embedded systems to be co-designed in order to increase their dependability and quality. They are not translated into machine code; instead, they are treated as directives for system programs (e.g.: configuration management programs, loaders, etc.).

The features of the specification language are:

– constructs for the description of hardware configurations,
– constructs for the description of software configurations,
– constructs for the specification of communication and its characteristics (peripheral and process connections, physical and logical connections, transmission protocols), as well as
– constructs for specifying both conditions and the method of carrying out dynamic reconfigurations in cases of failure.

The latest revision of PEARL carries the name PEARL90 and is still a procedural language. Some of the research on enhancing the predictability, safety and introducing object orientation into the PEARL language is described in [1, 3, 7]. This process was difficult because it was hard to sustain and improve the timely deterministic properties of PEARL together with the introduction of objects since by their dynamic allocation they are imposing non-determinism into the execution of PEARL programs. On the other hand the introduction of processes is not similar to C++ or Java threads, because PEARL TASKS have a different role in the program structure and additional scheduling parameters, requiring different status and handling of TASKs.

PEARL for distributed systems [6] has not been extended in an object-oriented fashion so far although it has the appropriate structure. It was addressed and in some extent further developed in the research of [1,3] with the intent to improve the safety of PEARL program execution.

In Specification PEARL [2] the standard has been extended in the foreseen manner in order to support the description of asymmetrical architectures as well as the parameterisation of the RTOS and schedulability analyser. It was meant to be used with the latest revision of PEARL. It was extended in its textual version and a corresponding graphical notation has been defined, used to build a CASE tool for the visual creation of specifications.

The description in Specification PEARL syntax consists of divisions, which describe different associated layers of the system design in considerable detail: station division, configuration division, net division and system division. The constructs from these layers may seem very disjoint on the first glance, but have common properties and can be structured in an object-oriented manner. In the following sections the structure of these layers and the properties of their constructs is given together with the idea on how to implement and use them in an object-oriented manner.

The article concludes with the description of the expected benefits from utilising the described HW/SW co-specification classes together with an idea on how to integrate them with current advances in real-time object-oriented languages and applications.

2. STATION DIVISION

Stations, being the processing nodes of the system are introduced here, stating their role in the distributed system and their structure. They are treated as black boxes with connections for their information exchange.

Several types of stations have been defined. Default is the "BASIC" station, which represents a general-purpose processing node. To be able to describe asymmetrical architectures, two additional types of processing nodes have been defined: "TASK" for application processors and "KERNEL" for operating system (kernel) processors. Since in embedded systems design (intelligent) peripheral devices are very important the "PERIPHERAL" station type was defined. A multiprocessor node is introduced by the "PART OF" attribute of the constituent processing nodes.

All stations have common properties of the "BASIC" station. Depending on their role in the distributed system they may have additional properties which leads to a good opportunity to derive a station from a similar station using the generalisation-specialisation concept. Because of multiprocessor nodes and station components there are also whole-part relations here. The class structure of the constructs from the station division is depicted in Figure 1 and their properties are given in the framed boxes below.

Each station in a system is associated with the state information for reconfiguration purposes. The basic components of a station are its processors (PROCTYPES), WORKSTORES and DEVICES.

The station division also carries information about the intelligent peripheral devices, attached to the system, which also have the role of stations, although they represent the inputs/outputs of the modelled system. Their connections to the devices in the system are described by the attributes of the peripheral station's components (e.g.: the direction of data flow, the protocol used and any additional signals which may be necessary for the communication). To support schedulability analysis every signal may be assigned its minimum inter-arrival time.

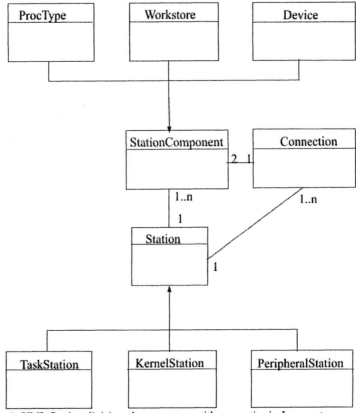

Figure 1: UML Station division class structure with properties in Java syntax

```
public class Station {
    StringBuffer name;
    String type={"BASIC", "KERNEL", "TASK", "PERIPHERAL"};
    boolean partOf;
    StringBuffer superStation;
    StateType states[];
    StateType stateRegister;
    StationComponent components;
    Connection connections;
}
public class PeripheralStation extends Station {
    int minStimuliPeriod;
}
```

```
public class TaskStation extends Station {
    StringBuffer supervisorName;
    Station supervisor;
}
public class KernelStation extends Station {
    int minTimeResolution;
    String schedulingPolicy={"RR","EDF","MLF","RM"};
    int minKernelRAM, minProcessRAM, minTaskRAM;
    int minIsrRAM, minQueueRAM;
    int maxTask, maxSema;
    int maxTaskSwitchTime, maxIntLatency;
    int maxQEvent, maxSchedEvent;
}
```

The station component's properties are limited to basic and timing information. They are uniquely identified by their IDs, which may be their HW device identifiers or logical names. Insignificant implementation details are omitted.

Station processors (PROCTYPEs) have speed descriptors, which tell their clock generator's frequencies. It is in general possible to generate multiprocessor stations and mix processors with different clock rates within the same station.

WORKSTORES are described by sizes and memory maps (they show the purpose of different areas of memory). The access time the different memory areas may also be specified (on-chip, RAM or ROM memories typically have different access times). This information is used by the compiler to determine the maximum execution times of tasks, which are loaded in these memory areas or access them during their execution.

DEVICES are identified by IDs (like stations, but they may be assigned a logical name for easier reference). The device types may vary and have different attributes assigned depending on their nature. Currently, interfaces, timers and shared variables are supported. The use of specific standard devices is supported through the generic device specification.

```
public class StationComponent {
    StringBuffer componentID;
    StationComponent NextComponent;
}
class Proctype extends StationComponent {
    int processorSpeed;
}
class Workstore extends StationComponent {
    int startAddress;
    int memoryAreaSize;
```

```
    boolean dualPort;
    String accessType={"RAM", "ROM", "XOM"};
    int accessTime;
}
class Device extends StationComponent {
    StringBuffer DeviceID;
    int baseAddress;
}
class Interface extends Device {
    StringBuffer driverID;
    int driverStartAddress;
    String dataDirection={"IN", "OUT", "INOUT"};
    String transferType={"DMA", "PACKAGE"};
    int transferSpeed;
    int packageSize;
    int intVector;
    int intLevel;
}
class Timer extends Device {
    int timerActivation;
    int timerPeriod;
    int timerDuration;
}
class SharedVariable extends Device {
    StringBuffer name;
    String signalTriggerCondition={"CHANGE", "EQUAL",
" GREATER", "LESS"};
    int referenceValue;
    int comparisonRegister;
}
public class Connection {
    StringBuffer connectionID;
    int connectionSpeed;
    int bandWidth;
    StationComponent endPoint1, endPoint2;
    Connection nextConnection;
}
```

Standard devices are identified only by their identifiers. Their behaviour is assumed to be known. Like in Full PEARL [4, 5] it is assumed that we have a database of standard devices with their relevant properties.

2.1   Configuration division

In the configuration division the software architecture is described. The largest executable program, which can be loaded to a station depending on its state is a "COLLECTION" of "MODULEs". It is also possible to specify under which conditions certain collections are removed from a station and which collections are loaded instead. These conditions are station state dependent.

Modules consist of "TASKs", which may communicate through "PORTS". Each program part has its unique name for reference. Modules are further described by their import and export definitions, in which it is stated, which data structures and tasks are shared with other modules.

Tasks are described by their trigger conditions and response times. Task alternatives, which serve the purpose of increasing fault-tolerance and enhance the feasibility of task scheduling, are given (during scheduling an alternative task with shorter run time or longer requested response time can be scheduled in order to maintain the feasibility of the schedule).

The connections between the ports are described by their directions and line attributes. Line attributes state which connections from the station division are used for the communication. It is stated which thereof are always followed ("VIA" attribute) and which can be chosen from a list based on the "PREFER" attribute.

The relations of configuration division components are depicted in Figure 2 and their properties are given in the framed box below. The software configuration constructs are given here with their mapping and references to the constructs from the station division.

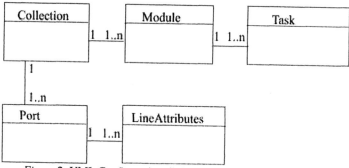

Figure 2: UML Configuration division class structure with properties in Java syntax

```
public class Collection {
    StringBuffer collectionID;
    Station station;
    StringBuffer state;
    Port ports;
```

```
}
class Module {
    StringBuffer moduleID;
    Collection collection;
    StringBuffer import;
    StringBuffer export;
}
class Task {
    StringBuffer taskID;
    Module module;
    String triggerCondition={"ON_DEMAND", "TIMER", "INT",
"SIGNAL", "SEMA"};
    int deadline;
    StringBuffer altTaskID;
}
class LineAttributes {
    Connection line;
    String attr[]={"VIA","PREFERED"};
    LineAttributes nextLine;
}
class Port {
    StringBuffer portID;
    String dataFlow={"IN", "OUT", "INOUT"};
    String transferType={PACKAGE, DMA};
    int bytesInPackage;
    String syncMechanism={"SEND-REPLY", "NOWAIT-SEND",
"BLOCKING-SEND"};
    LineAttributes lines;
    Port nextPort;
}
```

2.2   Net division

Any net topology of a distributed system can be described by point-to-point connections. Net division describes the physical connections between the station's components of the system by their logical names and directions.

The net division should become obsolete with the use of direct references to connections between the station division components and configuration division PORT mappings.

2.3   System division

System division encapsulates the hardware description and the assignment of symbolic names to hardware devices for their easier reference from the program or the net division. The described components from the station division are used.

By the object naming scheme this division would also become obsolete.

3. THE EXPECTED BENEFITS OF USING OO TECHNIQUES WITH SPECIFICATION PEARL

The dual representations (textual and graphical) of the same specification are difficult to manage and they introduce superfluous work for the designer who wants to transform the design from the desktop drawing into code. Hence it would mean a simplification if the constructs would represent target objects. Both net and system divisions are mainly present for backward compatibility to enable the output of textual specification code if needed. Otherwise the CASE tool would probably generate (references to) specification classes and objects in the target implementation language syntax.

The possible incompatibility of parameters is checked during the design process or while creating the architecture description in the Specification PEARL syntax. The modelled system is checked for completeness and parameter compatibility, since for subsequent design steps (e.g. SW/HW mapping), schedulability analysis or target language implementation a coherent, unambiguous description is needed. These checks would be simplified by the verification of the connections between the specified component objects during their creation.

Specification PEARL as a specification language needs a configuration manager or loader to be able to influence the loading scheme and execution of programs in a distributed system. Recently the specification for RT-Java and its reference implementation of the JVM have been issued [8]. In addition to previous releases they also incorporate the classes and attributes for RT operation. JVM is an ideal example of a configuration manager. Hence and since Java is an object oriented language it would be sensible to define Java classes for Specification PEARL constructs and use them to access resources of a distributed system through the JVM.

4. CONCLUSION

The method for real-time system's HW/SW co-specification Specification PEARL enables parallel design of the hardware and software parts and offers textual as well as graphical notations. For PEARL programmers it provides a good way to design the SYSTEM part of their program. On the other hand it is not strictly bound to PEARL and its output can be used as input of a configuration manager or loader. As mentioned in the pervious section the object-oriented Specification PEARL could be used with an object-oriented real-time language like RT Java. Its use in a CASE tool would be more straightforward than currently with the dual graphical and textual representations, although for compatibility reasons the possibility of the textual output should be retained.

Specification PEARL enables early reasoning about the system integration, but at the same time its hierarchical structure also enables top-down stepwise refinement in design. The designer first sets up the logical structure of the system, which is being detailed with time as well as implementation parameters. When at least the logical hardware architecture is set up, software units (COLLECTIONs) may be associated with it. The shell of the hardware architecture and the interconnections are sufficient to logically map the software onto hardware. The design can also be started from the software point of view and the mapping can then be done subsequently, when the stations are present.

Currently only the implementation of Specification PEARL for use with PEARL90 already exists, however with the advent of the RT Java specification with its reference implementation and the described specification language implementation, it seems to be a good idea to implement Java classes for Specification PEARL components. This would also ease the implementation of specifications and provide them with the appropriate loader and configuration manager.

REFERENCES

[1] A. H. Frigeri, W. A. Halang. Eine objektorientierte Erweiterung von PEARL 90. PEARL 97 - Workshop ueber Realzeitsysteme, Boppard, Germany, November 1997.

[2] R. Gumzej. Embedded System Architecture Co-Design and its Validation. Doctoral thesis, University of Maribor, Slovenia, 1999.

[3] W.A. Halang, C.E. Pereira and A.H. Frigeri: Safe Object Oriented Programming of Distributed Real Time Systems in PEARL. Comput. Syst. Sci. & Eng. (2002) 2: 85-94.

[4] Basic PEARL, DIN 66253, Part 1.

[5] Full PEARL, DIN 66253, Part 2.

[6] Multiprocessor PEARL, DIN 66253, Part 3.

[7] D. Verber, Object Orientation in Hard Real-Time System Development. Doctoral thesis, University of Maribor, Slovenia, 1999.

[8] The Real-Time Specification for Java (rtsj-V1.0), Addisson-Wesley, 2000, http://www.rtj.org.

Universal Plug and Play Machine Models
Modeling with Distributed Abstract State Machines

Uwe Glässer
glaesser@upb.de
Heinz Nixdorf Institute, Paderborn, Germany

Margus Veanes
margus@microsoft.com
Microsoft Research, Redmond, USA

Abstract: We present a high-level executable specification for the *Universal Plug and Play* (UPnP) standard illustrating the use of *Abstract State Machine* (ASM) technology as a practical tool for applied systems engineering. The concept of distributed real-time ASM allows us to combine both *synchronous* and *asynchronous* execution models in one uniform model of computation.

Key words: UPnP, ASM, Real-Time Behavior, TCP/IP networking

1. INTRODUCTION

We present here some results of using *Abstract State Machine* (ASM) technology [1] in a recent pilot project at Microsoft. This project was done in collaboration with a group that has developed the *Universal Plug and Play Device Architecture* (UPnP) [11], a distributed, open networking architecture enabling peer-to-peer network connectivity of various intelligent appliances, wireless devices and PCs. UPnP is an evolving industrial standard defined by the UPnP Forum [12].

We have developed a high-level executable specification of the UPnP protocol as basis for the communications software forming the core of Universal Plug and Play Device Architecture. Serving practical needs, we attempt to accurately reflect the abstraction level of the given informal requirements specification [11], where we focus on interoperability aspects rather than on internal details of UPnP components. The construction of a *distributed real-time ASM* allows us to combine both *synchronous* as well as *asynchronous* execution models within one uniform model of computation.

We introduce a discrete notion of global system time for dealing with real time behaviour and timing constraints such as delays and timeout events.

From our abstract ASM model of UPnP we have derived an executable version using the *ASM Language* (AsmL) [2]. An additional GUI serves for control and visualization of simulation runs making our abstract executable specification a useful practical tool for the UPnP developers and testers. A comprehensive description is given in [6]. Closely related to this work are ASM behavior models of various programming languages, e.g. Java [10], and modeling languages, e.g. SDL [5] and VHDL [3].[1]

Section 2 illustrates the UPnP protocol, and Section 3 briefly outlines the semantic model used here. Section 4 introduces overall concepts of the abstract protocol model, while Section 5 exemplifies the construction of the device model in some detail. Section 6 contains some concluding remarks.

2.   THE UPNP PROTOCOL

UPnP is a layered protocol architecture built on top of TCP/IP networks by combining various standard protocols, e.g. such as DHCP, SSDP, SOAP, GENA, etc. It supports dynamic configuration of some collection of *devices* offering various kinds of *services* requested by *control points*. To perform certain control tasks, a control point needs to know what devices are available, i.e. reachable over the network, what services a device advertises, and when those advertisements will expire. Services interact with entities in the external (physical) world through the actuators and sensors of a device. A sample UPnP device is illustrated in Figure 1.

General Restrictions: In general, the following restrictions apply. Control points and devices interact through exchange of messages over a TCP/IP network, where the specific network characteristics (like bandwidth, dimension, etc.) are left unspecified. Communication is considered to be neither predictable nor reliable, i.e. message transfer over the network is subject to arbitrary and varying delays, and some messages may never arrive. Furthermore, devices may come and go at any time with or without prior notice. Consequently, there is no guarantee that a requested service is available in a given state or that is will become available in a future state. Also, a service that is available need not remain available until a certain control task using this service has been completed.

Protocol Phases: The UPnP protocol defines 6 basic steps or phases. Initially, these steps are invoked one after the other in the order given below, but may arbitrarily overlap afterwards. (0) *Addressing* is needed for

---

[1] An ASM-based formal definition of SDL recently has been approved by the International Telecommunication Union (ITU) as part of the current SDL standard [5].

obtaining an IP address when a new device is added to a network. (1) *Discovery* informs control points about the availability of devices and their services. (2) *Description* allows control points to retrieve detailed information about a device and its capabilities. (3) *Control* provides mechanisms for control points to access and control devices through well-defined interfaces. (4) *Eventing* allows control points to receive information about changes in the state of a service at run time. (5) *Presentation* enables users to retrieve additional vendor specific information.

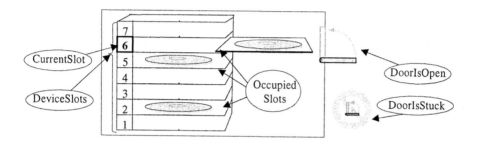

Figure 1. A generic *CD player* as a sample UPnP device. The picture illustrates the state information associated with one of the services, called *ChangeDisc*, associated with the CD player. This service provides functionality to add or remove discs from the CD player, to choose a disc to be placed on the tray, and to toggle (open/close) the door.

3.   ABSTRACT STATE MACHINES

This section briefly outlines the model of *distributed real-time ASM* at an intuitive level of understanding and in a rather informal style. For a rigorous mathematical definition, we refer to the theory of ASMs [8,9].

The Basic ASM Model. An abstract machine model A is defined over a fixed *vocabulary V*, some finite collection of function names and relation names. Formally, relations are treated as Boolean valued functions, i.e. *predicates*. States of A are *structures*[2] defining interpretations of V over a common base set. Starting from a given initial state, machine *runs* abstractly model executions of a system under consideration through finite or infinite sequences of state transitions.

The behavior of A is defined by its program P. Intuitively, P consists of one or more state transition *rules* specifying the runs of A. Each execution step computes some finite set of local function *updates* over a given state of A and fires all these updates simultaneously in one atomic action. We define

---

[2] We refer here to the notion of *structure* as it is used in first-order logic.

the rules of *P* inductively as composition of basic *update instructions* by means of simple rule constructors as illustrated in the subsequent sections.

The canonical rule constructor is the **do in-parallel**, which allows for the *synchronous* parallel composition of rules. In the below rule, the update set computed by R is defined to be the union of the individual update sets as associated with R1 and R2 respectively. The '**do in-parallel**' is optional (and usually is omitted).

$$R ::= \textbf{do in-parallel}\ R1\ R2$$

Concurrency. A distributed ASM is a generalization of the basic model. It consists of several autonomous ASM *agents* interacting with each other by reading and writing shared locations of global machine states. The underlying semantic model regulates such interactions so that potential conflicts are resolved according to the definition of *partially ordered runs* [8]. Agents come as elements of a dynamically growing and shrinking domain AGENT, where each agent has a *program* defining its behavior. The elements from a static domain PROGRAM collectively represent the distributed ASM program.

Real Time. Time values are modeled as real numbers by the elements of a linearly ordered domain Time. We define the relation "≥" on time values by the corresponding relation on real numbers. Another domain Duration represents finite time intervals as differences between time values.

domain Time, **domain** Duration

Global system time, as measured by some discrete clock, is represented by a *monitored*, nullary function now taking values in Time. A monitored function is an abstract interface to the system environment; as such, it changes its values depending on external actions and events. That is, one can only observe, but not control, how physical time evolves.

monitored now : TIME

As another integrity constraint on runs, we assume that agents react instantaneously, i.e. they fire a rule as soon as they reach a state in which the rule becomes enabled.

4.   ABSTRACT PROTOCOL MODEL

A reasonable choice for the construction of an abstract UPnP model is a distributed real-time ASM consisting of a variable number of concurrently operating and *asynchronously* communicating components. Intuitively, a component either represents a device, a control point or some fraction of the underlying communication network. Components have *interfaces* so that any interaction between a component and any other component is restricted to actions and events as observable at these interfaces.

The external world, i.e. the environment into which the system under consideration is embedded, affects the system behavior in various ways. For instance, the transport of messages over the communication network is subject to arbitrary delays and some messages may never arrive. Also, the system configuration itself changes as components come and go. Those external actions and events are basically unpredictable and as such they are modeled through a GUI allowing for user-controlled interaction with the external world. The overall organization of the model is illustrated in Fig. 2.

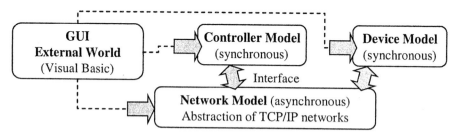

Figure 2. Overall organization of the distributed ASM model of UPnP.

4.1 Components and Interfaces

We formulate behavioral properties of UPnP protocol entities in terms of component interactions, where components are agents of a distributed ASM as identified by a given system configuration.

Conceptually, any interaction between the model and the external world involves two different categories of agents: (1) explicit agents of the model, namely control point agents, device agents or network agents, and (2) implicit agents living in the environment. The non-deterministic nature of environment agents faithfully reflects the system view of the environment.

At the component level, control points and devices are modeled as parallel compositions of *synchronously* operating machine models. Each component further decomposes into a collection of parallel ASMs, one for each protocol phase. In contrast, network components internally are based on an *asynchronous* model with decentralized control as explained below.

Communication Infrastructure. We define an abstraction of TCP/IP networks based on standard network terminology [4]. Our network model is based on a distributed execution model with asynchronous communication according to the view that a complex communication network usually consists of some (not further specified) collection of interconnected physical networks. The network model is described in greater detail in [7].

Transport Protocols. User level processes, or application programs, interact with each other by exchanging messages using the standard transport level protocols UDP and TCP. There may be several application programs running on a single host. Thus the *address* of an application program is given by the IP address of its host in conjunction with a unique protocol port number on this host. In our case, several control point programs may run on the same host. Devices, however, are considered as individual hardware units; therefore they are identified with the hosts on which they run. Collectively, we refer to control points and devices as *applications*.

DHCP Server Interface. The Dynamic Host Configuration Protocol (DHCP) enables automatic configuration of IP addresses when adding a new host to a network. We model interaction between a DHCP server and the DHCP client of a device explicitly only as far as the device side is concerned (cf. Section 5). The server side is implicitly given by one or more external DHCP server agents whose behavior is left abstract. In our model, a DHCP server represents another type of application program.

4.2   Basic Agent Types

We can now define AGENT as a derived domain, where we assume the four underlying domains COMMUNICATOR, CONTROL·POINT, DEVICE and DHCP·SERVER to be pairwise disjoint.

AGENT ≡ APPLICATION ∪ COMMUNICATOR
APPLICATION ≡ CONTROL·POINT ∪ DEVICE ∪ DHCP·SERVER

Depending on its type, agents either execute the program RunControlPoint, RunDevice, or RunNetwork. The behavior of DHCP server agents is not explicitly defined in terms of a program; rather it is determined by the respective actions of the external world.

domain PROGRAM ≡ {RunControlPoint, RunDevice, RunNetwork}

4.3   Abstract Data Structures

Mathematical modeling of complex system behavior requires appropriate abstractions for coping with the complexity and diversity of real-life systems. To simplify the formal representation of our model, we assume a rich background structure for *sets* and *maps* with sets of integers, maps from integers to strings, or even sets of such maps, etc. Both maps and sets may be viewed as aggregate entities and may be updated point-wise. We exemplify our approach below.

Messaging. Assume a static universe ADDRESS of *IP addresses* extended by *protocol port numbers* to refer to the global TCP/UDP address space and a unary function address associating with each application some element from ADDRESS. A distinguished address, called thisDevice, serves as a source address for devices that do not yet have an IP address.

address : APPLICATION → ADDRESS

Messages are uniformly represented as elements of a domain MESSAGE. Each message is of a certain type from the static domain MSG·TYPE. The message type determines whether a message is transmitted using UDP or TCP, though we do not make this distinction explicit. Further, a message identifies a sender, a receiver, and the actual message content, or payload.

An agent has a local mailbox for storing messages until these messages will actively be processed. The mailbox of an application represents its local input port as identified by the respective port number for this application.

mailbox : AGENT → Set of MESSAGE **initially** empty

Timeout Events. Agents have several distinct timers for different purposes. Each individual timer t has its own default duration effectively determining the expiration time when setting t. In a given state, a timer t is active if and only if its expiration time time(t) is greater than the value of now; otherwise, t is called *expired*.

duration : AGENT → Map of TIMER·TYPE to DURATION
time : AGENT → Map of TIMER·TYPE to TIME

For a given timer t of agent a, the operation of setting t is defined as follows: SetTimer(a,t) ≡ time(a)(t) := now + duration(a)(t).

In a given state, a predicate Timeout indicates for given timer instance t and agent a whether the timer instance is active or has expired.

Timeout : AGENT → Map of TIMER·TYPE to BOOL,
Timeout(a,t) = now ≥ time(a)(t)

5. DEVICE MODEL

We define the device model as *parallel composition* of six synchronously operating component ASMs, each of which runs a different protocol phase. For illustrating the approach, we restrict here on *Addressing* and refer to [6] for a comprehensive definition of the complementary protocol parts.

Device Status. In a given device state, [11] distinguishes three basically different situations: *inactive*–the device is not connected to a network; *alive*–the device is connected and may remain connected for some time; *byebye*–the device is connected but is about to be removed from the network. The device status is affected by actions and events in the external environment as expressed by an externally controlled function *status* defined on devices.

monitored status : DEVICE → { inactive, alive, byebye }

In the device model defined below, *me* refers to a device agent performing the program `RunDevice`. The component behavior is defined by the respective ASM rule macros specifying parallel operations of *me*.

```
RunDevice =
  if status(me) ≠ inactive then
    RunAddressing    //Component ASM for Addressing phase
    RunDiscovery     //Component ASM for Discovery phase
    RunDescription   //…
    RunControl
    RunEventing
    RunPresentation
```

Addressing. IP address management requires a DHCP server to assign an IP address when some new device (for which no IP address is specified manually) is added to the network. As reply to a DHCPDISCOVER message from a device's DHCP client, the server broadcasts a DHCPOFFER message identifying the IP address as well as the hardware address of the device.

When no DHCP server is available, a host may obtain a *temporary* IP address through auto IP addressing. This address can then be used until a DHCPOFFER message eventually is received (see [6] for details).

We abstract from any specific algorithms used for auto IP addressing by making a nondeterministic choice to determine a temporary IP address. For checking the validity of a chosen address, i.e. for testing whether this choice causes any conflicts, we assume to have some externally controlled decision procedure as represented by the predicate *ValidAutoIPAdr*.

monitored ValidAutoIPAdr : DEVICE × ADDRESS → BOOL

In the Addressing ASM below, `RunDHCPclient` models the interaction between the local DHCP client and the DHCP server. The client uses a timer for reissuing its IP address request repeatedly until it eventually receives a response from a server. The first timeout event also triggers the calculation of a temporary IP address in parallel to the execution of the DHCP client.

```
RunAddressing ≡
  if address(me) = thisDevice or AutoConfiguredAdr(me)
    then RunDHCPclient
  if address(me) = thisDevice and ¬DhcpOfferRcvd and
    Timeout(me,dhcpClientTimer)then
    choose adr ∈ ADDRESS: ValidAutoIPAdr(me,adr) do
```

```
    address(me):= adr
  AutoConfiguredAdr(me):= true
```
where
```
  DhcpOfferRcvd ≡ ∃ m ∈ mailbox(me): DhcpOffer(m)
```

6.   CONCLUSIONS

We illustrate here the construction of an abstract operational model of the *Universal Plug and Play* (UPnP) protocol. The concept of distributed real-time ASM allows us to combine synchronous and asynchronous execution models in one uniform model of computation. A notion of global system time allows for dealing with timing constraints.

For a comprehensive description of a fully executable model, including a GUI for control and visualization of simulation runs, sample control points and sample devices, see our technical report [6]. A more specific discussion on the role of the executable language AsmL as a domain-specific language for rapid prototyping in the UPnP project can be found in [7].

Conceptually, the abstract ASM model complements the informal requirements specification [11] serving as technical documentation, e.g. for further development, whereas the executable Asml model provides a basis for experimental validation, e.g. rapid prototyping and conformance testing.

REFERENCES

1. Abstract State Machine Web site. URL: http://www.eecs.umich.edu/gasm/
2. AsmL Web site. URL: http://www.research.microsoft.com/fse/asml/ Foundations of Software Engineering, Microsoft Research.
3. E. Börger, U. Glässer and W. Müller. Formal Definition of an Abstract VHDL'93 Simulator by EA-Machines. In C. Delgado Kloos and Peter T. Breuer, editors, *Formal Semantics for VHDL*, Kluwer Academic Pub., 1995, 107-139.
4. D. E. Comer. Internetworking with TCP/IP, *Principles, Protocols, and Architectures.* Prentice Hall, 2000.
5. R. Eschbach, U. Glässer, R. Gotzhein, M. von Löwis and A. Prinz. Formal Definition of SDL-2000 – Compiling and Running SDL Specifications as ASM Models. *Journal of Universal Computer Science*, 7 (11): 1025-1050, Springer Pub. Co., 2001.
6. U. Glässer, Y.Gurevich and M. Veanes, Universal Plug and Play Machine Models, Foundations of Software Engineering, Microsoft Research, Redmond, Technical Report, MSR-TR-2001-59, June 15, 2001.

7. U. Glässer, Y. Gurevich and M. Veanes. High-level Executable Specification of the Universal Plug and Play Architecture. In Proc. of *35th Hawaii International Conference on System Sciences*, Software Technology Track, IEEE 2002.

8. Y. Gurevich. Evolving Algebras 1993: Lipari Guide. *Specification and Validation Methods*, ed. E. Börger, Oxford University Press, 1995, 9-36.

9. Y. Gurevich. Sequential Abstract State Machines Capture Sequential Algorithms. ACM Trans. on Computational Logic, 1 (1): 77-111, July 2000.

10. R. Stärk, J. Schmid and E. Börger. Java and the Java Virtual Machine: Definition, Verification, Validation. Springer, 2001.

11. UPnP Device Architecture V1.0. *Microsoft Universal Plug and Play Summit, Seattle 2000*, Microsoft Corporation, Jan. 2000.

12. Official Web site of the UPnP Forum. URL: http://www.upnp.org

Analysis of Event-Driven Real-Time Systems with Time Petri Nets
A Translation-Based Approach

Zonghua Gu and Kang G. Shin
RTCL/EECS, University of Michigan, Ann Arbor, MI 48109 {zgu,kgshin}@eecs.umich.edu

Abstract: The growing complexity of modern real-time embedded systems makes it imperative to apply formal analysis techniques at early stages of system development. This paper considers formal modelling of event-driven real-time systems with Time Petri Nets, and subsequent analysis via model-checking by a simple, fully automatable translation into Timed Automata. The proposed approach is applied to a small application scenario taken from Avionics Mission Computing.

Keywords: real-time, embedded, Time Petri Net, Timed Automata, UPPAAL, model checking, CORBA

1. INTRODUCTION

Real-time embedded systems are ubiquitous in modern society, many of which perform safety-critical functions, and therefore, it is imperative to have tools and techniques that can guarantee a high degree of system correctness. In this paper, we consider application of Merlin and Farber's *Time Petri Net* (TPN) [12] to model event-driven real-time systems, and formally define a translation procedure from a TPN model into a semantically equivalent Timed Automata [7] model in order to perform model-checking on the TA model. This translation procedure also gives a formal semantics for TPN in terms of TA, and clarifies a number of semantic ambiguities in the original TPN definition. For example, we clearly define the semantics of multiple-enabledness of a transition as freshly enabling a transition after each firing, which is intuitively the behaviour of a task serving multiple queued execution requests.

As an example of our approach, we model and analyze an application scenario taken from Avionics Mission Computing [8]. Using the model checker UPPAAL, we were able to check the system timing properties such as end-to-end latency. In case a system timing property is violated, UPPAAL gives us an error trace leading to the violation state and allows us to gain more insight into the cause of the violation.

This paper is structured as follows: Section 2 considers TPN modelling of real-time scheduling. Section 3 describes a simple algorithm for mapping TPN into TA. Section 4 considers modelling and analysis of an application scenario taken from Avionics Mission Computing. Section 5 describes related work, and the paper concludes with Section 6.

2.   MODELLING OF REAL-TIME SCHEDULING WITH TPN

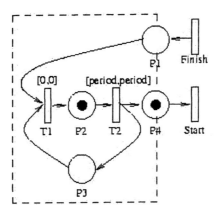

Figure 1. A periodic timer in TPN.

Figure 1 shows the TPN model for a periodic timer, and Figure 2 shows a TPN model for static priority, *non-preemptive* scheduling of two periodic tasks. The inhibitor edge from P11 to T22 models the fact that Task1 has priority over Task2: a non-empty P11 prevents T22 from firing.

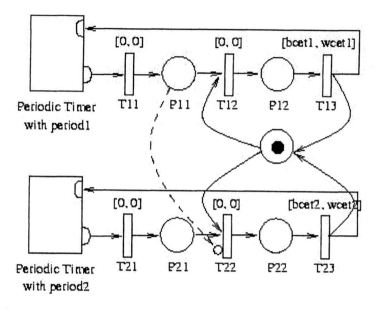

Figure 2. Static priority, *non-premptive* scheduling of two periodic tasks. The blocks marked *Periodic Timer* denote instantiations of the periodic timer model in Figure 1 with periods period1 and period2, respectively. The top part of the figure represents high-priority task Task1, and the bottom part represents low-priority task Task2. BCET stands for *best-case execution time* and WCET stands for *worst-case execution time*.

3. MAPPING TPN INTO TA

We formally define a translation algorithm for mapping a TPN model into a semantically equivalent TA model.

1. Declare a global urgent channel *go*. A transition with an urgent channel as its synchronization label is an urgent transition, and has to be taken whenever it is enabled without delay.

2. Create an automaton with a single location, and a transition with synchronization label *go!* starting and ending at that location, as shown in Figure 4.

3. For each TPN place $p \in P$, declare an integer global variable with the same name in the TA model.

4. Suppose a TPN transition $t \in T$ has an associated delay interval $[lb, ub]$, a pre-set of k input places $p_1^{in}, \ldots, p_k^{in}$, a post-set of m output places $p_1^{out}, \ldots, p_m^{out}$, and a set of n inhibitor arcs from places $p_1^{inh}, \ldots, p_n^{inh}$. Classify all the TPN transitions according to the number

of its input, output and inhibitor places. For example, all transitions with 1 input place, 2 output places, and 1 inhibitor place are put into the same class. For each transition class:

a) Define an automaton template with two locations *disabled* and *enabled*, one local clock c, and $k + m + n$ integer parameters named
$$p_1^{in}, \ldots, p_k^{in}, p_1^{out}, \ldots, p_m^{out}, p_1^{inh}, \ldots, p_n^{inh} .$$

b) Add an invariant condition $c \leq ub$ at the location *enabled*.

c) Add an edge from *disabled* to *enabled* with guard condition
$$p_1^{in} \geq B(p_1^{in}, t), \ldots, p_k^{in} \geq B(p_k^{in}, t), p_1^{inh} == 0, \ldots, p_n^{inh} == 0 ,$$
synchronization label *go?*, and assignment label $c := 0$.

d) Add $k + n$ edges from *enabled* to *disabled* with guard condition
$$p_1^{in} < B(p_1^{in}, t) \text{ on } edge_1, \ldots, p_k^{in} < B(p_k^{in}, t) \text{ on } edge_k ,$$
$$p_1^{inh} > 0 \text{ on } edge_{k+1}, \ldots p_n^{inh} > 0 \text{ on } edge_{k+n} , \text{ and synchronization}$$
label *go?* on every edge.

e) Add an edge from *enabled* to *disabled* with guard condition
$$p_1^{in} \geq B(p_1^{in}, t), \ldots, p_k^{in} \geq B(p_k^{in}, t), p_1^{inh} == 0, \ldots, p_n^{inh} == 0, c \geq lb ,$$
and assignment label
$$p_1^{in} := p_1^{in} - B(p_1^{in}, t), \ldots, p_k^{in} := p_k^{in} - B(p_k^{in}, t),$$
$$p_1^{out} := p_1^{out} + F(p_1^{out}, t), \ldots, p_m^{out} := p_m^{out} + F(p_m^{out}, t)$$

5. In the system configuration section, instantiate one automaton template for each TPN transition, with the appropriate global variables as parameters, representing the input, output and inhibitor places of that transition.

Figure 3. A dummy automaton with an urgent transition *go*.

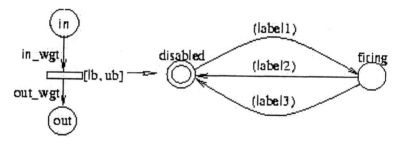

Figure 4. TA model of a TPN transition *t* with 1 input place *in*, 1 output place *out*, and time bounds *[lb,ub]*. The process template has argument list (int *in, out*; const *in_wgt, out_wgt*; const *lb, ub*), and a local clock *c*. The transition labels are: (label1) is *((in >= in_wgt; go? ;c := 0)*; (label2) is *(in < in_wgt; go?)*; (label3) is *(in >= in_wgt, c >= lb; in := in − in_wgt, out := out + out_wgt)*.

Figure 4 shows the mapping for a TPN transition *t* with 1 input place *in* and 1 output place *out*. The urgent channel *go* ensures that the automaton changes its state from *disabled* to *enabled* as soon as $in \geq in\_wgt$, that is, the input place in contains *in_wgt* or more tokens. The TPN transition's delay interval *[lb, ub]* is modelled by the state *enabled* in the TA model, which has an invariant condition $c \leq ub$, and a guard condition $c \geq lb$ on the lower outgoing transition that represents transition firing. The resulting semantics is that the automaton has to take the lower transition from *enabled* to *disabled* if it has been staying in state *enabled* continuously for at least *lb* time units, and at most *ub* time units. The automaton can also be disabled by condition $in < in\_wgt$, meaning that some other conflicting transition has been fired and removed one or more tokens from *t*'s input place *in* so that the number of tokens is now less than *in_wgt*.

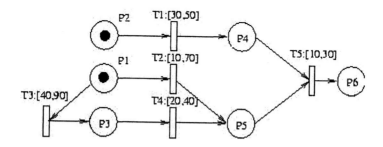

Figure 5. Simple TPN modeling concurency, competition and synchronization.

Figure 5 shows a simple TPN taken from [11]. In order to translate this TPN model into a TA model, it is simply a matter of instantiating the TA templates for TPN transitions with 1 input/1 output, and 2 input/1 output,

which happen to be the only two types of transitions present, as shown
below:

```
int p1 := 1,p2 := 1,p3 := 0,p4 :=0,p5 := 0,p6 := 0;
urgent chan go;
T1 := T1in_1out(p2, p4, 1, 1, 30, 50);
T2 := T1in_1out(p1, p5, 1, 1, 10, 70);
T3 := T1in_1out(p1, p3, 1, 1, 40, 90);
T4 := T1in_1out(p3, p5, 1, 1, 20, 40);
T5 := T2in_1out(p4, p5, p6, 1, 1, 1, 10, 30);
System Dummy, T1, T2, T3, T4, T5;
```

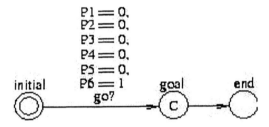

Figure 6. Observer automaton

Figure 6 shows an observer automaton that records the time t it takes to
reach the goal state (0, 0, 0, 0, 0, 1) from the initial state (1, 1, 0, 0, 0, 0),
where the state vector denotes marking of the TPN (p1, p2, p3, p4, p5, p6).
Using the model checker UPPAAL we can prove that t falls in the time
interval [40, 140]. In order to verify that this is a tight bound, it is necessary
to perform three queries, due to UPPAAL's lack of parametric analysis [6]
capability:

1. A[] observer.goal imply observer.c $\geq$ 40 and Observer.c $\leq$ 140. This
   is checked to be true.
2. A[] observer.goal imply observer.c $\geq$ 41. This is checked to be false.
3. A[] observer.goal imply observer.c $\leq$ 139. This is checked to be false.

4.   MODELLING AND ANALYSIS OF AN APPLICATION SCENARIO FROM AVIONICS MISSION COMPUTING

Software for Avionics Mission Computing [8] is the embedded software
onboard a military aircraft for controlling mission critical functions, such as,

navigation, target tracking and identification, weapon firing, etc. The software provided to us by Boeing as part of the DARPA MoBIES (Model-based Integration of Embedded Software) project is modelled with *Unified Modelling Language* (UML) [3], and runs on a distributed hardware platform on top of real-time CORBA TAO [4]. Its software architecture is publish/subscribe, using Real-Time CORBA Event Service [5] as its underlying communications substrate. Event publishers push events through the event channel to event consumers, whose execution is triggered by the arrival of events. The system runs at a number of different rates driven by timer event publishers, such as 40Hz, 20Hz, 10Hz, 5Hz, and 1Hz.

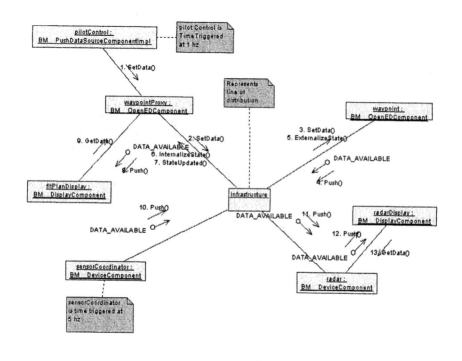

Multi-Rate Multi-Process...

Figure 7. *UML Collaboration Diagram for a multi-rate, multi-processor scenario.*

Figure 7 describes an execution scenario that is multi-rate (1Hz and 5Hz) and multi-processor. The 1Hz thread is initiated by the *pilotControl* component, which calls *SetData* on the *waypointProxy* component. The *waypointProxy* component, in turn, forwards the *SetData* call through the network to the master component *wayPoint* on another processor. Upon its wakeup, the *waypoint* component pushes a DATA_AVAILABLE event through the network, updating *waypointProxy* with fresh data and notifying *fltPlanDisplay* that fresh data is now available at the *waypointProxy* component. Upon notification, *fltPlanDisplay* calls *GetData* on *waypointProxy* to get the new waypoint data.

The 5Hz thread is initiated by the *sensorCoordinator* component, which pushes a DATA_AVAILABLE event through the network to the *radar* and *radarDisplay* components. Upon its wakeup, *radarDisplay* calls *GetData* on *radar* to get fresh data.

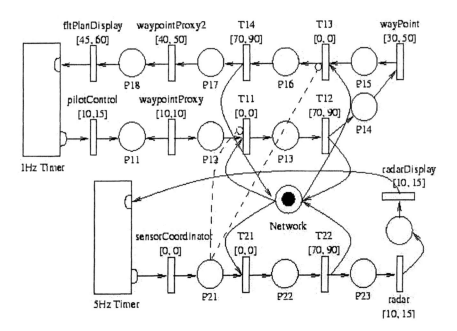

Figure 8. TPN model of the UML scenario in Figure 7.

The TPN model in Figure 8 is largely self-explanatory, with a few notable points. The three groups of transitions and places, *(T11, P13, T12), (T13, P16, T14), (T21, P22, T22),* model RT-CORBA infrastructure that processes message transmission across the network. The place *Network* models the non-preemptively scheduled network resource. The inhibitor arcs connecting *P12* to *T11* and *T13* express priorities in network resource arbitration.

By translating the TPN model into TA, we are able to use UPPAAL to check the following properties:
– The 5Hz thread has frame overrun. UPPAAL can give a diagnostic trace that shows the execution scenario that leads to the error condition, which is omitted due to space limitations.

- The end-to-end latency of the 1Hz transaction lies within [275,525]ms. UPPAAL can give execution scenarios for achieving the smallest and largest response times of the 1Hz transaction.

5.   RELATED WORK

Cortes [10] proposed a mapping algorithm from PRES+ model, which is a variant of TPN with additional data handling capabilities, into HyTech [6] models. Out mapping is simpler and more compositional because we take advantage of UPPAAL's capability of having guard conditions on urgent transitions, which is not present in Hytech. Cortes' mapping algorithm can only deal with 1-safe TPNs (where each place can contain at most one token), while our algorithm can deal with non-1-safe TPNs (each place can contain more than one token) and multiple-enabledness of transitions, which are required to model task queuing and preemptive scheduling.

Wang [11] described a reachability analysis algorithm for TPN that enables computation of end-to-end system timing properties. Our TPN-to-TA translation algorithm can perform verification of more complex system properties in the form of temporal logic specifications, not just reachability. Furthermore, tool support for the algorithms described in [11] is not available.

6.   CONCLUSIONS AND FUTURE WORK

In this paper we consider modelling of event-driven real-time systems with Time Petri Nets, and subsequent analysis via model-checking by defining a simple and fully-automatable mapping from TPN into Timed Automata.

A common complaint against formal methods in industry is that they are too hard to use for people without background in formal logic and mathematics. Even though graphical formalisms, such as Petri-Nets and Timed Automata, are generally easier to understand than text-based formalisms, they are usually not *broad-spectrum* models that can be applied throughout the system development life cycle. In order to use them, the designer has to manually map the regular software model into one of the *analysis specific* models, perform analysis, and then map the results back into the regular model. It is not realistic to expect industry to accept this pattern of usage in view of increasingly shorter time-to-market windows and product life-cycles, except in safety-critical industries such as the avionics and automotive industries. It also creates problems in maintaining consistency between multiple models of the same underlying system. In order to achieve broader acceptance of formal methods, we plan to investigate integration of formal analysis techniques with informal, widely-adopted techniques such as the Unified Modeling Language (UML) [3], by using UML as the user-visible modeling formalism, and use the formal techniques as back-end analysis engines that are largely invisible to the designer. As shown in this paper, it is natural to mapping UML Collaboration Diagrams into TPN models. We are also investigating adding timing annotations to UML *Activity Diagrams* and mapping them into TPN models.

REFERENCES

[1] Johan Bengtsson, Kim G. Larsen, Fredrik Larsson, Paul Pettersson, Wang Yi, "UPPAAL - A Tool Suite for Automatic Verification of Real-Time Systems", *Proceedings of the 4th DIMACS Workshop on Verification and Control of Hybrid Systems*, 22-24 October, 1995. LNCS 1066.

[2] S.Yovine. "Kronos: A Verification Tool for Real-Time Systems", *Springer International Journal of Software Tools for Technology Transfer*, Vol. 1, Nber. 1/2, October 1997.

[3] http://www.omg.org/uml

[4] D. Schmidt, D. Levine, S. Mungee, "The Design and Performance of Real-Time Object Request Brokers", *Computer Communications*, Volume 21, No. 4, April, 1998.

[5] D. Schmidt, D. Levine, T. Harrison, "The Design and Performance of a Real-time CORBA Object Event Service", *Proceedings of OOPSLA*, pp.434-763, 1997.

[6] T. Henzinger, P. Ho, H. Wong-Toi, "HYTECH: A Model Checker for Hybrid Systems" *Software Tools for Technology Transfer, special issue on timed and hybrid systems*, pp. 110-112, 1997.

[7] R. Alur, D.L. Dill, "A Theory of Timed Automata", *Theoretical Computer Science* 126:183-235, 1994.

[8] D. Sharp, "Object-Oriented Real-Time Computing for Reusable Avionics Software", *Proceedings of Fourth International Symposium on Object-Oriented Real-Time Distributed Computing*, pp. 185-192, 2001.

[9] H. Storrle, "An Evaluation of High-End Tools for Petri-Nets", *Technical Report, University of Munich*, June, 1998.

[10] L. Cortes, P. Eles, Z. Peng, "Verification of Embedded Systems Using a Petri Net Based Representation." *Proceedings of ISSS*, 2000, pp. 149-155

[11] J. Wang, Y. Deng, "Reachability Analysis of Real-Time Systems Using Time Petri Nets'" *IEEE Transactions on Systems, Man and Cybernetics*, Vol. 30, No. 5, October 2000.

[12] P. Merlin, D. Farber, "Recoverability of Communication Protocols - Implication of a Theoretical Study." *IEEE Transactions on Communications*, Vol. COM-24, pp.1036-1043, Sept. 1976.

Petri Net Based Design of Reconfigurable Embedded Real-Time Systems

Carsten Rust, Friedhelm Stappert and Reinhard Bernhardi-Grisson
University of Paderborn/C-LAB, Fuerstenallee 11, D-33102 Paderborn,Germany
Tel:. +49 5251 606126, Fax: + 49 5251 606065, Email: {car,fst,reinhard}@c-lab.de

Abstract: During the last years we have developed a methodology for the design of complex embedded real-time systems. The methodology supports the complete design flow reaching from modeling of embedded systems on a high level of abstraction over simulation and analysis down to the implementation on target platforms. In this paper, we describe our current work, which aims at opening the methodology for dynamically reconfigurable systems. We describe the main ideas for extending our formal model of High-Level Petri Nets in order to capture these systems. Furthermore, we describe our approach for timing analysis of these systems.

1.   INTRODUCTION

Embedded systems design is becoming more and more complicated. The reasons are manifold, e.g. limited resources, reliability requirements, or the fact that embedded systems usually are distributed and contain concurrent behavior. In addition, embedded systems are – under several aspects like target architecture, modeling paradigms, and demands concerning reliability – heterogeneous. A further factor raising complexity of embedded systems design is that they are to an increasing extent dynamically reconfigurable. As an example, we will consider an automotive system in Section 3. Obviously, dynamically changing system parts increase the heterogeneity of a system even more. Dynamically evolving subsystems – which imply a powerful basic model for specification – have to be consid-

ered together with basic controllers running under hard reliability constraints.

Several design methodologies for embedded systems based on different
formal models have been developed in recent years. Examples are the projects Ptolemy [5], which is based on several models of computation, and
Moses [6], which is based on High Level Petri Nets. The methodology for
our approach (cf. Section 2) is also based on Petri Nets. All mentioned
methodologies are devoted to the design of heterogeneous systems. However, to our knowledge existing methodologies do no support dynamic reconfiguration of systems at run-time. Hence, existing methodologies are not
well-suited for the above described systems, which we would like to characterize as heterogeneous embedded real-time systems including dynamically reconfigurable components. In this paper, we describe our approach for
the design of these systems. In the following sections, we will first give an
overview over the existing methodology and a typical application scenario
and then describe our main ideas for two subtasks of the design, namely
modeling and timing analysis.

2.   PREVIOUS WORK

The approach presented in this paper is based on an existing methodology for static embedded real-time systems [1]. The methodology proposes a
design flow divided into the three stages *Modeling, Analysis and Partitioning,* and *Synthesis* (cf. Figure 1). Within the stage of modeling, a heterogeneous model of the system under construction – specified using languages
from different application domains – is transformed into one unique High
Level Petri Net model, namely an extended Predicate/Transition-Net (Pr/T-
Net). In the second stage, Petri Net analysis and timing analysis methods are
applied in order to validate functional as well as temporal requirements and
furthermore in order to gather information for an effective implementation of
the system. The implementation is generated in the final stage of synthesis.

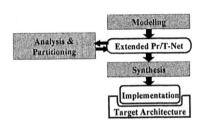

Figure 1: Design Flow

3.   APPLICATION SCENARIO

In *Figure 2*, several components of an application scenario - an automotive system - are depicted, e.g. an air conditioning system (*ClimateControl*) and a display unit. The components are interconnected via different busses. The specification is heterogeneous in several ways, e.g. in that it mixes continuous controllers with state based specifications. In addition, the specified system is dynamically reconfigurable, for instance for the handling of so called Fail-Over situations, that is in error situations, where functionality has to be relocated. Another potential reason for dynamic reconfiguration is an altering functionality of a component, e.g. for diagnosis purposes. In the future applications are conceivable, where certain tasks are assigned to a component at run-time. An example may be a part of a decentralized intersection management, which aims at guiding several convoys of vehicles through an intersection [2].

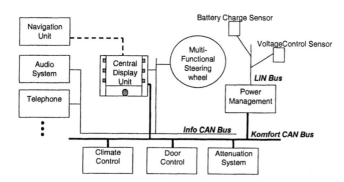

Figure 2. Application Example

4.   MODELING

Instead of a monolithic High-Level Petri Net model as before, our methodology now uses a set of Petri Net languages as formal model. For each part of the system under construction, an appropriate Petri Net model may be chosen for modeling it. For example, simple models like Place/Transition Nets may be chosen for the specification of small safety critical systems, that do not require high modeling power, but must support exhaustive analysis possibilities. On the other hand, for switching components between different modes, high-level self modifying Petri Net models are provided. Despite their different properties with respect to modeling power and analysis capabilities, all Petri Net models are compatible with each other and hence can be integrated into one model enabling global investigations of the system.

In *Figure 3*, the Petri Net specification for a component of our application scenario is depicted, namely the unit for controlling the air conditioning system (*ClimateControl*). The specification includes one input place (*Event*) as well as an output place (*Ready*). By means of the input place, messages are received from other components like the air conditioning operating unit, the central display unit, or by other control units. The Power Management may for instance send a message *OFF* when the battery's state of charge is critical causing the Climate Control to switch off the air conditioning. The output place *Ready* is marked in order to indicate when a reaction to a specific input has been computed. To control the air conditioning system, calls to API functions of the system are associated with the firing of transitions. A firing of transition T_5 results for instance in a deactivation of the system.

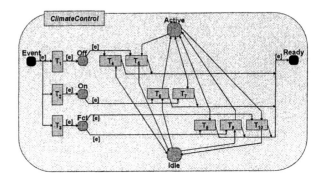

Figure 3: Specification of Climate Control

The depicted Petri Net results from an incremental design process starting with a simple model which is developed to a complete specification by means of refinement steps. An example for refining a specification is the replacement of the node *Active* in *ClimateControl* by the net depicted in *Figure 4*. Another example is a so called Type Refinement, that replaces the type of *Event* and its associated places like *On* and *Ready* with an enumeration of all possible event types. Besides extending the type, the refinement assigns guards like ($e = ON$) to the transitions $T_1, .., T_3$.

For the incremental modeling, we basically use the refinements summarized by Lakos in [3]. These are type refinement, node refinement (like that of node *Active*) and in addition a refinement adding a subnet to an existing net. Since we are dealing with real-time systems, we additionally need refinements introducing a notion of time. They allow for instance to annotate a transition with the execution time of its corresponding code in the implementation. Technically, a refinement introducing transition delays is similar to a type refinement. The types of places related to the timed transition are extended with a time-stamp. Transitions on the other hand are annotated in order to evaluate and manipulate the time-stamps.

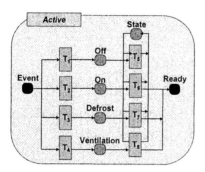

Figure 4: Refinement of node Active

For realizing dynamic reconfiguration, we propose to apply the mechanism of net refinement – usually only used during the specification of a system – at run-time. Technically, the refinement of components is associated to the firing of certain transitions.

As an example, consider a Fail-Over situation in our application scenario: The system is notified of a failure of the Power Management, which must be handled by relocating functionality from the Power Management to other components. One step of this error handling is to modify the above described *ClimateControl*. After the modification, the Climate Control itself includes the Power Management component, that observes the battery's state of charge and generates an event *OFF*, when the state becomes critical.

The modification is realized by a series of refinements, e.g. a subnet refinement for adding a node, which is further refined to the battery supervision. The refinements are triggered by the firing of transitions, which get concession to fire when a failure of the Power Management is signaled. Obviously, a couple of technical features in the target system is presumed for the described reconfiguration to work, e.g. the possibility to redirect values of battery sensors to the Climate Control. However, providing a sound formal framework for specifying the reconfiguration is a prerequisite for a proper design process.

The main advantage of using refinements is that they allow a well-structured development of models. The refinement mechanism can be used for creating a heterogeneous hierarchical Petri Net (heterogeneous in the sense of comprising different model classes), whose single components are classified rigorously. The Petri Net class of each subnet comprises for instance information over the datatypes used, whether the subnet is timed, and whether the subnets incorporate dynamic reconfiguration at run-time.

The classification is implicitly done during refinement: In addition to the usual mapping from an abstract net to a refined one, each refinement step determines the class of the refined net. The class is determined depending on the class of the abstract net as well as of the components added by the refinement step. As described above , the mechanism of net refinement is also used for specifying dynamical changes at run-time. Hence, at run-time the same classification is possible for dynamically evolving subsystems as for static subsystems at design time.

The result of the modeling process, a hierarchical Petri Net specification with classified subnets, is finally handed over to the further design steps, e.g. evaluation of the complete model by simulation or verification of single components in terms of functionality. The Petri Net class of each component determines which tools may be chosen for its analysis and synthesis. In this paper however, we will not discuss the entire analysis and synthesis stages, but concentrate on timing analysis, which is treated in the following section.

5.   TIMING ANALYSIS

When the final implementation of a model (or parts of it) is generated, it must be assured that it will run fast enough on the given target processor, i.e. that it will meet the given real-time constraints at run-time. Therefore, accurate estimates of the Worst-Case Execution Time (*WCET*) of the given Petri Nets are calculated. These estimates serve as input for a subsequent schedulability analysis. In this context, executing a net means that, starting from a specified initial marking, a defined end-marking of the given net is reached. For example, in *Figure 3* an end marking is reached when the place *Ready* is marked.

Traditional WCET analysis approaches (e.g. [4]) only analyze the code generated for a given specification as well as the corresponding processor-specific assembler code, but they have no knowledge of the original Petri Net. Thus, we propose to perform an additional analysis on the Petri Net Level.

For a motivation of the analysis on Petri Net Level, consider the code typically generated for the execution of a Petri Net in *Figure 5*. Analyzing source code only usually cannot yield an upper bound on the number of iterations of the while-loop. Furthermore, without any information about the run-time behavior of the code, a WCET analysis would assume the worst-case for each iteration of the loop, i.e. that each if-branch will be executed, although typically only a few transitions will fire during one iteration. An analysis of the Petri Net can yield both, a tight upper bound on the number of iterations and the required information about run-time behavior. In general, by means of the analysis on the Petri Net level we want to answer questions like '*How many steps will the net need at most to reach the end-marking?*', '*How often will transition T_i fire at most during all steps?*', or '*Which transition(s) will fire / not fire during the i-th step?*'. This information is handed over to a traditional source code based WCET analysis.

```
while net is alive
    get enabled transitions
    if T1 is enabled
        fire T1
    if T2 is enabled
        fire T2
    ...
end while
```

Figure 5: Petri Net Code

The analysis on Petri Net level is divided into the two phases *reachability analysis* and *behavioral analysis*. The reachability graph yielded by the reachability analysis is needed in order to find longest execution paths using standard graph algorithms (like Dijkstra's Algorithm). The structure of the reachability graph used in our analysis is different from graphs computed by common Petri Net analysis algorithms, as described in the following.

As we are primarily interested in the start- and end-states only, it is not important to investigate all possible intermediate states a net can reach. Therefore, we assume that the net is executed according to the *step-semantics*: For a given marking (i.e. state) of the net first the set of enabled transitions is determined and then all these transitions are assumed to fire in parallel. For example, in *Figure 6* c) we do not explicitly represent the states that are reached by firing t_1 or t_2 alone, but only the state that is reached after firing both t_1 and t_2 regardless of which transition fires first. Hence, the edges of the reachability graph are not labelled with a single transition only, but instead with the *firing set* of transitions firing concurrently in the corresponding step. This significantly reduces the size of the reachability graph.

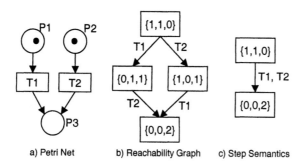

a) Petri Net   b) Reachability Graph   c) Step Semantics

Figure 6: Step Semantics

In addition, we not only need information about *which* states a net can reach, but also *how often* these states will be reached during net execution. States that are reached more than once are indicated by cycles in the reachability graph. Hence, additional information about how often these cycles will be taken must be provided, especially when these figures depend on the input data of the net. To bound the number of iterations of such a cycle, it is sufficient to specify an upper bound on the maximum number of executions of one or more transitions in it. This number can either be provided manually by the designer, or derived automatically by analyzing the net, e.g. using techniques known from program flow analysis [10].

In order to be able to apply Dijkstra's Algorithm for finding longest paths, the reachability graph must be a DAG (*Directed Acyclic Graph*), since the longest-path problem is *NP*-complete for graphs that contain cycles. To achieve this property, we use the information about the maximum number of executions of transitions described above to 'unroll' cycles in the reachability graph. Each transition with a maximum execution count gets an additional *count place* as input place that contains as many tokens as the execution count, and one of these tokens is consumed each time the transition fires. Due to these additional places, each execution of a cycle is identified with unique markings that differ only in the number of tokens on the corresponding count places. It is however not necessary to unroll all cycles completely. Instead, all edges inside a cycle can be multiplied with the number of times this cycle is taken in the worst case.

After computing the reachability graph, the behavioral analysis computes longest paths, whereby according weights are assigned to the edges so that the length of the path indicates the desired result. Some examples are:

Maximum number of steps: To bound the number of steps of the given net, all edges in the reachability graph are assigned the weight 1. The length of the longest path from the initial to the final state then is the maximum number of steps the net can execute.

Maximum number of firings: The total number of possible transition firings can be found by assigning n to each edge of the reachability graph, where n denotes the number of transitions that fire in the corresponding step. Then the length of the longest path indicates the desired number.

Maximum number of firings of a certain transition: Similar to the above, the number of times a certain transition T will fire at most can be calculated by giving the weight 1 to all edges whose firing set contains T, and 0 to all others. Again, the length of the longest path represents the sought value.

In order to exploit the information compiled above on the source code level, we use the *Flow Facts Language* introduced in [7], which can be utilized by our WCET analysis tool presented in [8]. The information about the behavior of a given Petri net described above can easily be converted to flow facts. As a simple example, consider *Figure 7* a), which depicts the reach-ability graph of the net in *Figure 4*. The nodes are characterized by the places that contain a token in the corresponding state. Obviously the net can make at most two steps to reach the end marking, and therefore the corresponding loop iterates twice. A set of flow facts is shown in *Figure 7* b): The first two facts specify that for the first loop iteration (i.e. the first step) none of $T4$, $T5$ and $T6$ will be executed, and that exactly one of the transitions $T1$, $T2$ and $T3$ will fire. The respective information for the second loop iteration is specified by the flow facts 3 and 4. Furthermore, the (redundant) information that all transitions can fire at most once during all iterations (denoted by '[]') is encoded in the set of facts in 5).

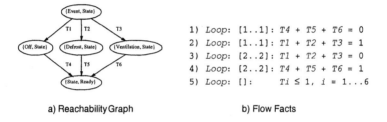

a) Reachability Graph   b) Flow Facts

Figure 7: Example Analysis

Since the models we investigate in our design environment are intended to be changing at run-time, a complete static timing analysis of the model at design time is not possible. Instead we additionally need an *online* timing analysis performed at run-time. Furthermore, in our intended scenario the set of available processors is changing dynamically at run-time, hence the online timing analysis must be processor-independent.

This is achieved by replacing the hardware-dependent back-end of the WCET tool with a more generic analysis that yields an estimate of the computational complexity of the source code by e.g. counting the arithmetic operations performed. Consequently, the low-level analysis will not yield a target-specific WCET for each basic block of the given program, but instead an estimate on the computational complexity of the corresponding code. The higher level analysis, like program flow analysis, is performed as usual and not affected by the different implementation of the low-level analysis part. An approach for generic analysis is presented by Carro et al. in [9]. There, the code for a given task is first translated to a universal 3-address code for a virtual machine. This code is then analyzed according to some performance characteristics like how many jumps, arithmetic operations or memory access operations it employs. Available processors are classified according to how fast they are able to perform these operations. Based on these figures together with the specified real-time constraints of the task (like period and deadline), an appropriate processor can be chosen for the given task.

6.   CONCLUSION

We have presented our current work towards a methodology for the design of dynamically reconfigurable systems embedded systems. The main ideas for extending our formal model of High-Level Petri Nets in order to capture these systems were described. Furthermore, we presented our approach for a timing analysis of such systems.

REFERENCES

[1]   C. Rust, J. Tacken, C.Böke, *"Pr/T--Net based Seamless Design of Embedded Real-Time Systems"*. In Proc. of 22nd Int. Conference on Application and Theory of Petri Nets (ICATPN'2001) Newcastle upon Tyne, UK, June, 2001, volume 2075 of Lecture Notes in Computer Science, pages 343-362.

[2]   R. Naumann, R. Rasche, and J. Tacken, *"Managing autonomous vehicles at intersections"*. IEEE Intelligent Systems & Their Applications, Vol. 13, No. 3, May/June 1998.

[3]   C.A. Lakos, *"Composing Abstractions of Coloured Petri Nets"*. In Proc. of 21st Int. Conference on Application and Theory of Petri Nets (ICATPN'2000) Aarhus, Denmark, June, 2000, volume 1825 of Lecture Notes in Computer Science, pages 323-342.

[4]   F. Stappert, P. Altenbernd. "Complete Worst-Case Execution Time Analysis of Straight-line Hard Real-Time Programs". *Journal of Systems Architecture*, 46(4): 339-355. Kluwer Academic Publishers 2000.

[5]   E. Lee et al., "Overview of the Ptolemy Project". Technical Memorandum UCB/ERL M01/11, Dept. EECS, University of California, Berkeley, 2001.

[6]   "The Moses Project". http://www.tik.ee.ethz.ch/~moses/.

[7]   Jakob Engblom, Andreas Ermedahl. "Modeling Complex Flows for Worst-Case Execution Time Analysis". *Proc. 21st IEEE Real-Time Systems Symposium (RTSS'00)*. 2000.

[8]   Jakob Engblom, Andreas Ermedahl, Friedhelm Stappert. "A Worst-Case Execution-Time Analysis Tool Prototype for Embedded Real-Time Systems". *Workshop on Real-Time Tools*. Aalborg, Denmark. 2001.

[9]   Luigi Carro, Flavio R. Wagner, Marcio Kreutz, Marcio Oyamada. "A Design Methodology For Embedded Systems Based On Multiple Processors". *Proc. Distributed And Parallel Embedded Systems, Paderborn, Germany*. Kluwer Academic Publishers. 2001.

[10]   J. Gustafsson. *Analyzing Execution-Time of Object-Oriented Programs Using Abstract Interpretation*. PhD thesis, Department of Computer Systems, Information Technology, Uppsala University, May 2000.

Model checking robustness to desynchronization

Jean-Pierre Talpin

INRIA *project* ESPRESSO - IRISA, *Campus de Beaulieu, 35042 Rennes cedex, France*

Abstract   The engineering of an everyday broader spectrum of systems requires reasoning on a combination of synchronous and asynchronous interaction, ranging from co-designed hardware-software architectures, multi-threaded reactive systems to distributed telecommunication applications. Stepping from the synchronous specification of a system to its distributed implementation requires to address the crucial issue of desynchronization: how to preserve the meaning of the synchronous design on a distributed architecture ? We study this issue by considering a simple SCCS-like calculus of synchronous processes. In this context, we formulate the properties of determinism and of robustness to desynchronization. To check a specification robust to desynchronization, we consider a canonical representation of synchronous processes that makes control explicit. We show that the satisfaction of the property of determinism and of robustness to desynchronization amounts to a satisfaction problem which consists of hierarchically checking boolean formula.

1.   INTRODUCTION

Synchronous programming [1, 3, 8] has been proposed as an efficient approach for a trusted design of reactive systems. It has been widely publicized, using the idealized model of zero-time computation and instantaneous broadcast communication. Distributed systems do not, however, obey this idealized picture of perfect synchrony: computations and communications take time, interaction topologies evolve during service. Synchrony and asynchrony are fundamentally different concepts in nature. Asynchrony is traditionally relevant for reasoning on distributed algorithms and for modeling non-determinism, failure, mobility. It meets a natural implementation by networked point-to-point communication. Synchrony is specific to the design of reactive systems and digital circuits. In this context, timeless logical concurrency and determinism are suitable hypothesis. A synchronous design hypothesis consists of assuming that communications and computations are instantaneous between successive execution steps of a system. Making this hypothesis allows one to focus on the logics of the system, which is characterized by synchronization and causal relations between events. By contrast, time prevail in an asynchronous design. Communication time is to be taken into account at every level of the system under design. Nonetheless, an everyday broader range of software development areas requires reasoning on a combination of synchronous and asynchronous interaction at the different architectural levels of the system under design. Relevant practical examples are co-designed hardware-software architectures, reconfigurable embedded devices, multi-threaded reactive systems components on real-time virtual machines and operating systems, distributed and reactive telecommunication applications on fault-tolerant middle-ware. In summary, every system whose design requires robustness to latency, to distribution, to threading. In the present article, we formulate the issue of robustness in the algebraic and operational setting of a calculus of synchronous processes. We start by giving a structured operational semantics of synchronous processes. Then, we characterize the synchronous and desynchronized traces of synchronous processes. We probe the minimality and adequacy of this setting by formulating the properties of determinism (defined by the equivalence between the synchronous (internal) and asynchronous (external) observations) and of robustness to desynchronization (defined by the mutual acceptability of desynchronized traces by synchronous processes). To check desynchronization correct, we consider a representation of processes in terms of polynomials dynamical equations over the ring $\mathbb{Z}/3\mathbb{Z}$. We show that the satisfaction of the properties of determinism and of robustness to desynchronization is amenable to model-checking the corresponding invariant expressed as a (vector of) constraint(s) over $\mathbb{Z}/3\mathbb{Z}$.

2.   COMMUNICATING SYNCHRONOUS PROCESSES

In the signal calculus, a process p consists of elementary actions await $x(u)$ and emit $x(u)$ combined using synchronous composition $p \times q$ and non-deterministic choice $p+q$. We use an infinite countable set of names to denote processes $f \in \mathcal{F}$, signals $x, y \in \mathcal{X}$ and variables $v, w \in \mathcal{V}$ (we assume $\mathcal{F}$, $\mathcal{X}$ and $\mathcal{V}$ disjoint). Meta-variables are noted $c \in \mathbb{B} = \{tt, ff\}$ for constants, $m, n \in \mathcal{N} = \mathcal{X} + \mathcal{V}$ for names and $u \in \mathcal{U} = \mathcal{V} + \mathbb{B}$ for parameters. We write $\tilde{n}$ for a sequence of names. The actions await $x(u)$ and emit $x(u)$ implement synchronous broadcast communications (a denotes the prefix await or emit of an action). The action emit $x(u)$ immediately broadcasts the value u along the signal x. The action await $x(u)$ instantaneously receives a value along the signal x and expect this value to match u. The silent action nil is defined by rec $f()$.next $f()$. Simultaneous actions p and q are combined using synchronous composition $p \times q$ and non-deterministic choice $p+q$. Restriction $(n)p$ limits the scope of a signal or variable n to a process p. The evolution of a process in time is modeled by recursion and unit delay. A recursive process rec $f(v).p$ consists of a process p, a parameter (v) and a name f. Its recursive call with the actual parameter u is written $f(u)$ and prefixing it by next delays its execution in time.

$$p, q ::= \text{nil} \mid \text{await } x(u) \mid \text{emit } x(u) \mid p \times q \mid p{+}q \mid (n)p \mid (\text{rec } f(v).p)(u) \mid f(u) \mid \text{next } p$$

We write $p[x/y]$ for the substitution of y by x in p and dom S for the domain of a substitution S. We write $\text{fv}(p) \subset \mathcal{N}$, $\text{dv}(p) \subset \mathcal{X}$ and $\text{rv}(p) \subset \mathcal{V}$ for the set of free names, defined signals and receiving variables of a process. In particular, $\text{rv}(\text{await } x(v)) = \{v\}$, $\text{rv}(\text{emit } x(u)) = \text{rv}(\text{await } x(c)) = \text{rv}(f(u)) = \emptyset$ and $\text{dv}(\text{await } x(u)) = \text{dv}(\text{emit } x(u)) = \{x\}$. The *operational semantics* of processes p is formally defined by the structural relation $p \equiv q$ and by the transition relation $p \overset{e}{\to} q$. The structural equivalence relation $p \equiv q$ gives a structure of sets to $(\mathcal{P}, +)$ and of monoid to $(\mathcal{P}, \times, \text{nil})$.

$$
\begin{array}{lll}
p \times (q \times r) \equiv (p \times q) \times r & p{+}q \equiv q{+}p & (m)p \equiv (n)(p[n/m]) \quad {}^{n \notin \text{fv}(p)} \\
p{+}(q{+}r) \equiv (p{+}q){+}r & p \times q \equiv q \times p & p \times (n)q \equiv (n)(p \times q) \\
(n)\text{nil} \equiv \text{nil} \quad p \times \text{nil} \equiv p{+}p \equiv p & (n)(m)p \equiv (m)(n)p & p{+}(n)q \equiv (n)(p{+}q)
\end{array}
$$

In the present article, we exclusively consider tail-recursive processes, by syntactically limiting the number of guarded recursive calls next $f\tilde{u}$ which may occur within the body p of a recursive process definition rec $f\tilde{v}.p$. The relation $\mathcal{T}_1$ (resp. $\mathcal{T}_0$) accepts exactly the processes p which have at most one (resp. zero) delayed recursive call per choice branch.

$$
\begin{array}{llllll}
\dfrac{}{\mathcal{T}_0[\text{await } x(u)]} & \dfrac{}{\mathcal{T}_0[\text{nil}]} & \dfrac{\mathcal{T}_0[p] \; \mathcal{T}_0[q]}{\mathcal{T}_0[p \times q]} & \dfrac{\mathcal{T}_0[p] \; \mathcal{T}_1[q]}{\mathcal{T}_1[p \times q]} & \dfrac{\mathcal{T}_0[p]}{\mathcal{T}_1[p]} & \dfrac{\mathcal{T}_i[p]}{\mathcal{T}_i[(n)p]}
\end{array}
$$

$$
\begin{array}{llll}
\dfrac{}{\mathcal{T}_0[\text{emit } x(u)]} & \dfrac{}{\mathcal{T}_1[\text{next } f(u)]}
\end{array}
$$

$$
\begin{array}{llll}
\dfrac{\mathcal{T}_i[p] \quad p \equiv q}{\mathcal{T}_i[q]} & \dfrac{\mathcal{T}_i[p]}{\mathcal{T}_i[\text{next } p]} & \dfrac{\mathcal{T}_i[p]}{\mathcal{T}_i[(\text{rec } f\tilde{v}.(\text{next } f(v){+}p))(u)]} & \dfrac{\mathcal{T}_i[p] \; \mathcal{T}_i[q]}{\mathcal{T}_i[p{+}q]} \quad {}^{\forall i \in \{0,1\}}
\end{array}
$$

The term e in the transition relation $p \overset{e}{\to} q$ is a partial function of $\mathcal{E} = \mathcal{X} \rightharpoonup (\mathbb{B} + \{\bot\})$ which represents the *context or environment* of a process at the instant at which an execution step from p to q takes place. It defines the *events* that occur at that instant. An event $x \mapsto u$ of e (also written $e(x) = u$) denotes the value u of the signal x at the (logical) instant denoted by e. The signal x can alternatively be regarded as absent at a given instant. This is denoted by associating x to the mark $\bot$ in e (i.e. $e(x) = \bot$). The rule **(eqv)** embeds the structural equivalence relation in the operational semantics. It allows for the syntactic recombination of processes. The semantics of $(n)p$ depends on whether n is a receiving variable or a defined signal of p. In **rule (sub)**, the variable v is substituted by a value c in p. The meaning of restriction $(x)p$, **rule (let)**, is to limit the scope of the signal x to the expression p. We write e_x for e without x (i.e. $x \notin \text{dom } e_x$). **Rule (com)** is the axiom of communication. An atomic action await $x(c)$ or emit $x(c)$ reduces to nil by associating x to c in the environment. **Rule (or)** is the choice rule. It enables a transition from $p{+}q$ to r with e if a transition from the branch p to r with e is possible. **Rule (and)** implements synchronous composition. It stipulates that the simultaneous transitions from p to p' with e and from q to q' with f are valid if and only if the environments e and f agree on the assignment to all signals shared by

p and q (they behave like p and q for all other signals). This is specified by the side-condition to the construction of the composition $e \uplus f$ of the partial functions e and f, which requires $e(x)$ and $f(x)$ to be equal for all x shared by $\mathrm{dom}\, e$ and $\mathrm{dom}\, f$, and by further requires e and f to be defined at least on all defined signals of p and q. **Rule (fix)** handles the call $(\mathrm{rec}\, f(v).p)(c)$ to a recursive process f. As in SCCS, it requires a transition of p where (v) is substituted by (c) and f is unfolded by $\mathrm{rec}\, f(v).p$. **Rule (nxt)** is the axiom for unit delay $\mathrm{next}\, p$. Its sole purpose is to put off the execution of p until the next step. It requires an empty environment.

$$
\text{(eqv)} \;\; \frac{p \equiv p' \;\; p' \xrightarrow{e} q' \;\; q' \equiv q}{p \xrightarrow{e} q} \qquad
\text{(sub)} \;\; \frac{p[c/v] \xrightarrow{e} q}{(v)p \xrightarrow{e} q} \qquad
\text{(let)} \;\; \frac{p \xrightarrow{e} q}{(x)p \xrightarrow{e_x} (x)q}
$$

$$
\text{(or)} \;\; \frac{p \xrightarrow{e} r}{p+q \xrightarrow{e} r} \qquad
\text{(and)} \;\; \frac{p \xrightarrow{e} p' \;\; q \xrightarrow{f} q'}{p \times q \xrightarrow{e \uplus f} p' \times q'} \;\; \forall x \in dv(p) \cap dv(q) \begin{pmatrix} x \in \mathrm{dom}\, e \cap \mathrm{dom}\, f \\ e(x)=f(x) \end{pmatrix}
$$

$$
\text{(fix)} \;\; \frac{(p[c/v])[\mathrm{rec}\, f(v).p/f] \xrightarrow{e} q}{(\mathrm{rec}\, f(v).p)(c) \xrightarrow{e} q} \qquad
\text{(com)} \;\; \mathrm{await}\, x(c) \xrightarrow{x \mapsto c} \mathrm{nil} \quad \mathrm{emit}\, x(c) \xrightarrow{x \mapsto c} \mathrm{nil}
$$

$$
\text{(nxt)} \;\; \mathrm{next}\, p \xrightarrow{\emptyset} p \qquad \text{(nil)} \;\; \mathrm{nil} \xrightarrow{e} \mathrm{nil} \;\; {}^{(\forall x \in \mathrm{dom}\, e,\, e(x)=\perp)}
$$

Example 1 *In order to understand the semantics of the signal calculus, let us for instance consider a simple counting process* even, *which samples every even occurrence of the signal* x *by emitting the signal* y. *The state of the counter is stored in place of the actual parameter of the process. The process* even *makes use of the syntax* $[u = v]$ *for guards. A transition across a guard* $[u = v]$ *is allowed iff the names* u *and* v *match. A guard can be defined using a receiving name* w *and a pair of intermediate ports* x *and* y: $[u = v] \equiv (w, x, y)(\mathrm{emit}\, x(u) \times \mathrm{emit}\, y(v) \times \mathrm{await}\, x(w) \times \mathrm{await}\, y(w))$. *If the signal* x *is present (e.g.* $e = x()$) *then the process* even *reacts to it by unfolding its definition (by substituting the name* even *by the term* f_{even}) *and by substituting its formal parameter* u *by its actual parameter* ff. *Then, the only possible choice of the process* even *is to match* e_1 *with the action of awaiting* x *and to cross the process* p_1 *guarded by the tautology* $[ff = ff]$, *yielding* $\mathrm{nil} \times (\mathrm{nil} \times \mathrm{next}\, f_{even}(tt)) \equiv \mathrm{next}\, f_{even}(tt)$. *Finally, the process becomes* $f_{even}(tt)$ *after stepping the* next *statement, changing the value of its actual parameter to* tt, *in order to emit* y *next time the signal* x *occurs, by forcing the selection of the branch* p_2.

$$
\overbrace{\mathrm{rec}\, \mathrm{even}(u). \left(\mathrm{next}\, \mathrm{even}(u) + \left(\mathrm{await}\, x() \times \left(\begin{matrix} ([u = ff] \times \mathrm{next}\, \mathrm{even}(tt)) \\ + ([u = tt] \times \mathrm{next}\, \mathrm{even}(ff) \times \mathrm{emit}\, y()) \end{matrix} \right) \right) \right)}^{f_{even}} (ff)
$$

$$
\underbrace{}_{p_1} \qquad \underbrace{}_{p_2}
$$

$$
\mathrm{next}\, f_{even}(ff) + (\mathrm{await}\, x() \times (([ff = ff] \times \mathrm{next}\, f_{even}(tt)) + ([ff = tt] \times \mathrm{next}\, f_{even}(ff) \times \mathrm{emit}\, y())))
$$

3.   DETERMINISM AND ROBUSTNESS

In order to determine under which properties the synchronous design of a system can safely be distributed on an asynchronous network, we establish formal connections between synchrony and asynchrony. We start by giving a formal definition of the properties under consideration. A *synchronous trace* consists of an infinite countable series of events that correspond to the successive transitions of a process in time.

Definition 1 (trace) *If $p_0 = p$ and $p_i \overset{e_i}{\to} p_{i+1}$ for all $i > 0$ then the series $t = (e_i)_{i \geq 0}$ is a* synchronous trace *of p. We say that p and q are* synchronously equivalent, *written $p \simeq q$, iff p and q accept the same synchronous traces.*

An *desynchronized trace* $T \in \hat{\mathcal{E}}^*$ is obtained from a synchronous trace t by removing absence: $E, F \in \hat{\mathcal{E}} = \mathcal{X} \rightharpoonup \mathbb{B}$. Formally, $\hat{\emptyset} = \emptyset$, $\widehat{e, x \mapsto \bot} = \hat{e}$, $\widehat{e, x \mapsto c} = (\hat{e}, x \mapsto c)$. Hence $\hat{t} = (\hat{e_i})_{i \geq 0}$ is the asynchronous abstraction of a trace $t = (e_i)_{i \geq 0}$. Intuitively, a desynchronized trace respects the ordering of events along signals in time, but discards reference to absence. We relate desynchronized traces T with the partial order relation $\leq$. The ordering of traces under the relation $\leq$ renders the loss of a global reference of time incurred by the removal of absence yet preserves the causal ordering between successive events. For all $T = (E_i)_{i \geq 0}$, we write $\mathrm{dom}\, T = \cup_{i \geq 0} \mathrm{dom}\, (E_i)$.

Definition 2 (desynchronization) *T' is a* desynchronization *of T, written $T \leq T'$, iff $T \leq^x T'$ holds for all $x \in \mathrm{dom}\, T \cap \mathrm{dom}\, T'$. We write $ET \leq^x FT'$ iff, either $x \notin \mathrm{dom}\, F$ and $ET \leq^x T'$, or $E(x) = F(x)$ and $T \leq^x T'$.*

It is useful to relate synchronous traces under the equivalence relation of stuttering. A transition $p \overset{e}{\to} q$ is stuttering iff it is silent i.e. $\mathrm{im}\, e = \{\bot\}$. We write $t \lesssim t'$ iff t and t' only differ by silent transitions e. In the remainder, we write $\mathcal{S}[\![p]\!]$ for the set of synchronous traces of a process p, $\hat{\mathcal{S}}[\![p]\!] = \{\hat{t} \mid t \in \mathcal{S}[\![p]\!]\}$ for its asynchronous abstraction and $\mathcal{S}_{\lesssim}[\![p]\!]$ for its equivalence classes for the relation of stuttering $\lesssim$. We write $\mathcal{A}[\![p]\!] = \{T \mid t \in \mathcal{S}[\![p]\!] \wedge \hat{t} \leq T\}$ for the set of desynchronized (or admissible) traces of a process p.

Definition 3 *Traces et and $e't'$ are* stuttering-equivalent, *written $et \lesssim e't'$ iff $\mathrm{im}\, e = \{\bot\}$ and $t \lesssim e't'$; or $\mathrm{im}\, e' = \{\bot\}$ and $et \lesssim t'$; or $e = e'$ and $t \lesssim t'$.*

The property of determinism is defined by the equivalence between the internal (synchronous) and external (asynchronous) observations of a process. A process is said deterministic iff, given an asynchronous trace T of p, it is possible to reconstruct a synchronous trace t that is unique modulo stuttering and such that $\hat{t} \leq T$ (i.e. the trace t of p accepts T). This means that every asynchronous trace of the process corresponds to a synchronous trace in which the successive instants of the execution have been reconstructed from the values of signals present in the asynchronous trace. Concretely, a deterministic process forms a unit of compilation: interaction with a deterministic process does not require any knowledge on its internal clock.

Definition 4 *p is deterministic iff $\forall T \in \mathcal{A}[\![p]\!]$, $\exists! t \in \mathcal{S}_{\lesssim}[\![p]\!]$, $\hat{t} \leq T$.*

The property of robustness to desynchronization is defined by the considering the desynchronized traces of p, q and $p \times q$. The desynchronized composition of p and q can be modeled by $\mathcal{A}[\![p]\!] \cap \mathcal{A}[\![q]\!]$ because the intersection of $\mathcal{A}[\![p]\!]$ and $\mathcal{A}[\![q]\!]$ corresponds to the traces T which are both desynchronizations of a synchronous trace t of p (i.e. $t \in \mathcal{S}[\![p]\!]$ and $\hat{t} \leq T$ hence $T \in \mathcal{A}[\![p]\!]$) and of a synchronous trace of trace t' of q (i.e. $t' \in \mathcal{S}[\![p]\!]$ and $\hat{t}' \leq T$ hence $T \in \mathcal{A}[\![q]\!]$). If $\mathcal{A}[\![p \times q]\!] = \mathcal{A}[\![p]\!] \cap \mathcal{A}[\![q]\!]$ holds, this means that all desynchronized traces T of $p \times q$ uniquely correspond via the relations $\hat{t} \leq T$ and $\hat{t}' \leq T$ to a pair of synchronous traces of p and q. Hence, the desynchronized interaction between p and q is deterministic, just as it is for synchronous composition, and no global synchronization is not required to achieve it. The property of robustness ensures that the synchronous design of a system supports the distribution of its components over an asynchronous network without loss of semantics.

Definition 5 *$p \times q$ is robust to desynchronization iff $\mathcal{A}[\![p \times q]\!] = \mathcal{A}[\![p]\!] \cap \mathcal{A}[\![q]\!]$*

In order to verify that a synchronous process is deterministic, or that a pair of synchronous processes is robust to desynchronization, we make use of the tool SIGALI [9]. SIGALI is a model-checker that implements resolution techniques on systems of equations expressed in the $\mathbb{Z}/3\mathbb{Z}$ ring. In SIGALI, a system equations characterizes a set of solutions for the states and events of a process. The resolution technique consists of manipulating the equation system, instead of the solution sets, in order to avoid the enumeration of state-spaces. In order to model the behavior of a synchronous process, we encode each of its actions by an equation $\phi = \psi$ over $\mathbb{Z}/3\mathbb{Z}$. In either arms of this equation, a signal or variable n is encoded by its possible states: 0 if it is absent, 1 if it is present and true, -1 if it is present and false. Formula ϕ and ψ are composed by multiplication $\phi.\psi$ (ϕ and ψ), addition $\phi + \psi$ (ϕ or ψ) and subtraction $\phi - \psi$ (ϕ and not ψ). We write $x^2 = x.x$ for the clock of the signal x (it tells whether x is present or absent). A primed variable v' denotes the next value of v. A scored name v_0 denotes the initial value of v. Composition $\Phi \wedge \Psi$ and scope-restriction $\exists n.\Phi$ define the translation of a synchronous process into a system of equations in $\mathbb{Z}/3\mathbb{Z}$ that describes the evolution of the defined signals $\tilde{x} = \mathrm{dv}(p)$ and receiving variables $\tilde{v} = \mathrm{rv}(p)$ of a process p in time. In this section, we identify the term $\tilde{x}$ (resp. $\tilde{v}$) to an event represented by a vector of $\mathbb{Z}/3\mathbb{Z}^{|\mathrm{dv}(p)|}$ (resp. a state of $\mathbb{Z}/3\mathbb{Z}^{|\mathrm{rv}(p)|}$). We write $X \subset \mathbb{Z}/3\mathbb{Z}^{|\mathrm{dv}(p)|}$ (resp. $V \subset \mathbb{Z}/3\mathbb{Z}^{|\mathrm{rv}(p)|}$) for a set of events and states. The function $G_p(\tilde{x})$ defines the guard or clock of the process p. The process p is active iff its clock $G_p(\tilde{x})$ equals 1. The function $I_p(\tilde{v})$ defines an initial assignment of values to variables $\tilde{v}$ which must equal 0. The constraint $C_p(\tilde{x}, \tilde{v})$ defines an assignment of values to signals $\tilde{x}$ and variables $\tilde{v}$ which must always equal 0. The transition function $T_p(\tilde{x}, \tilde{v})$ defines the next values $\tilde{v}'$ of the variables $\tilde{v}$ in p as a function of the current values of signals $\tilde{x}$ and variables $\tilde{v}$.

$$\phi, \psi ::= 0 \mid 1 \mid -1 \mid n \mid v' \mid v_0 \mid \phi.\psi \mid \phi + \psi \mid \phi - \psi \quad \text{(formula)}$$
$$\Phi, \Psi ::= (\phi = \psi) \mid \Phi \wedge \Psi \mid \exists n.\Phi \quad \text{(equation)}$$
$$(I_p(\tilde{v}) = 0, \; T_p(\tilde{x}, \tilde{v}) = \tilde{v}', \; G_p(\tilde{x}) = 1, \; C_p(\tilde{x}, \tilde{v}) = 0) \quad \text{(constrained transition system)}$$

SIGALI [9] uses the theory of algebraic geometry and, in particular, operations on varieties, ideals and morphisms, in order to define and prove properties of systems such as liveness and invariance. Let $X \subset \mathbb{Z}/3\mathbb{Z}^{|\mathrm{dv}(p)|}$ a set of events, $V \subset \mathbb{Z}/3\mathbb{Z}^{|\mathrm{rv}(p)|}$ a set of states and consider the quotient ring of polynomial functions $\mathcal{A}[XV] = \mathbb{Z}/3\mathbb{Z}[XV]/(X^3 - X, V^3 - V)$. An ideal of the sets of events X and states V in $\mathcal{A}$ is defined by $\mathcal{I}(XV) = \{\phi \in \mathcal{A}[XV] \,|\, \forall(\tilde{x}, \tilde{v}) \in X \times V, \phi(\tilde{x}, \tilde{v}) = 0\}$. It represents the set of equations which have the solution XV. Reciprocally, to any system of equations Φ, the variety $\mathcal{V}(\Phi) = \{(\tilde{x}, \tilde{v}) \in X \times V \,|\, \forall\phi \in \Phi, \phi(\tilde{x}, \tilde{v}) = 0\}$ represents the set of states and events acceptable by Φ. There exists a direct correspondence between ideals and variety: $\mathcal{V}(\mathcal{I}(XV)) = XV$ and $\mathcal{I}(\mathcal{V}(\langle\Phi\rangle)) = \langle\Phi\rangle$ where $\langle\Phi\rangle$ is the set of linear combinations of the system of equations Φ. As a consequence, an ideal can be represented by a single equation, its principal generator. To capture the evolution of a system, one regards the transition function T as a morphism of $(\mathbb{Z}/3\mathbb{Z})^{|\mathrm{fv}(p)|} \to (\mathbb{Z}/3\mathbb{Z})^{|\mathrm{rv}(p)|}$ that defines post-conditions. The associated comorphism $T^* \in (\mathbb{Z}/3\mathbb{Z})^{\mathrm{rv}(p)|} \to (\mathbb{Z}/3\mathbb{Z})^{|\tilde{\mathrm{fv}}(p)|}$ defines the pre-conditions by $T^*(\phi(\tilde{v})) = \phi(T_i(\tilde{x}, \tilde{v}))_{1 \le i \le \|\mathrm{rv}(p)|}$ for any $\phi \in (\mathbb{Z}/3\mathbb{Z})^{|\mathrm{rv}(p)|}$ (The series $(T_i)_{0 < i \le |\mathrm{rv}(p)|}$ are the components of T). Many properties of systems of equations can be verified using operations of varieties, ideals, morphisms and comorphisms. One important is liveness. We say that a system is alive iff it cannot reach a state from which no transition can be taken (a deadlock). We henceforth restrict the study of further properties to such systems, in which all trajectories are infinite. It is proved in [9] that the liveness of a system under the set of constraints C can be stated as $T^*(\langle C\rangle \cap \mathbb{Z}/3\mathbb{Z}[V]) \subseteq \langle C\rangle$. It is implemented by a fixed-point iteration algorithm.

Definition 6 (liveness) *Let p be a process characterized by (I, T, G, C). A state $\tilde{v} \in (\mathbb{Z}/3\mathbb{Z})^{|\mathrm{rv}(p)|}$ is alive if there exists an event $\tilde{x} \in (\mathbb{Z}/3\mathbb{Z})^{|\mathrm{dv}(p)|}$ s.t. $C(\tilde{x}, \tilde{v}) = 0$. A set of states W is alive iff every state $\tilde{v} \in W$ is alive. A system is alive iff, for all $(\tilde{x}, \tilde{v})$ s.t. $C(\tilde{x}, \tilde{v}) = 0$, $T(\tilde{x}, \tilde{v})$ is alive.*

The second property of interest in the present article is invariance. The tool SIGALI allows to verify other properties, such as invariance under control, reachability and attractivity [9]. It is proved in [9] that the invariance of a property represented by a set of states W can be stated as $T^*(\mathcal{I}(W)) \subseteq \langle C\rangle + \mathcal{I}(W)\mathbb{Z}/3\mathbb{Z}[XV]$.

Definition 7 (invariance) *Let p be a process characterized by (I, T, G, C). A subset of state $W \subset (\mathbb{Z}/3\mathbb{Z})^{|\mathrm{rv}(p)|}$ is invariant iff for every $\tilde{v} \in W$ and every $\tilde{x} \in (\mathbb{Z}/3\mathbb{Z})^{|\mathrm{dv}(p)|}$ s.t. $C(\tilde{x}, \tilde{v}) = 0$, the state $T(\tilde{x}, \tilde{v})$ is in W.*

The recursive function $\Phi[\![p]\!]$ translates a tail-recursive process p into the system of equations (I, T, G, C) that characterizes its control. It is defined by induction on the structure of p. For a recursive definition rec $f(v).p$, we associate the formal parameter v to f by scoring v with f. The system of equations $\Phi[\![p]\!]$ is a point-wise translation of the meaning of the process p, as specified by the relation $p \rightarrow^e q$. In the rule for synchronous product $p \times q$, we write $T_{p\uparrow\tilde{x}}$ for the completion of T_p to the signals $\tilde{x}$ which are present in q and absent from p. Since T_p is, by construction, of the form $\wedge_i(\phi_i.T_p^i)$, the completion of T_p by the signals $\tilde{x}$ is defined by the completion of all T_p^i with $y = 0$, for all $y \in \tilde{x}$ and not referenced in T_p^i: $(\wedge_i\phi_i.(T_p^i))_{\uparrow\tilde{x}} = \wedge_i\phi_i.(T_p^i \wedge (\wedge_{y \in \tilde{x}\backslash fv(T_p^i)}(y = 0)))$. In the rule for non-deterministic choice $p+q$, we identify $\phi.(\psi = \psi')$ to $\phi.\psi = \phi.\psi'$ for ϕ a clock and $v = \phi \wedge v = \psi$ to $v = \phi.\psi$. The requirement of determinism between the branches p or q of the choice is rendered by imposing the constraint $\phi_p.\phi_q = 0$. We write $[\![u]\!]$ for the encoding of a parameter u in $\mathbb{Z}/3\mathbb{Z}$: $[\![v]\!] = v$, $[\![tt]\!] = 1$, $[\![ff]\!] = -1$.

$$\Phi[\![\text{await } x(c)]\!]=((), x = [\![c]\!], 1 - (x - [\![c]\!])^2 = 1, ())$$
$$\Phi[\![\text{await } x(v)]\!]=((), x = v, x^2 = 1, ())$$
$$\Phi[\![\text{emit } x(u)]\!]=((), x = [\![u]\!], x^2 = 1, ())$$
$$\Phi[\![p \times \text{next } f(u)]\!]=\Phi[\![p]\!] \wedge ((), v^{f\prime} = [\![u]\!], (), ())$$
$$\Phi[\![((\text{rec } f(v^f).(\text{next } f(v^f)+p))(u)]\!]=\Phi[\![p]\!] \wedge \left(v_0^f = [\![u]\!], (), (), ()\right)$$

$$\Phi[\![p \times q]\!] = \exists\tilde{m}\tilde{n}.\begin{pmatrix} I_p \wedge I_q \\ T_{p\uparrow\tilde{x}} \wedge T_{q\uparrow\tilde{x}} \\ \phi_p = 1 \\ C_p \wedge C_q \wedge (\phi_p - \phi_q = 0) \end{pmatrix} \qquad \Phi[\![(n)p]\!]=\exists n.(\Phi[\![p]\!])$$

where

$$\Phi[\![p+q]\!] = \exists\tilde{m}\tilde{n}.\begin{pmatrix} \phi_p.I_p \wedge \phi_q.I_q \\ \phi_p.T_p \wedge \phi_q.T_q \\ \phi_p + \phi_q = 1 \\ C_p \wedge C_q \wedge (\phi_p.\phi_q = 0) \end{pmatrix}$$

$$\Phi[\![p]\!]=\exists\tilde{m}. (I_p, T_p, \phi_p = 1, C_p)$$
$$\Phi[\![q]\!]=\exists\tilde{n}. (I_q, T_q, \phi_q = 1, C_q)$$
$$\tilde{x}=\text{dv}(p) \cap \text{dv}(q),$$
$$\tilde{m} \cap \tilde{n}=\emptyset$$

The function $\Phi[\![p]\!]$ is sound because any synchronous trace t of p satisfies Φ_p. We write $\vec{e}$ the representation of e as a vector of $\mathbb{Z}/3\mathbb{Z}^{|\text{dv}(p)|}$ of indexes in $\text{dv}(p)$, so that for all $x \in \text{dv}(p)$, $\vec{e}_x = [\![e(x)]\!]$.

Theorem 1 (soundness) *If $t \in S[\![p]\!]$ then, for all $i \geq 0$ and transition $p_i \xrightarrow{t_i} p_{i+1}$, the state $T_{p_i}(\vec{t_i}, \tilde{v})$ is alive for any $\tilde{v}$ s.t. $I_{p_i}(\tilde{v}) = 0$.*

Checking determinism of a live process p and the robustness of a pair of deterministic processes p and q to desynchronization reduces to checking the invariants $\mathcal{D}_p$ and $\mathcal{R}_{p \times q}$. The criterion $\mathcal{D}_p$ for checking that a process p is deterministic consists of ensuring that the clock of every signal y in p is computable starting from the clock of the main signal x (i.e. $y^2 \leq x^2$). This allows for a unique flow of control to be iteratively reconstructed from the value of the boolean signals present at a given instant. The criterion $\mathcal{R}_{p \times q}$ for checking robustness to desynchronization consists of ensuring that, whenever a shared signal x is present in p (resp. q), then there is enough control expressed by the master clock ϕ_q (resp. ϕ_q) of q to ensure that it cannot be absent from q (resp. p), hence the assertion $(\phi_p.\phi_p^x).(\phi_q.(1 - \phi_q^x)) = 0$. We write ϕ_p^x for the clock of x in p (i.e. either ϕ s.t. C_p implies $x^2 = \phi$ or else x^2).

Theorem 2 (determinism and robustness) *A live process p is deterministic if there exists $x \in \mathrm{dv}(p)$ s.t. C_p implies $x^2 = \phi_p$ and s.t. T_p satisfies the invariant $(\mathcal{D}_p)$. The product of deterministic processes $p \times q$ is robust to desynchronization if $T_{p \times q}$ satisfies the invariant $(\mathcal{R}_{p \times q})$.*

$$(\mathcal{D}_p) : C_p \wedge \left(\bigwedge_{y \in \mathrm{dv}(p)} (y^2 \leq x^2) \right) \qquad (\mathcal{R}_{p \times q}) : \bigwedge_{x \in \mathrm{dv}(p) \cap \mathrm{dv}(q)} \left(\begin{array}{l} ((\phi_p . \phi_p^x) . (\phi_q . (1 - \phi_q^x)) = 0) \\ \wedge ((\phi_q . \phi_q^x) . (\phi_p . (1 - \phi_p^x)) = 0) \end{array} \right)$$

Example 2 (determinism and robustness) *Let us reconsider the process* even *and its synchronous composition with the process* if *below. Using the criterion* $\mathcal{D}$, *one can checks that each process is deterministic: the signals y and z satisfy $y^2 \leq x^2$ and $z^2 \leq x^2$ (i.e. x is the main clock of* even *and* if*); the choice branches of* even *and* if *have exclusive clocks (i.e. $y^2.(1 - (v + 1)^2) = 0$ or $(1 - (v - 1)^2).(1 - (v + 1)^2) = 0$ for* even *and $y^2.z^2 = 0$ or $(1 - (w - 1)^2).(1 - (w + 1)^2) = 0$ for* if*). To check that the composition of* even *and* if *is robust to desynchronization, it is additionally necessary to check that the criterion $\mathcal{R}$ is meet. This amounts to showing that y is present in* even *iff it is present in* if*, i.e. that $(x^2.\phi_p^y).(x^2.(1 - \phi_q^y)) = 0$ and that $(x^2.\phi_q^y).(x^2.(1 - \phi_p^y)) = 0$ (i.e. that $(x^2).(1 - (v - 1)^2).(w - 1)^2 = 0$ and $(x^2).(1 - (w - 1)^2).(v - 1)^2 = 0$) is an invariant of* $p \times q$. *This requires fixed-point iteration using the method proposed in the previous section.*

$$\mathrm{rec\ even}(v).\mathrm{next\ even}(v) + \left(\mathrm{await}\ x() \times \left(\begin{array}{l} [v = \mathit{ff}] \times \mathrm{next\ even}(\mathit{tt}) \\ + [v = \mathit{tt}] \times \mathrm{next\ even}(\mathit{ff}) \times \mathrm{emit}\ y() \end{array} \right) \right) (\mathit{ff})$$

$$\mathrm{rec\ if}(v).\mathrm{next\ if}(w) + \left(\mathrm{await}\ x() \times \left(\begin{array}{l} [w = \mathit{tt}] \times \mathrm{next\ if}(\mathit{ff}) \times \mathrm{emit}\ y() \\ + [w = \mathit{ff}] \times \mathrm{next\ if}(\mathit{tt}) \times \mathrm{emit}\ z() \end{array} \right) \right) (\mathit{ff})$$

4.   RELATED WORK

The first formal address of *desynchronization* can be found in [6], where precise relations between well-clocked synchronous functional programs and the subset of Kahn-networks are established, and shown to be amenable to bufferless evaluation. In [7], the author considers the distribution of synchronous automata on asynchronous networks using FIFO-buffered broadcast communications. In [4], a model for the distribution of synchronous programs on distributed architectures is introduced which uses low-level non-blocking one-place buffers. In [2], Ban extensive analysis of the links between synchrony and asynchrony is presented in the context of synchronous transition systems (STS) and the general notion of isochrony is introduced. In [12], an implementation of communicating reactive systems with multiple clocks using ESTEREL is presented. In [5], the theory of latency-insensitive designs is resented as a foundation of a new methodology to design very large digital systems by assembling blocks of existing *intellectual property* (IP).

5.   CONCLUSION

We have formulated the problem of checking the robustness of synchronous processes to desynchronization in the algebraic and operational setting of a calculus of communicating synchronous processes: the signal calculus. We have shown that this problem reduces to model-checking invariants expressed as constraints in the algebraic framework of $\mathbb{Z}/3\mathbb{Z}$. Relevant applications for this method are found in the synchronous engineering of systems whose design requires attention on robustness to latency, to distribution, to threading: co-designed hardware-software architectures, (reconfigurable) embedded devices, multi-threaded reactive systems components on real-time virtual machines, distributed and reactive telecommunication applications.

References

[1] A. BENVENISTE, P. LE GUERNIC, C. JACQUEMOT. Synchronous programming with events and relations: the SIGNAL language and its semantics. In *Science of Computer Programming*, v. 16, 1991.

[2] A. BENVENISTE, B. CAILLAUD, P. LE GUERNIC. From synchrony to asynchrony. *International Conference on Concurrency Theory*. Lectures Notes in Computer Science. Springer, 1999.

[3] G. BERRY, G. GONTHIER. The ESTEREL synchronous programming language: design, semantics, implementation. In *Science of Computer Programming*, v. 19, 1992.

[4] G. BERRY, E. SENTOVICH. An Implementation of Constructive Synchronous Constructive Programs in Polis. *Formal Methods in Systems Design 17(2)*. Kluwer Academic Publisher, 2000.

[5] L.P. CARLONI, K.L. MCMILLAN, A.L. SANGIOVANNI-VINCENTELLI. Latency Insensitive Protocols. In *International conference on computer-aided verification*. Lectures Notes in Computer Science n. 1633. Springer, 1999.

[6] P. CASPI. Clocks in dataflow languages. In *Theoretical Computer Science*, v. 94. Elsevier, 1992.

[7] P. CASPI, A. GIRAULT, C. JARD. Distributed reactive systems. In *International Conference on Parallel and Distributed Computing Systems*. ISCA, 1994.

[8] N. HALBWACHS, P. CASPI, P. RAYMOND, D. PILAUD. The synchronous data-flow programming language LUSTRE. In *Proceedings of the IEEE*, v. 79(9). IEEE, 1991.

[9] H. MARCHAND, E. RUTTEN, M. LE BORGNE, M. SAMAAN. Formal Verification of SIGNAL programs: Application to a Power Transformer Station Controller. *Science of Computer Programming*, v. 41(1), pp. 85–104, 2001.

[10] R. MILNER. Calculi for synchrony and asynchrony. In *Theoretical Computer Science*. Elsevier, 1983.

[11] PNUELI, A., SHANKAR, N., SINGERMAN, E. Fair transition systems and their liveness proofs. In *International Symposium on Formal Techniques in Real-time and Fault-tolerant Systems*. Lecture Notes in Computer Science. Springer, 1998.

[12] RAJAN, B., SHYAMASUNDAR, R., K. Modeling distributed embedded systems in multiclock ESTEREL. In *Conference on Formal Description Techniques for Distributed Systems and Communication Protocols*. Kluwer, October 2000.

A Semi-Formal Method to Verify Correctness of Functional Requirements Specifications of Complex Systems

Nihal Kececi
Department of Computer Science
Université du Québec à Montréal
Software Engineering Management Research Laboratory
nkececi@lrgl.uqam.ca

Wolfgang A. Halang
Computer Engineering and Real Time Systems
Faculty of Electrical Engineering FernUniversitat
Wolfgang.Halang@FernUni-Hagen.de

Alain Abran
École de Technologie Supérieure - ETS
1100 Notre-Dame Ouest, Montréal, Canada H3C 1K3
abran.alain@uqam.ca

Abstract: Many standards mandating verification of requirements correctness do not comprehensively state what information should be captured and used for verification and quality assurance activities. Therefore, a wide range of methods, from simplistic checklists to comprehensive formal methods, is used to verify correctness of system and software requirements. In this paper, a semi-formal method to verify functional requirements using a graphical logic-based structured architecture referred to as Graphical Requirement Analysis is proposed and illustrated with a case study. Its architecture allows to trace functional system requirements and to show correctness (non-ambiguity, consistency, completeness) of specifications. The support of graphical system engineering descriptions greatly facilitates to simulate requirement specifications and designs. Such capability is believed by many to be an essential aspect of developing and assuring the quality of highly complex systems requiring high integrity.

Keywords: Requirements engineering; functional correctness, verification; quality; modular programming; functional decomposition; modeling of complex embedded systems specifications.

1.   INTRODUCTION

To deal with inconsistent and incomplete requirements, many approaches to software requirement analysis have been developed over the last few years. According to a survey and assessment of conventional software V&V methods [1], requirements and design techniques consist of four major classes and various subclasses. These major classes of techniques and the total number of individual techniques are as follows:

Formal methods are based on a translation of requirements into mathematical form. Eight different techniques were discovered.

Semi-formal methods are based on the expression of requirement specifications in a special requirement language. Eleven different individual techniques were discovered.

Reviews and Analysis (informal method) are based on reviews by special personnel of the adequacy of the requirement specification according to a pre-established set of criteria and detailed checklists and procedures. Seven different techniques were identified.

Tracing and Analysis Techniques of the requirements are based on matching of each unique requirement element to design elements and then to the elements of the implementation. Two different techniques were identified.

However, there are some common problems not fully tackled by most of these techniques:
Formalizing the requirements (in total or in part) presents a new viewpoint. But formalization itself cannot guarantee to detect error, nor can it prove that the requirement specification is correct.
Mathematical verification of requirements does not seem to greatly simplify development.

Testing a specification will not find all the possible errors. For instance, combinatory effects are unlikely to be encountered.

Also, the ultimate interrelationship of the various aspects of the specification may not be known until the implementation is complete.

Graphical Requirement Analysis (GRA) is a framework that describes a function into graphical logic based with a structured form. To build a module (functional block) it requires identifying inputs, outputs and logic into multilevel hierarchy. The architecture of GRA methodology provides for functional system requirements traceability as well as correctness (ambiguity, consistency, completeness) of specification. GRA support of system-engineering descriptions in a graphical mode greatly facilitates simulating requirements specification and designs [2-3]. Such capability is believed by many to be an essential aspect of developing and assuring the quality of highly complex systems requiring high integrity. In this paper benefits of such a graphical functional module, and lessons learned from implementation is presented.

Summary: In this section, we highlight some limitations of the V&V Requirements and Design Methods. In section 2, we present the key aspects of the proposed GRA approach, in section 3, a case study of its implementation, and observations in section 4.

2.   GRAPHICAL REQUIREMENT ANALYSIS (GRA)

The GRA framework [3-4] was proposed as a verification and integration tool for software and system specification as well as design specification. It aims to visualize functional specifications (input-process-output-interfaces) using a logic-based graphical framework. Figure 1 illustrates the framework's modelling philosophy for complex embedded systems. A software module performing a specific action is invoked by the appearance of its name in an expression; it may receive an input value and return a single value. When a module (function) is decomposed, sub-modules (functions) can be identified. The GRA framework's core concept is derived from the functional modelling methodology and a function's basic characteristics as defined in the standard IEEE 610.12 [5]. However, it also captures some system and software engineering approaches such as hierarchy theory, success failure mechanism, function block diagram paradigm, modular programming, and the COSMIC-FFP [6] functional size measurement procedure.

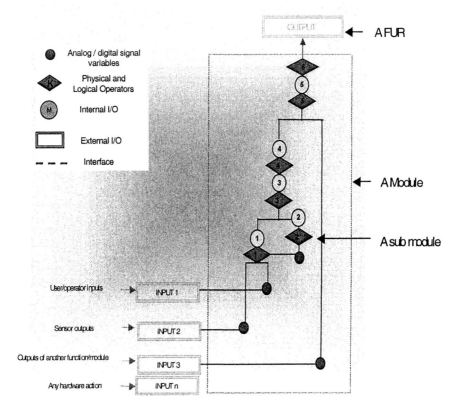

Figure 1. Modelling philosophy of the GRA framework for complex embedded systems.

1. Identifying a functional user requirement FUR (effort at requirement specification level)

* Hierarchy theory and the success-failure paradigm are used to break a FUR into sub-modules (components) to facilitate design and development (design level effort).

* Inputs/outputs and algorithms of modules are identified (architectural level effort).

2. Defining the relationships in the hierarchies, which show connections between different nodes of a hierarchy or between nodes of two different hierarchies. The relations can be characterized as:
* Logical (Boolean) connectivity relationships are used to show the redundancy and connectivity between various components; in a logical relationship the states of the input and output nodes are binary.

* Physical connectivity relationships refer to node relations described by some physical laws, and are mostly represented by a continuum of values; accordingly, physical relationships are analogue in nature.

* Uncertain (fuzzy) connectivity relationships are appropriate when relationships are not fully known, or physical descriptions are either not available or uncertain.

3. Defining the operators based on the relationships between sub-modules

* Physical operators are presented in the GRA framework with a macro function such as mathematical, data/time, string, aggregate, data type conversion, array, system, graph, hierarchy and database functions.

* Logical operators in an expression describe the type of action the expression should perform, or how the expression should compare or relate two values, e.g., arithmetical, text, comparison, and conditional or loop control operators.

Summary: Graphical Requirement Analysis (GRA) is a methodology *for translating textual functional requirements to logic based graphical format* that may or may not be understood exactly, where the user is responsible for telling the developer what the functional requirements should do or vice versa (where the developer is responsible for verifying correctness of functional requirements).

3.   CASE STUDY

The detailed FUR descriptions for a pressure controller were transformed from textual to graphical form. This process captured functional traceability as well as data and component traceability analysis. To build the pressure control function within the GRA architecture, the following documents had to be reviewed to ensure that all related functions were indeed included (and traceable backward and forward): the "Software Requirements Specification" (SRS) to understand what the function was supposed to do, the "Software Design specification" (SDR) to identify the control blocks to be used, the "Theory Manual" to understand the pressure control system procedure, and the "User Guide" to identify the system variables and the I/O of the pressure controller. The main purpose of this reviewing process is to identify typical characteristics of functional user requirements: outputs, inputs (user inputs, system variables, other function outputs), arithmetical operators or algorithms describing how these input variables provide desired output values, and the control procedure defining the relationships between inputs, outputs and logical operators. Figure 2 illustrates the results of this review process for a FUR of a pressure control system: user inputs are identified from the SRS, system variables and the function's output are identified from the User Guide, algorithms are identified from the Software Design Specification, and the control procedure is identified from the Theory   Manual.

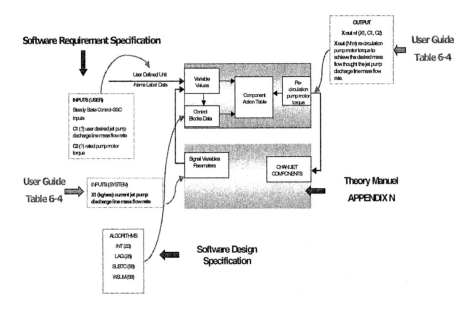

Figure 2. Pressure Control Function Procedure

The pressure control function detects the main steam line pressure X1, and adjusts the main steam line valve to achieve the pressure set point. Its implementation is composed of so-called control blocks, which are operators producing output parameter signals out of input parameter signals. Output signals can then be used as input parameters to other control blocks. Thus, a control procedure for a component action can be constructed by coupling control block operators in series and in parallel. Here, five control blocks are used to compose the pressure controller. Their types and identification numbers are Integration-INT23, Subtraction-SUBTC56, First-order lag-LAG26, weighted summation-WSUM59 and Addition-ADD3 yielding the Pressure controller-204. Figure 3 presents the functionality of the pressure control system within the GRA framework. It clearly shows all attributes of a Functional User Requirement.

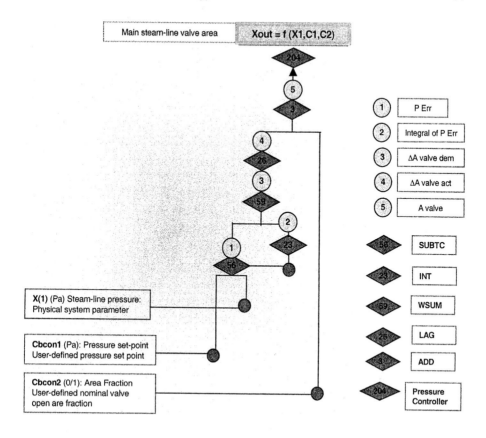

Figure 3. Verification of pressure control FUR within the GRA framework

4. LESSON LEARNED

From this case study one can draw several conclusions beneficial in addressing the problems of functional requirements correctness. Being based on checking listed items and criteria, formal review and inspection techniques are able to identify functional information at certain levels, but not functionalities in full detail. Table 1 states the levels of information detectable by GRA and by review and inspection. Review and Inspection criteria are selected from [7-8]. Software quality engineers, configuration managers, and project managers evaluating products and projects can all use the information provided within the GRA framework. Even though we emphasize here verification of software requirements specifications, software never runs alone, but always as part of a larger system consisting of other software products with which it has interfaces, of hardware, humans and workflow. The GRA framework captures both system and software specifications and design attributes. Therefore, it lends itself as an alternative method to establish the requirements' correctness of embedded systems.

Table 1. Formal review and inspection versus GRA

REVIEW & INSPECTION "Criteria"	GRA Analysis Functional Description	GRA Analysis Graphical Description
Inputs	External Inputs	
Output	External Output	
Algorithms -	Logic, Control Block	
-	Internal Input	
-	Internal Output	
Interfaces	Interfaces	
Time	Data Flow Sequence	

REFERENCES

1. Groundwater E.H., Miller L.A., Mirsky S.M. 1995. *Guidelines for the Verification and Validation of Expert System Software and Conventional Software. Survey and Document of Expert System Verification and Validation Methodologies* NUREG/CR-6316, SAIC-95/1028. Vol.1-7.

2. Kececi N., Abran A., *"An Integrated Measure for Functional Requirements Correctness"*. IWSM2001, 11th International Workshop on Software Measurement, August 28-29, 2001 Montréal (QC) Canada

3. Kececi, N., M. Modarres, and C. Smidts. "System Software Interface for Safety-Related Digital I&C Systems", European Safety and Reliability – ESREL'99 Conference, TUM Munich- Garching, September 13-17, 1999. http://www.lrgl.uqam.ca/team/membres.html

4. Kececi N., Abran A. "Analyzing, Measuring and Assessing Software Quality in a Logic Based Graphical Model" 4th International Conference on Quality and Dependability-QUALITA 2001, 22-23 March 2001 Annecy France.

5. Kececi N., M. Li, C. Smidts, C. "Function Point Analysis: An Application to a Nuclear Reactor Protection System," International Topical Meeting on Probabilistic Safety Assessment –PSA'99, Washington, DC, August 22-25, 1999.

6. IEEE Std. 610.12-1990. *IEEE Standards Glossary of Software Engineering Standards.*

7. Abran, A., Desharnais, J.M., Oligny, S., St-Pierre, D. and Symons, C. "COSMIC-FFP Measurement Manual, version 2.1", Software Engineering Management Research Laboratory, Université du Québec à Montréal, Montreal, Canada, 2001. Downloadable at http://www.lrgl.uqam.ca/ffp.html

8. IEEE 830-1998, "IEEE Guide to Software Requirements Specification".

9. IEEE 1012-1998, "IEEE Standards for software Verification and Validation Plan"

Towards Design Verification and Validation at Multiple Levels of Abstraction[*]
Correct Design of Distributed Production Control Systems

Holger Giese, Martin Kardos, and Ulrich Nickel
University of Paderborn, Germany

Abstract: The specification of software for distributed production control systems is an error prone task. The ISILEIT project aims at the development of a seamless methodology for the integrated design, analysis and validation of such embedded systems. Suitable subsets of UML and SDL for the design of such systems are therefore identified in a first step. The paper then focuses on how we use a series of formal semantics of our design language to enable the effective evaluation of software designs by means of validation and verification. We will further explain how the use of multiple Abstract State Machine meta-models permits simulation and model checking at different levels of abstraction

Key words: embedded system design, UML, SDL, formal semantics meta-models, ASM, formal verification, model-checking, validation, code generation

1.   INTRODUCTION

In today's embedded systems, the fraction of hardware, which realizes the functionality of the system is decreasing and replaced by decentralized and complex software systems. Modeling approaches and software development processes and techniques for the production of correct, stable and flexible adjustable distributed embedded software systems are thus required. Integrating software development into the overall system engineering process is one step. Moreover, analysis techniques, that fulfill the additional requirements system engineering brings into the game, have to be embedded.

[*]   This work has been supported by the German Research Foundation (SPP1064, GA 456/7).

The ISILEIT project [1] aims at the development of a seamless methodology for the integrated design, analysis and validation of distributed embedded production control systems. Its focus is the (re-)use of accepted techniques which should be improved with respect to formal analysis, simulation and automatic code generation.

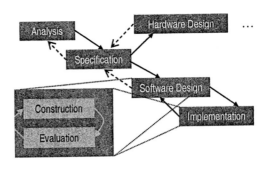

Figure 1. Construction and evaluation during design

The methodology defined in the ISILEIT project consists of several consecutive design steps. Together, they form a consistent development process that covers all aspects of system design, i.e. analysis, specification, design and implementation (see partially Figure 1). At the beginning of every system design process, a core system specification has to be developed. This specification then further serves as an input to the design process for the different system elements including the software. In the overall process, effects backwards are somehow required to be minimal (dashed arrows), because changes in hardware would result in high costs. In contrast, in the later phases of the software design and implementation, we have a more iterative process where construction and evaluation alternates to ensure that the specification is met (see Figure 1).

To describe embedded system software during the _construction_ phase with UML [2] and SDL [3], we integrated SDL block diagrams, UML statecharts and collaboration diagrams [4] to form an executable specification language that allows us to specify reactive behaviour as well as complex application specific object structures.

The _evaluation_ of a particular possible incomplete software model against the requirements imposed on its behaviour is also part of the design. A number of informal techniques, such as reviews or walkthroughs can be used. However, informal approaches often fail to identify the misconceptions related to the complex interplay of multiple processes and timing effects present in distributed embedded systems. Therefore, in our approach also the formal system evaluation is supported in form of (1) verification by means of model-checking and (2) validation by means of simulation or testing. We adapted Abstract State Machine (ASM) [5] as a formalism that helps us to tailor the system models to any given or desired level of abstraction by means of different meta-models. This allows us to manipulate the designed system state-space and its size. The *validation* in our approach is based on this series of formal semantics with different levels of abstraction or running the generated executable code. For the automatic *formal verification* of a designed system model, a transformation is used, that generates a corresponding low-level model-checking description based on its ASM model and it's meta-model. Such a low-level model description can be model-checked and the results are propagated back to the design view.

In Section 2 the design language and modelling activities during the construction are described. The support for multiple levels of abstraction and the verification are then considered in Section 3. In Section 4 the validation of a design at different abstraction levels and the implementation model are presented. The paper closes with an overview about related work in Section 5 and a conclusion and outlook on future work (Section 6).

2.   CONSTRUCTION

The major emphasis of the ISILEIT project lies on (re-)using existing techniques, which are used by engineers in industry for the specification of the control software of a material flow system (MFS). Thus, during the first phase of the project, we analysed our case study to identify which specification technique is most suitable for which part of the system specification with respect to the domain of production control systems. Figure 2 shows the schematic overview of the regarded system.

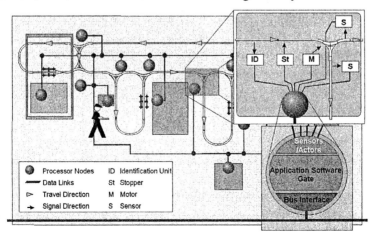

Figure 2. Schematic overview of the material flow system (MFS)

The material flow system, which connects several manual working stations and robots, is track based. The MFS is controlled by processor nodes, which are connected by a field bus. Every node is responsible for a part of this distributed system. In Figure 2, a processor node is depicted, which controls a gate. The sensors and actors are connected with the node by the process interface.

The here described system can be seen as a system of asynchronously communicating automata. Therefore, we decided to take SDL block diagrams to specify the overall static communication structure. SDL is a design language, which is well known from the area of telecommunication engineering. It has a well defined formal semantics, which captures the asynchronous communication aspects of our system [6]. We integrated parts of the available ASM specification of SDL into the formal semantics of our design language. Figure 3 shows the result of the first step. It is a simple SDL block diagram showing the system as a network of logical control nodes – processes running in parallel and communicating via signal channels.

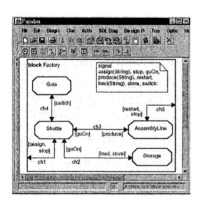
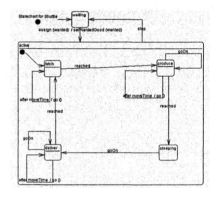

Figure 3. SDL block diagram of the   *Figure 4.* Simple statechart describing the
       sample factory   shuttle control

We derive the initial (UML) class diagram of the desired system. At this, each process(type) identified in the SDL block diagram generates a class in the class diagram. In addition, each signal received by a process in an SDL block diagram creates a signal method in the corresponding class. In the next step, we can now refine this class diagram by adding further classes, which the active classes use to implement their functionality.

SDL block diagrams (and the derived class diagrams) specify the number of signals which are understood by the different processes. Now, we have to define how each process will react on these signals. Thus, for each process class, one has to provide a statechart modelling the general process behaviour. These statecharts should at least cover all signals that are understood by/declared in the corresponding process class. In the engineering field, usually SDL process diagrams are used for this purpose. However, we prefer statecharts here, due to the additional expressive power of nested states and history states. Following this idea, we assign to every active class (process) one UML statechart that describes its behaviour. Figure 4 shows the statechart that specifies the behaviour of the process (or active class) shuttle.

In current practice, when the detailed behaviour of the system needs to be specified, pseudo-code or statements of the target language are used. To avoid this in our approach, we decided to use a well defined subset of activity and collaboration diagrams which are combined to so called story diagrams. We use this visual programming language for the specification of do, entry, exit, and transition actions within the statecharts.

To conclude, we integrate SDL block diagrams, statecharts and collaboration diagrams to form an executable design language that allows us to specify reactive behaviour as well as complex application specific object-structures. A more detailed description of the presented methodology can be found in [4].

3.   VERIFICATION

ASM serves in our approach as method that integrates all modelling languages combined in our graphical modelling language at one common semantic base. In other words, it models the semantics of this language. In our approach, we model distributed control systems with possibly complex behaviours that imply large system state spaces. Therefore, different levels of abstraction can be achieved using multiple ASM meta-models and only a single ASM encoding of the concrete system model (see Figure 5). The ASM meta-models are operating as interpreters of the specific ASM encoding of the concrete system model and automatically abstract from not required details.

The verification of a designed system model is based on the generation of an ASM encoding of the system model. This is done by filling in the unspecified data structure (domains and functions) of an ASM meta-model. For example, the sets of states, transitions and events of the statechart from Figure 4 form the data structure that will be filled in ASM meta-model I. The required complete ASM model is derived by combining an ASM meta-model with the specific ASM encoding of a concrete system. This complete ASM model is further fed into a transformation process that generates a corresponding low-level model-checking description, e.g., a description in a specific model-checker language [7] or a particular BDD representation. Finally, this low-level model description can be model-checked and the results can be propagated back to the system design.

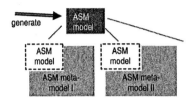

Figure 5. Constructing the ASM model

In the most abstract view (meta-model I), we consider the processes just in a black box view. We abstract from the concrete communication behavior assuming only the non deterministic occurrence of events that are accepted by the process, i.e. the rule *selectEvent* in Figure 6 left-hand-side non-deterministically choose one element from the set of all events acceptable by the process (cf. pessimistic abstraction [8]). Also the state representation together with actions and guards are ignored in order to hide any implementation details. Therefore, the guard evaluation rule *evalGuard* chooses non-deterministically between true or false and action evaluation rule *executeAction* executes just an empty rule *skip*. Thus, the result is an ASM meta-model describing the semantics of a statechart ignoring all implementation details related to events, guards and actions.

```
                I                    │                  II

// evaluate specified guard          │// evaluate specified guard
evalGuard(g as Guard) as Boolean     │evalGuard(g as Guard) as Boolean
= choose v in {true, false}          │= choose v in {true, false}

// select event for dispatching      │// select event for dispatching
// chose any possible one            │// take first event (FIFO queue)
selectEvent() as Event =             │selectEvent(a as Agent) as Event =
choose e in acceptable_events        │a.events:= tail(a.events)
                                     │return a.events(0)
// execute specified action          │
executeAction(a as Action) = skip    │// execute specified action
                                     │executeAction(a as Action) = skip
```

Figure 6. Sample of abstractions in ASM meta-model I and II

It is obvious that this level is sometimes too abstract and restricts the set of verifiable properties to a small subset working just without any bounds to implementation (e.g., the object hierarchy), but it serves as a good base for the further refinement going down from this very high-level ASM meta-model to more detailed ones. This abstract view can be step by step refined taking into account more and more details of the implementation: variables, the object structure etc.

In Figure 6 right-hand-side the *selectEvent* rule of the refined meta-model II is presented. In contrast to the version of the meta-model I, this time the concrete event queue is contained in the model and therefore the statechart is evaluated in a more detailed context. The rule extracts the first element *e* of the event queue *events* and returns it. Note that the *selectEvent* rule of the meta-model II is indeed a refinement of that one of the meta-model I, because for any event *e* stored as first element in the event queue *events* will hold *e* ∈ *acceptable_events*. This refinement only holds w.r.t. safety properties, because the abstraction does not include the question whether an event occurs at all.

The rather abstract view of each component provided by the meta-model I occurs during the system design, when the internal component behavior is designed. For the overall architecture and coordination between shuttles and the rest of the system at least the possible event processing has to be added. While in the first case the supported abstraction levels permit to verify each object independently as an autonomous process reacting to the stimuli of its environment, the more detailed view requires that the process for a reasonable subset of all objects are embedded into a network of interconnected, communicating processes. Therefore, the processes will be mapped to a set of distributed ASM agents which are interconnected (see Agent parameter *a* of *selectEvent* in Figure 6 right-hand-side). At the more detailed levels the communication is therefore refined by replacing the non-deterministic occurrences of event by explicit managed event queues. In the end, we refine the base ASM meta-model by taking into account all implementation details, such as objects and their hierarchy, action execution semantics, guard evaluation against object attributes and their values. All these features extend our basic ASM, i.e. its data structure by defining new ASM domains and functions and its operation set in terms of new ASM rule definitions.

Other ASM meta-models may take other details into account that cover the dynamic semantics of statecharts and the non active local OO data structures and would therefore allow verifying properties which depend on the particular objects and their attribute values. Also, the communication can be refined by additional ASM agents that cover the more sophisticated behavior of communication channels. Note, we will adapt parts of the already existing ASM semantics for SDL [6]. The resulting lattice of different abstraction levels w.r.t. refinement permits to verify specific properties at an appropriate abstraction level. These different views also reflect the transition from an architectural design (coarse-grain design) to a fine-grain-design and the details of an implementation.

4.   VALIDATION

The design phase is characterized as the alternation of the construction and evaluation activities. To allow the designer to evaluate his or her system model in practice, besides verification validation in form of simulation and testing is common. To also support the evaluation of abstract and incomplete designs, we can use the same lattice of abstractions built by our ASM meta-models. Simulation of our ASM generated models is possible, because we use the AsmL [9] specification language, which supports the transformation of AsmL specifications into C++ code. Therefore, the executable ASM models permit the designer to validate his or her intermediate designs using the same abstraction levels presented for the verification.

When the final system should be simulated including all implementation details, it is however not useful to use a full ASM formalization with all its inherent overhead. Instead, the execution and debugging of the generated code is more appropriate (cf. [10]). Such an approach closes the gap between the simulation system (interpretation) and the software running on the real system following the "test what you run, run what you test" philosophy. Our attempt is to use the same code both, for the simulation as well as for the running system. So, the generated code has to be free from any kind of debug information and could be optimised for *special* issues, i.e. speed or space optimisations. To observe the running system, we developed a graphical debugging tool called 'Dobs' (Dynamic Object Browsing System). Dobs is able to display the internal object structure of a running Java virtual machine by various graphical representations [11].

5.   RELATED WORK

The verification of software by means of model-checking is usually only feasible, when instead of the full system model of the software system an abstraction with reasonable state space size is considered. This process usually happens in an additional abstraction step that precedes the application of model-checking tools (cf. [12]). Therefore, experimenting with multiple abstraction levels to identify a one, which provides the required feasible model containing the relevant properties, is rather cumbersome without tool support.

Several projects exist, that deal with SDL or UML based design and verification by means of model-checking (e.g., [13][14][15][16][17]). For example, an approach dealing with model-checking SDL specifications can be found in [13]. It also transforms the SDL code into an intermediate representation which can be further verified using a model-checker. However, these approaches, in contrast to the presented work, support only a single abstraction level.

Concerning simulation as the validation method, in contrast to other tools and simulation environments, e.g. STATEMATE [18], PROGRES [19], which simulate the specified model like an interpreter, our approach is to generate source code out of the specification and observe the running system.

In commercial sphere, there are already some tools available that allow the user to check his or her UML or SDL specification on a very high abstraction level. The case tool Telelogic TAU [20] is an example for the practical use of different abstraction levels for the validation of SDL specifications. On the highest abstraction level for example, only atomic transitions between the states of a process diagram are considered. The validation can then be refined by considering more details, like intermediate states or signals that take an undefined amount of time for their transmission. However, the focus of TAU lies on the verification of SDL specifications with limited possibilities concerning complex object structures and their modification.

6.   CONCLUSION AND FUTURE WORK

In this paper, we presented an approach, of how to construct and evaluate distributed and embedded systems. The construction of the system is realized by using a well defined design language, which employs a subset of UML and SDL. The presented support for multiple levels of abstractions by means of different ASM meta-models enables the validation and verification during the ongoing design. Therefore, it permits analysis of even incomplete models of complex distributed embedded system software and thus helps to cope with the state-space explosion problem. The presented approach is further embedded into the overall design methodology developed within the ISILEIT project for distributed production control systems.

REFERENCES

[1] Integrative Specification of Distributed Control Systems for the Flexible Automated Manufacturing (ISILEIT), German Research Foundation (DFG) program "integrative specification of engineering applications".: http://www.upb.de/cs/isileit/

[2] Booch, G., Rumbaugh, J., Jacobson, I.: The Unified Modeling Language User Guide. Addison-Wesley, Reading, Massachusetts, 1999.

[3] ITU-T Recommendation Z.100, Specification and Description Language (SDL), International Telecommunication Union (ITU), Geneva, 1994 + Addendum 1996.

[4] H.J. Köhler, U. Nickel, J. Niere, and A. Zündorf. Integrating UML Diagrams for Production Control Systems. In Proc. of the 22th Int. Conf. on Software Engineering (ICSE), Limerick, Irland. ACM Press, 2000.

[5] Y. Gurevich: Evolving Algebras 1993: Lipari Guide; E. Börger (Eds.): Specification and Validation Methods; Oxford University Press, 1995.

[6] R. Eschbach, U. Glässer, R. Gotzhein, M. von Löwis and A. Prinz: Formal Definition of SDL-2000 - Compiling and Running SDL Specifications as ASM Models. Journal of Universal Computer Science (J.UCS), October 2001.

[7] G. del Castillo and K. Winter: Model checking support for the ASM high-level language. In S. Graf and M. Schwartzbach, editors, Proc. on 6th Int. Conf. TACAS 2000, volume 1785 of LNCS, pages 331-346, 2000.

[8] H. Giese, M. Kardos and U. Nickel: Integrating Verification in a Design Process for Distributed Production Control Systems. Second International Workshop on Integration of Specification Techniques for Applications in Engineering (INT 2002). Grenoble, France, April 2002. (to appear)

[9] http://www.research.microsoft.com/fse/AsmL/default.html

[10] James D. Arthur, Markus K. G"oner, Kelly I. Hayhurst, and C. Michael Holloway. Evaluating the Effectiveness of Independent Verification and Validation. IEEE Computer, 32(10):79-83, October 1999.

[11] U. Nickel and J. Niere, 'Modelling and Simulation of a Material Flow System', in Proc. of Workshop 'Modellierung' (Mod), Bad Lippspringe, Germany, Gesellschaft für Informatik, 2001.

[12] William Chan, Richard J. Anderson, Paul Beame, Steve Burns, Francesmary Modugno, David Notkin, and Jon D. Reese. Model Checking Large Software Specifications. IEEE Transactions on Software Engineering, 24(7):498-520, 1998.

[13] M. Bozga, J.Cl. Fernandez, L. Ghirvu, S. Graf, J.P. Krimm, L. Mounier, J. Sifakis. IF: An Intermediate Representation for SDL and its Applications. Proceedings of SDL-FORUM 1999 (Montreal, Canada) June 1999..

[14] Gihwon Kwon. Rewrite Rules and Operational Semantics for Model Checking UML Statecharts. In Andy Evans, Stuart Kent, and Bran Selic, editors, Proceedings of the third International Conference on the Unified Modeling Language (UML 2000), York, UK, volume 1939, page 528ff. Springer Verlag, October 2000.

[15] Johan Lilius and Iván Porres Paltor. vUML: a Tool for Verifying UML Models. In Proceedings of the 14th IEEE International Conference on Automated Software Engineering, Cocoa Beach, Florida, USA, 1999.

[16] Prasanta Bose. Automated Translation of UML Models of Architectures for Verification and Simulation Using SPIN. In Proceedings of the 14th IEEE International Conference on Automated Software Engineering, Cocoa Beach, Florida, USA, 1999.

[17] http://www-omega.imag.fr/.

[18] D. Harel, H. Lachover, A. Naamad, A. Pnueli, M. Politi, R. Sherman, A. Shtull-Tauring, and M. Trakhtenbrot. STATEMATE: A Working Environment for the Development of Complex Reactive Systems, IEEE Trans. Soft. Eng., 16, 403-414, 1990, Paderborn, 1999.

[19] A. Schürr, A. J. Winter, A. Zündorf. Graph grammar engineering with PROGRES. In W. Schäfer, Editor, Software Engineering - ESEC '95, LNCS 989, Springer Verlag, 1995.

[20] Telelogic Tau SDL Suite: http://www.telelogic.com

Modeling and Verification of Pipelined Embedded Processors in the Presence of Hazards and Exceptions

Prabhat Mishra, Nikil Dutt
Architectures and Compilers for Embedded Systems (ACES), Center for Embedded Computer Systems, University of California, Irvine, CA 92697, USA

Abstract: Embedded systems present a tremendous opportunity to customize designs by exploiting the application behavior. Due to increasing design complexity deeply pipelined high performance embedded processors are common today. In the presence of hazards and exceptions the validation of pipelined embedded processors is a major challenge. We extend a Finite State Machine (FSM) based modeling of pipelined processors to verify the pipeline specification in the presence of hazards and multiple exceptions. Our approach leverages the system architect's knowledge about the behavior of the pipelined processor, through Architecture Description Language (ADL) constructs, and thus allows a powerful top-down approach to pipeline verification. We applied this methodology to the DLX processor to demonstrate the usefulness of our approach

Key words: Pipeline Verification, Architecture Description Language.

1.   INTRODUCTION

Verification is a major challenge in design and development of programmable embedded systems. It is especially difficult for deeply pipelined high performance processors in the presence of hazards and multiple exceptions. System architects critically need modelling techniques that allow rapid exploration, customization and validation of different processor pipeline configurations, tuned for a specific application domain. Recent approaches on language-driven Design Space Exploration (DSE) [4, 7], use ADL to capture the processor architecture, generate automatically a software toolkit for that processor, and provide feedback to the designer on the quality of the architecture. While some of these approaches [4, 5, 7] captures hazards and interrupts in ADL for specific types of architectures, to our knowledge no previous approach has an explicit way of describing hazards and interrupts for a wide variety of processor and memory architectures [6], and the attendant task of verifying the processor pipeline in the presence of hazards and multiple exceptions. It is important to verify the ADL description of the architecture to ensure the correctness of the software toolkit. The benefits of verification are two-fold. First, the process of any specification is error-prone and thus verification techniques can be used to check for correctness and consistency of specification. Second, changes made to the processor during DSE may result in incorrect execution of the system and verification techniques can be used to ensure correctness of the modified architecture.

The rest of the paper is organized as follows. Section 2 presents related work addressing verification of pipelined processors. Section 3 outlines our approach and the overall flow of our environment. Section 4 presents our FSM based modeling of processors in the presence of hazards and exceptions. Section 5 proposes our verification technique followed by a case study in Section 6. Section 7 concludes the paper.

2.   RELATED WORK

Several approaches for formal or semi-formal verification of pipelined processors have been developed in the past. Theorem proving techniques, for example, have been successfully adapted to verify pipelined processors [2, 14, 16]. However, these approaches require a great deal of user intervention, especially for verifying control intensive designs. Burch and Dill presented a technique for formally verifying pipelined processor control circuitry [1]. This technique has been extended to handle more complex pipelined architectures by several researchers [15, 17]. All the above techniques attempt to formally verify the implementation of pipelined processors by comparing the pipelined implementation with its sequential (ISA) specification model, or by deriving the sequential model from the implementation. On the other hand, in our verification approach, we define a set of properties, and verify the correctness of pipelined processors by testing whether the properties are satisfied using a FSM-based model.

An architecture description language (ADL) driven modeling and validation technique is presented in [11]. Mishra et al. [9] presented an FSM based modeling of pipelined processors with in-order execution and is closest to our approach. Our work extends this model to verify the processor pipeline in the presence of hazards and multiple exceptions.

3.   OUR APPROACH

Figure 1 shows the modeling and validation flow. In our IP library based exploration and verification scenario, the designer starts by specifying the processor description in an ADL. The FSM model of the pipelined processor description is automatically generated from this ADL description. We have defined several properties such as determinism, in-order execution, and finiteness, to ensure that the ADL description of the architecture is well-formed in the presence of hazards and multiple exceptions. Our automatic property checking framework determines if all the necessary properties are satisfied or not. In case of failure, it generates traces so that designer can modify the ADL specification of the architecture. If the verification is successful, the software toolkit (including compiler and simulator) can be generated for design space exploration.

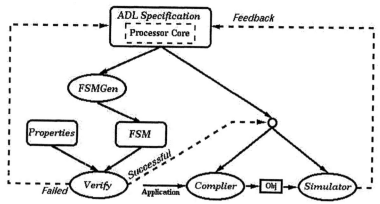

Figure 1. The flow in our approach

4.   MODELING OF PROCESSOR PIPELINES

In this section we describe how we derive the FSM model of the pipeline from the ADL description of the processor. We first explain how we specify hazards, stalls, exceptions, interrupts, and flow conditions in ADL, then we present the FSM model of the processor pipeline using the information captured in the ADL. The detailed description can be found in [13].

4.1   Processor Pipeline Description in ADL

We have chosen the EXPRESSION ADL [8] that captures the structure, behavior, and the mapping between them for the processor pipeline. The ADL description can be used to detect hazards. Structural hazards are captured using reservation tables [3]. Using the same constraint information (regarding sources and destinations) available in RTs the data hazards viz., read-after-write (RAW), write-after-write (WAW), and write-after-read (WAR), can be detected. Control hazards due to branches can have different outcomes depending on how the branch is handled for that architecture. In our framework we treat branch mis-prediction as an exception and the necessary flushing can happen during exception handling.

A functional unit can be *stalled* due to external signals or due to conditions arising inside the processor pipeline. For units, with multiple children the stalling conditions due to internal contribution may differ. For example, the unit $UNIT_{i-1, j}$ in Figure 2 with q children can be stalled when *any* one of its children is stalled, or when *some* of its children are stalled, or when *all* of its children are stalled; or when *none* of its children are stalled. During specification, designer selects from the set (ANY, SOME, ALL, NONE) the internal contribution along with any external signals to specify stall condition for each unit.

A unit is in *normal flow* if it can receive instruction from its parent unit and can send it to its child unit. Typically, a unit performs *nop insertion* when it does not receive any instruction from its parent and its child unit is not stalled. The Program Counter (PC) unit can be *stalled* due to external signals such as cache miss or when the fetch unit is stalled. When a branch is taken the PC unit is said to be in *branch taken* state. The PC unit is in *sequential execution* mode when the fetch unit is in normal flow, there are no external interrupts, and the current instruction is not a branch instruction. A unit is in *exception* condition when it receives an exception or due to internal contribution. We specify exceptions and interrupts in ADL [13].

4.2   FSM Model of Processor Pipelines

This section presents an FSM-based modeling of controllers in pipelined processors. Figure 2 shows a fragment of a processor pipeline. The oval boxes represent units, rectangular boxes represent pipeline latches, and arrows represent pipeline edges. We assume a pipelined processor with in-order execution as the target for modeling and verification. The pipeline consists of N stages. Each stage can have more than one pipeline register. In this paper we call these pipeline registers instruction registers (IR). Let $Stage_i$ denote the i-th stage where $(0 \le i \le N-1)$, and N_i the number of pipeline registers between $Stage_{i-1}$ and $Stage_i$. Let $IR_{i,j}$ denotes an instruction register between $Stage_{i-1}$ and $Stage_i$ $(1 \le j \le N_i)$. During execution the instruction stored in $IR_{i,j}$ is executed at $Stage_i$ and then stored into the next instruction register $IR_{i+1, s+k}$ $(1 \le k \le q)$. In this paper, we define a state of the N-stage pipeline as values of PC and $(N-1) \times \Sigma_{i=1}^{N-1} N_i$ instruction registers.

Let PC(t) and $IR_{i,j}(t)$ denote the values of PC and $IR_{i,j}$ at time t, respectively. Then, the state of the pipeline at time t is defined as

$$S(t) = < PC(t), IR_{1,1}(t), ..., IR_{N-1,N_{N}-1}(t) > \qquad (1)$$

We first describe the conditions for exception (XN), stalling (ST), normal flow (NF), nop insertion (NI), sequential execution (SE), and branch taken (BT) in the FSM model, then we describe the state transition functions possible in the FSM model using these conditions.

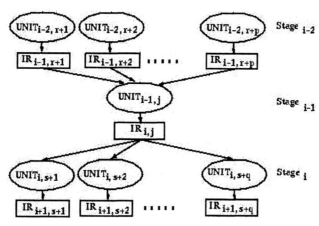

Figure 2. A fragment of a processor pipeline

4.2.1   Modeling Conditions in FSM

Let us assume, every instruction register $IR_{i,j}$ has an exception bit $XN_{IR_{i,j}}$, which is set when the exception condition ($cond^{XN}_{IR_{i,j}}$ say) is true. $XN_{IR_{i,j}}$ has two components as shown in Equation 2. Similarly, the conditions for stall, normal flow, nop insertion (for instruction registers), sequential execution, and branch taken (for PC) are shown in Equation 3-8. Let us assume, BT_{PC} bit is set when the unit completes execution of a branch instruction.

$$cond^{XN}_{IR_{i,j}} = XN_{IR_{i,j}} = XN^{child}_{IR_{i,j}} + XN^{self}_{IR_{i,j}} \qquad (2)$$

$$cond^{ST}_{IR_{i,j}} = ST_{IR_{i,j}}.\overline{XN_{IR_{i,j}}} = (ST^{child}_{IR_{i,j}} + ST^{self}_{IR_{i,j}}).\overline{XN_{IR_{i,j}}} \qquad (3)$$

$$cond^{NF}_{IR_{i,j}} = NF^{parent}_{IR_{i,j}}.NF^{child}_{IR_{i,j}}.\overline{ST^{self}_{IR_{i,j}}}.\overline{XN_{IR_{i,j}}} \qquad (4)$$

$$cond^{NI}_{IR_{i,j}} = NI^{parent}_{IR_{i,j}}.NI^{child}_{IR_{i,j}}.\overline{ST^{self}_{IR_{i,j}}}.\overline{XN_{IR_{i,j}}} \qquad (5)$$

$$cond^{SE}_{PC} = NF^{child}_{PC}.\overline{ST^{self}_{PC}}.\overline{BT_{PC}}.\overline{XN_{IR_{1,j}}} \qquad (6)$$

$$cond^{ST}_{PC} = (ST^{child}_{PC} + ST^{self}_{PC}).\overline{BT_{PC}}.\overline{XN_{IR_{1,j}}} \qquad (7)$$

$$cond^{BT}_{PC} = BT_{PC} + XN_{IR_{1,j}} \qquad (8)$$

4.2.2   Modeling State Transition Functions

In this section, we describe the next state function of the FSM. Let f^{NS}_{PC} and $f^{NS}_{IR_{i,j}}$ $(1 \le i \le N\text{-}1, 1 \le j \le N_i)$ denote next state functions for PC and $IR_{i,j}$ respectively. For PC, we define three types of state transitions as follows.

$$PC(t+1) = f^{NS}_{PC}(S(t), I(t)) = \begin{cases} PC(t) + L & if \quad cond^{SE}_{PC}(S(t), I(t)) = 1 \\ t\arg et & if \quad cond^{BT}_{PC}(S(t), I(t)) = 1 \\ PC(t) & if \quad cond^{ST}_{PC}(S(t), I(t)) = 1 \end{cases} \quad (9)$$

Here, I(t) represents a set of external signals at time t, L represents the instruction length, and *target* represents the branch target address, which is computed at a certain pipeline stage. Similarly, for the instruction registers, $IR_{i,j}$, we define four types of state transitions as follows.

$$IR_{i,j}(t+1) = f^{NS}_{IR_{i,j}}(S(t), I(t)) = \begin{cases} IR_{i-1,r+l}(t) & if \quad cond^{NF}_{IR_{i,j}}(S(t), I(t)) = 1 \\ IR_{i,j}(t) & if \quad cond^{ST}_{IR_{i,j}}(S(t), I(t)) = 1 \\ nop & if \quad cond^{NI}_{IR_{i,j}}(S(t), I(t)) = 1 \\ nop & if \quad cond^{XN}_{IR_{i,j}}(S(t), I(t)) = 1 \end{cases} \quad (10)$$

In the above formulas, *nop* denotes a special instruction indicating that there is no instruction in the instruction register. For the first instruction register the data comes from the instruction memory pointed by the PC.

5.   VERIFICATION OF IN-ORDER EXECUTION

Based on the FSM modeling presented in Section 4, we propose a method to verify the correctness of pipeline controllers with in-order execution. A pipelined processor with in-order execution is correct if all instructions, which are fetched from instruction memory flow from the first stage to the last stage while maintaining their execution order. In this section we describe the properties needed for verifying the in-order execution.

5.1   Determinism Property

The next state functions for all state registers must be deterministic. This property is valid if all the following equations (Equation 11-14) hold. The first two equations mean that, in the next state function for each state register, the flow conditions must cover all possible combinations of processor states S(t) and external signals I(t). The last two guarantee that any two conditions are disjoint for each next state function. Informally, exactly one of the conditions should be true in a cycle for each state register.

$$cond_{PC}^{SE} + cond_{PC}^{BT} + cond_{PC}^{ST} = 1 \qquad (11)$$

$$cond_{IR_{i,j}}^{NF} + cond_{IR_{i,j}}^{ST} + cond_{IR_{i,j}}^{NI} + cond_{IR_{i,j}}^{XN} = 1 \qquad (12)$$

$$\forall x, y(x, y \in \{SE, BT, ST\} \cap x \neq y) \quad cond_{PC}^{x}.cond_{PC}^{y} = 0 \qquad (13)$$

$$\forall x, y(x, y \in \{NF, ST, NI, XN\} \cap x \neq y) \quad cond_{IR_{i,j}}^{x}.cond_{IR_{i,j}}^{y} = 0 \qquad (14)$$

5.2   In-Order Execution Property

In order to guarantee in-order execution, state transitions of adjacent instruction registers must depend on each other. All illegal state transitions of adjacent pipeline stages are described below using Figure 2. An instruction register cannot be in normal flow if all the parent instruction registers (adjacent ones) are stalled. If such a combination of state transitions are allowed, the instruction stored in $IR_{i-1, r+l}$ ($1 \leq l \leq p$) at time t will be duplicated, and stored into both $IR_{i-1, r+l}$ and $IR_{i,j}$ at the next cycle. Therefore, the instruction will be executed more than once. More formally, the Equation 15 should be satisfied.

$$\left| \right|_{l=1} cond_{IR_{i-1,r+l}}.cond_{IR_{i,j}} = \cup \qquad (15)$$

Similarly, if $IR_{i,j}$ flows normally, at least one of its child latches should also flow normally. If all of its child latches are stalled, the instruction stored in $IR_{i,j}$ disappears. The Equation 16 should be satisfied. Similarly, if $IR_{i,j}$ is in nop insertion, at least one of its child latches should not be stalled. The Equation 17 should be satisfied. Similarly, an instruction register cannot be in nop insertion, if previous instruction register is in normal flow. The Equation 18 should be satisfied.

$$cond_{IR_{i,j}}^{NF} \cap_{k=1}^{q} cond_{IR_{i+1,s+k}}^{ST} = 0 \quad (16) \qquad cond_{PC}^{ST}.cond_{IR_{1,j}}^{NF} = 0 \qquad (23)$$

$$cond_{IR_{i,j}}^{NI} \cap_{k=1}^{q} cond_{IR_{i+1,s+k}}^{ST} = 0 \quad (17) \qquad cond_{PC}^{SE} \cap_{j=1}^{N_1} cond_{IR_{1,j}}^{ST} = 0 \qquad (24)$$

$$cond_{IR_{i-1,r+l}}^{NF}.cond_{IRi,j}^{NI} = 0 \quad (18) \qquad cond_{PC}^{BT} \cap_{j=1}^{N_1} cond_{IR_{1,j}}^{ST} = 0 \qquad (25)$$

$$cond_{IR_{i-1,r+l}}^{NI}.cond_{IRi,j}^{NI} = 0 \quad (19) \qquad cond_{PC}^{SE}.cond_{IR_{1,j}}^{NI} = 0 \qquad (26)$$

$$cond_{IR_{i-1,r+l}}^{NF}.cond_{IRi,j}^{XN} = 0 \quad (20) \qquad cond_{PC}^{BT}.cond_{IR_{1,j}}^{NI} = 0 \qquad (27)$$

$$cond_{IR_{i-1,r+l}}^{ST}.cond_{IRi,j}^{XN} = 0 \quad (21) \qquad cond_{PC}^{SE}.cond_{IR_{1,j}}^{XN} = 0 \qquad (28)$$

$$cond_{IR_{i-1,r+l}}^{NI}.cond_{IRi,j}^{XN} = 0 \quad (22) \qquad cond_{PC}^{ST}.cond_{IR_{1,j}}^{XN} = 0 \qquad (29)$$

Similarly, an instruction register cannot be in nop insertion, if previous instruction register is also in nop insertion. The Equation 19 should be satisfied. Finally, an instruction register cannot be in normal flow, stall, or nop insertion if next (child) instruction register is in exception. The Equation 20-22 should be satisfied. Similarly, the state transition of PC must depend on the state transition of $IR_{1,j}$ as shown in Equation 23-29. All the equations (Equation 15-29) must hold to ensure correct in-order execution.

6.   A CASE STUDY

In a case study we successfully applied the proposed methodology to the single-issue DLX [10] processor. We have chosen DLX processor since it has been well studied in academia and has few interesting features viz., fragmented pipelines, multicycle units etc. The DLX processor has five pipeline stages viz., *Fetch* (IF), *Decode* (ID), *Execute*, *Memory* (MEM), and *WriteBack* (WB). The *Execute* stage consists of four parallel execution paths viz., integer ALU (EX), seven-stage multiplier (M1-M7), four-stage floating-point adder (A1-A4) and a multicycle division unit (DIV).

We used the EXPRESSION ADL [8] to capture the structure and behavior of the DLX processor. We captured the conditions for exception, stalling, normal flow, branch taken and nop insertion in the ADL [12]. Using the ADL description, we automatically generated the equations for flow conditions for all the units [12]. The necessary equations for verifying the properties viz., determinism, in-order execution etc., are generated automatically from the given ADL description. The *Eqntott* tool converts these equations in two-level representation of a two-valued Boolean function. We have used *Espresso* to minimize the equations. These minimized equations are analyzed to verify whether the properties are violated or not. The complete verification took 45 seconds on a 333 MHz Sun Ultra-5 with 128M RAM.

Our framework determined that the in-order execution is violated in the presence of an exception in A2 stage of the floating-point adder and generated a simple instruction sequence which violates in-order execution: floating-point addition followed by integer addition. The decode unit issued floating point addition I_{fadd} operation in cycle *n* to floating-point adder pipeline (A1 - A4) and an integer addition operation I_{iadd} to integer ALU (EX) at cycle *n+1*. Due to the exception in A2 stage and our exception model the A1, ID and IF stages got flushed whereas the I_{iadd} operation continued its execution.

We modified the ADL description to incorporate the notion of in-order relationship among units. For example, for EX unit the in-order children are

M2 and A2. Note that, when M3 stage is in exception condition, the M2 stage and it's parent (normal parent M1 and in-order parents EX and A1) stages will be flushed. Similarly, the in-order child for M2 stage is A2 and so on. However, this modeling is not good enough in the presence of multicycle functional units (e.g., DIV unit). The in-order children (parent) information will change depending on how many cycles the division operation is in DIV unit. So we model division unit with n-stages $(D_1, D_2, .., D_n)$, where n is the latency of the division operation, with the assumption that the stage D_i will have the division operation after i cycles and only one stage will have a valid operation at a time. Now we can extend the in-order child concept for multicycle units as well. Now, the in-order children for EX unit are M2, A2 and D2. Similarly, the in-order children for D1 unit are A2 and M2. Since we are considering single-issue machine, two units in the same level will not have valid instruction at the same point in time. For example, M1 and A1 cannot have valid instructions at the same point in time. The in-order execution was successful for this modeling in the presence of a single exception. This modeling is sufficient to handle multiple exceptions where the exception closer to completion has the higher priority. This is due to the fact that the exception closer to completion will flush all the operations above and thereby masks all the exceptions generated at the earlier stages in the pipeline. For example, if there are exceptions in M3 and A1, the exception in M3 will mask the exception in A1 stage. However, this modeling will not work when the exceptions have a fixed priority. If the exception in A1 has higher priority than the exception in M3 and if the current modeling is used, the exception in M3 will be incorrectly selected. To solve this problem we modeled the interrupt handler as described in [13]. Only one interrupt will be selected at a time. Hence, in the presence of fixed priority based multiple exceptions the DLX processor can be verified.

7. CONCLUSION

Embedded systems present a tremendous opportunity to customize designs by exploiting the application behavior. A major challenge has been to efficiently model and verify the complex pipeline behavior during the rapid exploration and customization of embedded systems. This paper proposed an ADL driven modeling and verification technique for pipelined embedded processors in the presence of hazards and multiple exceptions. The FSM model of the pipeline controller is generated automatically from this modeling. Based on the modeling we presented a set of properties that are used in our framework to verify the correctness of the in-order execution of the pipeline. We used the DLX processor as an example to demonstrate the usefulness of our approach. We are extending our modeling and verification technique towards VLIW and superscalar processors.

8.   ACKNOWLEDGMENTS

This work was partially supported by grants from DARPA(F33615-00-C-1632), Hitachi Ltd., and Motorola Inc. We would like to acknowledge Dr. Hiroyuki Tomiyama for his contribution to the validation work.

9.   REFERENCES

[1] J. Burch and D. Dill. Automatic Verification of Pipelined Microprocessor Control. CAV, 1994.

[2] D. Cyrluk. Microprocessor Verification in PVS: A Methodology and Simple Example. Technical Report, SRI-CSL-93-12, 1993.

[3] P. Grun et al. RTGEN: An Algorithm for Automatic Generation of Reservation Tables from Architectural Descriptions. ISSS, 1999.

[4] C. Siska. A Processor Description Language Supporting Retargetable Multi-pipeline DSP Program Development Tools. ISSS, 1998.

[5] M. Freericks. The nML Machine Description Formalism. TR SM-IMP/DIST/08, TU Berlin CS Dept., 1993.

[6] P. Mishra et al. Functional Abstraction driven Design Space Exploration of Heterogeneous Programmable Architectures. ISSS, pages 256-261, 2001.

[7] V. Zivojnovic et al. LISA - machine description language and generic machine model for HW/SW co-design. IEEE Workshop on VLSI Signal Processing, 1996.

[8] A. Halambi et al. EXPRESSION: A language for architecture exploration through compiler/simulator retargetability. DATE, 1999.

[9] P. Mishra et al. Automatic Verification of In-Order Execution in Microprocessors with Fragmented Pipelines and Multicycle Functional Units. DATE, pages 36--43, 2002.

[10] J. Hennessy and D. Patterson. *Computer Architecture: A quantitative approach*. Morgan Kaufmann Publishers Inc, San Mateo, CA, 1990.

[11] P. Mishra et al. Automatic Modeling and Validation of Pipeline Specifications driven by an Architecture Description Language. ASP-DAC/VLSI Design, pages 458--463, 2002.

[12] P. Mishra et al. Architecture description language driven verification of in-order execution in pipelined processors. UCI-ICS TR 01-20, UC, Irvine, 2001.

[13] P. Mishra et al. Specification of Hazards, Stalls, Interrupts, and Exceptions in EXPRESSION. UCI-ICS Technical Report 01-05, University of California, Irvine, 2001.

[14] J. Sawada and J. W.A. Hunt. Trace table based approach for pipelined microprocessor verification. CAV, 1997.

[15] J. Skakkebaek, R. Jones, and D. Dill. Formal verification of out-of-order execution using incremental flushing. CAV, 1998.

[16] M. Srivas and M. Bickford. Formal verification of a pipelined microprocessor. IEEE Software; 1990; 7(5):52--64.

[17] M. Velev and R. Bryant. Formal verification of superscalar microprocessors with multicycle functional units, exceptions, and branch prediction. DAC, 2000.

Statistical Analysis of a Hybrid Replication Model

Emerson Rogério de Oliveira Junior, Ingrid Jansch Porto
e-mail: emerson@inf.ufrgs.br, ingrid@inf.ufrgs.br
Phone: (+55)5133166161 Fax: (+55) 5133167308
Federal University of Rio Grande do Sul – Instituto de Informática
Caixa Postal 15064   Zip Code 91501-970 Porto Alegre   BRAZIL

Abstract: Replication is a technique commonly used to provide high-availability and fault tolerance in distributed systems. With multiple copies of the entities, a service can keep operation even when some copies are inaccessible because of a crash of the computer where a copy was stored, for instance. There are two main classes of replication techniques: passive and active replication. Passive replication suffers from a high reconfiguration cost in case of failure on the primary, and active replication has permanent processing redundancy.

The hybrid replication technique presented in this paper has the same advantages of the passive replication in good runs, and has much less processing overhead than the active replication. In this paper, we demonstrate the efficiency of our replication model by the comparison among the response time (for the client) of the passive, active and hybrid replication scenarios using statistical analysis.

Key words: Distributed systems, replication, statistical analysis, high-availability

1.   INTRODUCTION

One of the potential benefits of distributed systems is their use in providing high-available services, that is, services that are likely to be up and accessible when needed. Availability is a desirable metric to fault-tolerant systems. However, fault-tolerant systems always introduce redundancy in the system. With redundant copies, a replicated entity can continue providing services in spite of the failure of some copies, without affecting their clients. One example of redundancy is replication.

The replication technique can be used in different computing science areas. Some of them are databases, where the proposals of Kemme [6,7], Pedone [8], Helal [9], Patinõ-Martínez [10] and Wiessman [11] are good examples. Additionally, Baker´s work in cluster computing [12] and Zhou´s research [13] in real-time systems are also good references.

In embedded systems, it is very common the use of diskless systems. This implies the use of other stations to store data, mainly when we need stable memory (fail safe environment). In distributed systems, instead of using specially implemented stable memory systems, other nodes may be used as secondary memory hosts. However, conventional disks (used in most of the distributed nodes) may not be considered as stable memory - a set of nodes may be used with this goal, using replication management techniques.

In distributed systems, the literature distinguishes two main classes of replication techniques: passive replication [1] and active replication [2]. In passive replication, the client's request is sent to the primary replica that handles this request, sends messages to the other replicas in order to update their state, and sends back the response to the client. In active replication, the client's request is sent to all the replicas, every replica handles the request and sends back the reply to the client (just one reply is enough depending on the supposed failure modes). One drawback of the passive replication is to significantly increase the response time in case of failure in the primary copy. By other way, the active replication presents redundancy of processing (because all replicas handle the client's request) as a significant overhead.

Motivated by these drawbacks, this paper proposes the use of a combination on these techniques - passive replication and active replication - constituting a hybrid replication model. The hybrid replication has no increased response time presented by passive replication, in case of the primary failure and has much less processing usage than active replication model. Some experiments show some preliminary results that illustrate our ideas.

The rest of the paper is organized as follows. Section 2 introduces background concepts and related work about the replication models found in literature. We briefly present the statistical concepts used in the analysis in Section 3. Section 4 describes the specification of the hybrid replication model proposed in this paper, with the algorithm used and a discussion about the failure scenarios. Section 5 presents the results obtained about validation of the hybrid replication model, using statistical analysis. In section 6, we present our conclusions and some points to improve our research.

2. REPLICATION MODELS

Fault-tolerance in distributed systems is typically achieved through replication. The main replication techniques are passive replication and active replication. Other hybrid replication techniques, derived from the main techniques, are found in literature. These hybrid replication techniques are known by semi-passive replication [4] and semi-active replication [5].

In passive replication - also called primary-backup replication [1] - one replica, called primary, plays a special role: it receives the request from the client process, and sends the response back. The invocation is handled as follows (Figure 1):
- The client sends the request to the primary. Then, the primary receives the request and handles it. At the end of the operation, the state of the primary is updated and the primary sends the update message to the backups. Upon reception of this message, the backups update their states and send an acknowledgement (*ack*) back to the primary. Once the primary has received the *ack* from all (non-crashed backups, the response is sent to client.

The passive replication technique makes no assumption on the determinism of the requests – it allows for non-deterministic operations as it ensures the linearizability through the primary replica. The main disadvantage is that the implementation of passive replication requires a mechanism to agree on the primary (e.g., a group membership service). This leads to an increased response time in the case of primary failure [5].

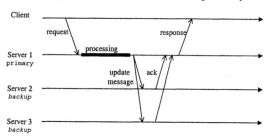

Figure 1. Passive replication.

In the active replication, also called state-machine approach [2], all replicas handle the client request. There is no centralized control, as in the passive replication. The request is handled as follows (Figure 2):
- The client's request is sent to all replicas and each replica processes the request, updates its state, and sends the response back to client. The client waits until it receives the first response or waits until it receives a majority of identical responses.
- To a client, all correct replicas should appear as having the same state. In order to guarantee this, all invocations sent by the clients should be

treated in the same order by all correct replicas. This is ensured by a total order multicast primitive – also called atomic multicast – that provides total ordering of messages multicast to a set of destination [15].

Active replication requires the operations on the replicas to be deterministic and waste extra resources through redundant processing, which is not the case of passive replication [3].

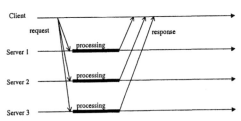

Figure 2: Active replication.

3.   DEFINITION OF THE HYBRID REPLICATION MODEL

We consider an asynchronous system augmented with unreliable failure detectors and assume that the processors fail only under crash model. There are neither Byzantine failures nor link failures. The channels are reliable and the processes do not recover after a crash, as assumed by Chandra and Toueg [16]. In fact, as this system is to be implemented on a local network, the communication delays should be estimated with good results.

Similarly to passive replication, in the hybrid replication, the primary handles the requests and, after processing of each request, it sends an update message to the backups. In our solution, there are two primaries. We argue that the probability that one primary fail is smaller than the probability that two primaries fail simultaneously (before the system reconfigures and recovers from the last failure).

The hybrid replication model, illustrated in figure 3, has two primaries – named $primary_1$ and $primary_2$ and two (or more) backups. There is no restriction about the number of backups.

The actions performed by the hybrid replication model are:
- The client sends a request to both primaries ($primary_1$ and $primary_2$);
- Both, $primary_1$ and $primary_2$ handle the request and send an update message to the backups;
- When the backup states have been updated, an ack message is sent to primaries;

– The primaries send a response to the client. The client discards the second answer.

In this model, it is verified that there is more processing than the passive replication, but there is less than in active replication. The main advantage of the hybrid replication model is that, in case of crash failure of one primary, the other primary will send the response message to the client. This is not done by the passive replication because there is only one primary to process the client requisition.

We can assume that in the absence of server crash or failure suspicion, the client's request is handled at the same time with the hybrid replication as it was handled with the passive replication.

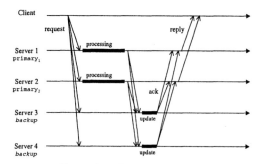

Figure 3: Hybrid replication model.

Six failure scenarios can occur in the hybrid replication:
1. One of the primaries fails before the client request is processed: in this case, the hybrid replication is equal to the passive replication in the sense that one of the backups will be elected to be the next primary and the client request processing will be finished.
2. One of the primaries fails during the processing of the client request: while in passive replication the client must resend the request to a new primary, in our hybrid replication is not necessary because the other primary processes the request.
3. One of the primaries fails after processing the request, but before sending the response to the client: the remaining primary receives the *ack* signal that was sent by the backups, and transmits the response to the client.
4. One of the primaries fails after sending the response to the backups: the other primary will continue the actions of the replication.
5. Both primaries fail: the new primaries will be elected among the remaining backups and the client must re-send the request to them.
6. One or more backups fail: the replication will proceed without interruptions because the primaries process the client request. In this case, new backups could be created. Notice that, in fact, as there are two

primaries, under one single faulty node assumption, even the acknowledgement of the backups is necessary to continue operation on the primaries (or to send the answer to the client).

4.   STATISTICAL CONCEPTS

We use some statistical parameters to analyze our proposal. A statistic is a measure on the items in a random sample. Since the only reason to ever draw a random sample is to infer something about the population from which it came, it should be clear that when we calculate a given statistic we only do so in order to estimate a corresponding parameter of the population from which the sample was drawn.

When the evaluated values present a normal distribution, we can use the mean and the standard deviation as statistical parameters. Besides, if the distribution is not normal, we can use the Central Limit Theorem to prove our goals with statistics [14]. This allowed us to approximate the distribution of sample means with a normal distribution. This means that once we have the mean and standard deviation of the sample mean, we can construct a Z variable and compute probabilities using the standard normal distribution.

Another statistical evaluation is the hypothesis testing. In hypothesis testing, we start with a null hypothesis, H_0, which represents the status quo, or our default belief: it is what we continue to believe unless we judge that there is sufficient evidence to discard it [14].

5.   VALIDATION OF THE HYBRID REPLICATION

In this section, we present the statistical analysis about the execution of the experiments with replication. To demonstrate the efficiency of our hybrid replication model, we have executed seven different experiments, which are:
- passive replication without failure;
- passive replication with failure in the primary;
- active replication without failure;
- active replication with failure in one of the servers;
- hybrid replication without failure;
- hybrid replication with one failure affecting the primary; and
- hybrid replication with two failures affecting both primaries.

The executions were performed using Linux, C language (gcc compiler) and sockets for the communication between the processes evolved. The experiments, with and without failures, were executed 1000 times each one and we get the response time to the client request of each execution. So, we had 7000 response times for the client request.

The distribution obtained from the experiments was not a normal curve. All the histograms presented more than one mode. We believe that this occurs because the scheduling time used by the processor to execute the experiments is not a controllable variable, presenting random values. It causes a great response time variation. Because the distribution is not normal, we have used the Central Limit Theorem to evaluate the values presented in our experiments. Table 1 presents the statistical values observed about the response times obtained in our experiments without the occurrence of failures. Table 2 indicates the values obtained in executions with failures.

Table 1: Execution of the experiments without failures (in seconds).

Replication	Passive	Active	Hybrid
Amount of values (N)	1000	1000	1000
Mean (μ)	1,9054	1,1100	2,1155
Standard deviation (σ)	0,2541	0,4754	0,0452

Table 2: Execution of the experiments with failures (in seconds).

Replication	Passive	Active	Hybrid with failure in one primary	Hybrid with failure in both primaries
Amount of values (N)	1000	1000	1000	1000
Mean (μ)	5,9713	1,1113	2,2295	6,0371
Standard deviation (σ)	0,5720	0,0142	0,2938	0,8162

<u>passive replication</u> : mean = 1,9054s, standard deviation = 0,0008s;
<u>active replication:</u>   mean = 1,1100s, standard deviation = 0,0150s;
<u>hybrid replication:</u>   mean = 2,1155s, standard deviation = 0,0014s.

With the mean and standard deviation values, and using the probability of 95%, we have calculated the confidence interval (CI):
<u>passive replication</u> : CI = [1,9053s ; 1,9055s];
<u>active replication:</u>   CI = [1,1091s ; 1,1109s];
<u>hybrid replication:</u>   CI = [2,1154s ; 2,1156s].

From the presented values, we can be sure that, in 95% of the cases, the calculated means are in the presented confidence intervals. As it occurs in the execution with no failures, we observe that the response times obtained with the experiments with failures demonstrate that the distribution is not normal, either. The means are those presented in Table 2, but the standard deviation had to be modified according the Central Limit Theorem. So, we have that:

<u>passive replication:</u> mean = 5,9713s, standard deviation = 0,0181s;
<u>active replication:</u> mean = 1,1113s, standard deviation = 0,0004s;
<u>hybrid replication with one failure primary:</u> mean = 2,2295s, standard deviation = 0,0093s;
<u>hybrid replication with two failure primaries:</u> mean = 6,0371, standard deviation = 0,0258s.

With the mean and standard deviation values, and using the probability of 95%, we have calculated the confidence interval (CI):

passive replication: CI = [5,9702s ; 5,9724s];

active replication: CI = [1,1112s ; 1,1114s];

hybrid replication with one failure primary: CI = [2,2289s ; 2,2301s];

hybrid replication with two failure primaries: CI = [6,0355s ; 6,0387s].

As indicated by the presented values, in 95% of the cases, the calculated means of the measured times are in the presented confidence intervals.

5.1   Comparing execution with failures

As presented, it can be seen that the mean time needed to execute active replication with no failure is the smallest of all, and the biggest time is the observed in hybrid replication with no failure. It has happened before a very optimistic situation has been considered: just one client. In a concurrent scenario, order properties have to be considered and the numbers will be really different. In the case of executions with failure, the time presented by active replication is the smallest of all, again, and the hybrid replication with failure, in both primaries, is the biggest of all types of replication.

It can be observed that the mean time of hybrid replication with failure in both primaries is almost the same that the mean time needed with passive replication. Other interesting observation that can be considered is that the mean time needed to execute in hybrid replication with one failure is smaller than the mean time in passive replication. This is a goal that we have achieved with our replication model.

We argue that our hybrid replication model has much less processing usage than active replication model. To prove this, we have extracted the CPU time utilization needed to process the client's request in the experiments. The mean time to process the client's request was 0,2172s and the mean time to update the state of the servers was 0,0005s. Table 3 indicates the CPU mean time utilization of all seven experiments, considering how much times was processed the request and how much times it was necessary to update server states.

Table 3: CPU mean time utilization (in seconds).

Replication	CPU mean time processing	CPU mean time updating	Total CPU mean time
passive	1 x 0,2172s	2 x 0,0005s	0,2182s
active	3 x 0,2172s	0 x 0,0005s	0,6516s
hybrid	2 x 0,2172s	1 x 0,0005s	0,4349s
passive with failure	1 x 0,2172s	1 x 0,0005s	0,2177s
active with failure	2 x 0,2172s	0 x 0,0005s	0,4344s
hybrid with one failure primary	1 x 0,2172s	1 x 0,0005s	0,2177s
hybrid with two failure primaries	1 x 0,2172s	0 x 0,0005s	0,2172s

6.   CONCLUDING REMARKS

Some observations can be extracted from the statistical analysis presented in this paper.

We can prove that the hybrid replication model with one failure uses the same amount of processing time that the passive replication model with no failure. To do this, we use the hypothesis test with values of Z distribution in passive replication with no failures *vs.* hybrid replication with one failure. The null hypothesis H0 is that the mean time of the experiments is the same. The Z observed value (Zo) is equal to $-1,2142$ and the Z critical value (Zc) is equal to 1,96. Comparing the absolute values achieved, we get that the relation $|Zo| < |Zc|$ is true, indicating that the null hypothesis must be accepted. This means that the mean time of passive replication with no failure and the hybrid replication with one failure is statistically the same.

The mean time needed to execute the hybrid replication with one failure was less than the mean time needed to execute the passive replication with one failure. It happens because in hybrid replication there is no intervention of the failure detector: the failure detector was only used in passive replication and in hybrid replication with failure in both primaries.

Another observation is that the mean time to execute the hybrid replication with two failure primaries is almost equal to the time to execute the passive replication. Comparing with the active replication, the hybrid replication needed less CPU time to process the request than the necessary in active replication.

In comparison with the active replication, the statistical analysis demonstrates that the response times, in mean, is greater than the response time observed in the hybrid model. However, our model executed the replication in less time than the necessary to execute the same replication, in active replication model.

The hybrid replication model presented can be used in an embedded system if the multicast primitives needed to reach replica consistency are inserted in this system. These primitives are necessary to guarantee the message changes between the replicas. In the same way, this replication model can be used in hard real time systems, too. In this case, if one primary fails to process the client request, the second one will continue with the replication action, preserving the time limits imposed by the hard real time system.

We observed that the use of the statistical analysis is a good manner to prove hypothesis. However, it was observed that a few papers found in literature, present their results using some type of statistical analysis.

At present, we are implementing the necessary framework to guarantee the consistency in our replication model. We expect that, with the replica consistency, we will be able to run the experiments again with the same good results obtained until now.

7.   REFERENCES

[1]   BUDHIRAJA, N.; MARZULLO, K.; SCHNEIDER, F.; TOUEG, S. Optimal Primary-Backup Protocols. In: Int. Workshop on Distributed Algorithms (WDAG´92), Haifa – Israel, Proceedings, p. 362-378, 1992.

[2]   SCHNEIDER, F.B. Replication Management using the State-Machine Approach, In Distributed Systems. p.169-198. Addison-Wesley. 1993.

[3]   GUERRAOUI, R.; SCHIPER, A. Failure Tolerance by Replication in Distributed Systems. In Reliable Software Technologies. ADA-Europe´96, Proceedings, LNCS 1088, p. 38-57, Springer-Verlag, June 1996.

[4]   DÉFAGO, X. Agreement-Related Problems: From Semi-Passive Replication to Totally Ordered Broadcast. n. 2229, 2000. 158p. (Ph.D. Thesis).

[5]   POWELL, D. Delta-4: A Generic Architecture for Dependable Distributed Computing. ESPRIT Research Reports. Project 818/2252. Springer Verlag. 1991.

[6]   KEMME, B.; ALONSO, G. A New Approach to Developing and Implementing Eager Database Replication Protocols. In ACM Trans on Database Systems, Sept. 2000.

[7]   KEMME, B.; BARTOLI, A.; BABAOGLU, Ö. Online Reconfiguration in Replicated Databases Based on Group Communication. In: IEEE International Conference on Dependable Systems and Networks (DSN 2001), Proceedings, p.117..126. Goteborg, Sweden. July 2001.

[8]   PEDONE, A.; KEMME, B. Exploiting Atomic Broadcast in Replicated Databases. In EUROPAR, Proceedings, Sep 1998.

[9]   HELAL A. A.; HEDDAYA, A. A.; BHARGAVA, B. B. Replication Techniques in Distributed Systems. Kluwer Publishers, Boston-London-Dordrecht, 1996, 156p.

[10] PATIÑO-MARTÍNEZ, M.; JIMENEZ-PERIS, R.; KEMME, B.; ALONSO, B. Scalable Replication in Database Cluster. In: 14th Int. Symposium on Distributed Computing Systems (DISC2000), Proceedings, Toledo, Spain, Oct. 2000.

[11] WIESMANN, M.; PEDONE, F.; SCHIPER, A. Understanding Replication in Databases and Distributed Systems. In: 20th Int. Conf. on Distributed Computing Systems (ICDS2000), Proceedings, p.264-274, Taipei – R.O.C., Apr. 2000.

[12] BAKER, M. Cluster Computing White Paper. Univ. of Portsmouth, UK, July 2000.

[13] ZOU, H.; JAHANIAN, F. Optimization of a Real-Time Primary-Backup Replication Service. In: 17th IEEE Symp. on Reliable Distributed Systems (SRDS´98), Proc., West Lafayette, USA, p.177-185, 1998.

[14] SPIEGEL,M. Estatística. Coleção Schaum, McGraw-Hill do Brasil, RJ, 1980, 580p.

[15] FELBER, P. The CORBA Object Group Service: A Service Approach to Object Groups in CORBA. (Ph.D. Thesis). EPFL. 1998.

[16] CHANDRA, T. D.; TOUEG, S. Unreliable Failure Detectors for Reliable Distributed Systems. Journal of the ACM, 43(2). pp.225-267, 1996.

Building Embedded Fault-Tolerant Systems for Critical Applications: An Experimental Study

Paul Townend, Jie Xu and Malcolm Munro
Dept. of Computer Science, University of Durham, DH1 3LE, UK

Abstract: An increasing range of industries have a growing dependence on embedded software systems, many of which are safety-critical, real-time applications that require extremely high dependability. Two fundamental approaches – fault avoidance and fault tolerance – have been proposed to increase the overall dependability of such systems. However, the increased cost of using the fault tolerance approach may mean that this increase in dependability is not worth the extra expense involved. We describe an experiment undertaken in order to establish whether or not software redundancy (or the multi-version design method) can offer increased dependability over the traditional single-version development approach when given the same level of resources. The results of this and a subsequent follow-up study are then given. The analytic results from these experiments show that despite the poor quality of individual versions, the multi-version method results in a safer system than the single-version solution. It is evident that regarding the single-version method as a "seem-to-be" safer design decision for critical applications is not generally justifiable.

Key words: Detected and undetected failures, embedded fault-tolerant systems, multi-version programming, safety-critical applications, software development cost

1. INTRODUCTION

According to [SCI00], an embedded system is "*a data processing system which is 'built-in' or 'embedded' within a machine or a system. It partly or wholly controls the functionality and the operation of this machine. The data processing system and the enclosing system are dependent on each other in such a way that one cannot function without the other.*" In recent years, the number of embedded systems in usage has grown at an enormous rate; this has been especially evident with the rise of handheld computers, network computers and intelligent devices.

With this growth, the role of software dependability within such systems has become increasingly important. Dependability is usually referred to as *the property of a software system such that reliance can justifiably be placed on the service it delivers* [LAP95], and it subsumes the attributes of reliability, availability, safety, and security etc. These attributes have their own definitions, e.g. software reliability is defined as the probability of *failure-free* software operation for a specified period of time in a specified environment, whilst software safety emphasizes the non-occurrence of *catastrophic* consequences on the environment of the software.

Of greatest concern is the dependability of embedded systems within the safety-critical domain, examples of which include factory control systems, heart pacemaker monitors, and radar systems. Systems such as these all have the scope of potentially disastrous failure, including loss of human life and property. Dependability is also important when considering the economic implications of developing embedded software, as the cost of replacing systems with faulty firmware can be huge, especially where software has been burned directly onto ROM. Many devices, such as those in consumer electronics, simply do not justify the cost of replacement, and so may instead pick up a reputation of poor quality – both in terms of product and company.

Given the clear need for dependability within such systems, an unacceptably high level of faults still occur; indeed, some commentators (e.g. [HAT97]) point out that although techniques that supposedly promote the goal of improved dependability have come and gone, the defect density of software has remained similar for more than fifteen years. It is therefore critical that methods be found for increasing the dependability of embedded software. [KEL91] states that "*...while complete fault removal in sequential software is difficult, it becomes effectively impossible in real-time, concurrent software. Current testing methodologies, while useful to detect and localize errors in sequential software are inadequate when applied to highly concurrent and asynchronous real-time software.*" It can therefore be seen that traditional, single-version methods may not be advisable during the implementation and testing of many embedded systems. By contrast, the *fault-tolerance* approach accepts the existence of faults but seeks to allow errors to be recovered without affecting the running of a system.

There are a number of different ways this can be achieved. Most approaches, such as recovery blocks [RAN95] and multi-version design [AVI77], are based on the use of functionally equivalent software components (i.e. software alternates or versions). **Recovery block systems** work on the principle of acceptance testing and backward error recovery. Unfortunately, there are situations in which backward recovery is not appropriate; many embedded systems cannot simply "roll back" the system to a previous state. Also, recovery-block systems are less predictable due to their dynamical recovery operations, and so may not be suitable for many real-time systems. Because of this, the most popular form of fault tolerance within such systems is based on the concurrent execution of multiple diverse components. **Multi-version design** works on the principle of independently implementing n channels of a program, which are then executed in parallel with a single input (although conceptually, parallel execution is not necessary – channels may be executed separately). The outputs of these channels are then compared under a voting system, which forwards a single output based on the majority agreement.

In principle, multi-version design provides a general way of allowing a software system to operate successfully in the presence of software design faults. Some researchers have concluded that the dependability of software developed using this approach increases dramatically; for example, [HAT97] concludes that a three-channel system, governed by majority polling, would have a dependability improvement ratio of 45:1 over a single version of the system. This is not a new finding; earlier papers, such as [AVI84] have also argued that multi-version produces highly dependable software. However, such massive increases in dependability have been drawn into question. [KNI90] argue that these gains in dependability are under the assumption that there are no correlated failures within two or more channels of the system – in other words, no faults will occur in the same place and produce the same results. Numerous studies have shown that this is simply not the case. [ECK85] has shown that even small probabilities of correlated faults can reduce the dependability of an multi-version system dramatically, and [LEV95] further argues that every experiment with the approach of using separate teams to write software versions has found that independently written software routines do not fail in a statistically independent way.

It appears to be the case that such massive dependability gains can only be assumed on a theoretical level; in real-world applications, the overall cost/dependability ratio of a multi-version system is likely to be much lower than theoretical models suggest. The question of cost therefore becomes increasingly important; if the increased cost of developing a multi-version system were to always result in an extremely dependable system then the increased development budget may be justified. However, if this increased budget does not lead to significant dependability gains, then the additional spending may not be justified.

Despite this, it is generally accepted that when each channel of such a system has high dependability, the overall system will be more dependable than an equivalent high-dependability single-version (i.e. fault avoidance) system [HAT97]. It is also generally accepted that when the budget and available resources are so limited that each channel of the multi-version system is of poor quality, the single version method will produce more dependable results based on the same budget. When the dependability of individual channels is in-between these two extremes, it is unknown which of the approaches will produce the most dependable system.

The question of which approach produces the more dependable system when given a fixed and limited budget has never previously been investigated. This is important, as the finite budgets that many organizations are faced with means that a large number of realistic applications fall between these two extremes. In such cases it is unclear which design method will achieve higher dependability; for example, the lack of current understanding is one of the major reasons why the Boeing Corporation made the decision not to use the multi-version approach in the Primary Flight Control system in its 777 aircraft. Although it is dangerous to rely on the multi-version approach without theoretical and empirical support evidence, relying on the single-version approach just because it has been used traditionally for years is equally unjustifiable.

We therefore ask: *Given a limited budget (e.g. money, people and time) for a given application, which development method for building a reliable system should we choose in order to achieve the maximum possible level of software reliability?*

2.   AN EXPERIMENTAL STUDY

At the University of Durham, we have begun to address this issue by performing an ongoing series of experiments to compare the two approaches when given a fixed development budget. We describe here our initial experiment for a realistic industrial application (detailed in [TOW01]), and combine these results with the results of a follow-up study.

In [TOW01], both a multi-version system and single-version system were developed to control the simulation of a factory production cell, both using a fixed amount of development resources. Resources were defined as *the total means available to a company for increasing production or profit.* In the real world, this encompasses a number of different elements, such as system cost and employee wages. In this experiment, the resource measured was time; in other words, the accumulative resources (time) allocated to the development of the multi-version system was to be the same as that allocated to the single-version system.

The factory production cell application [LOT96] was chosen as it was necessary to implement an application that was both small enough to construct within the development budget allocated, and also complex enough to have the potential for faults to be present within the system code. It was also desirable for the application to be real-time and embedded, as such systems invariably involve high reliability and safety requirements, as well as high timing constraints. The production-cell simulation, detailed in figure 1, consists of two conveyor belts, one of which delivers the raw units (blanks) into the system, and one of which moves the blanks out of the system once they have been fully processed. The unit also consists of four separate workstations, each of which has its own number. Depending on the type of a workstation, it can either be switched on and off by the controller software, or is permanently on. Two cranes are mounted on a racking which prevents them from occupying the same horizontal position at the same time, and are used to transport blanks around the system. Each blank has its own bar-code, which identifies which workstations it needs to be placed in, and the minimum and maximum amounts of time that it can spend within each workstation. Blanks may be processed either in specific (preserved) order, or in any (non-preserved) order, depending on the instructions in the bar-code.

The software controllers were needed to control the operations of the simulation; they needed to allow the simulation to process up to two blanks at any one time, whilst ensuring that the blanks were processed correctly within the appropriate time constraints. It was also necessary to ensure that the system remained safe; for example, it was imperative to ensure that the two cranes never collided with each other, and that no blank was placed in a workstation that already contained a blank. Also, the feed belt needed to be controlled by the software in order to ensure that no more than two blanks entered the system at any given time, and that none fell off the end of the belt. The simulation and the controller software communicated via a first-in-first-out pipe mechanism, with communications being sent as ASCII text.

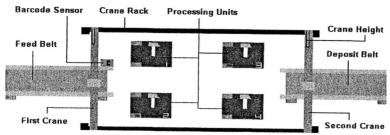

Figure 1 - The flexible production cell [LOT96]

Three programmers were used to develop the controller systems, with development separated into three equal time phases. The first time phase was used by each programmer to develop a working version of the controller software; at the end of this phase, the three programs were used as channels in the multi-version system. The second and third time phases were then used by each programmer to refine their respective versions and to exploit various methods and tools for improving the dependability of those versions. There was no differentiation between these two phases – they are merely noted in order to demonstrate that the additional time spent developing the multi-version systems was twice that of the original development time. These additional time phases resulted in each of the single-version systems having had the same amount of resources spent on them as the 3-version voter system. At the conclusion of this development process, an extensive testing plan was implemented in order to ascertain the dependability of the single-version systems and the 3-version system. An analysis was then performed to determine which of the methods had resulted in the most dependable software.

Unlike many other experiments of its type, this study did not make use of a pre-written requirements document; rather, the document's production was considered to be part of the development process for which resources were allocated, and was produced jointly by the three programmers. Apart from this, there was no further interaction between programmers. In order to encourage diversity, each channel was developed using different development environments; these are shown in figure 2.

Channel	Operating System	Language
A	Sun Solaris 2.7	GNU C++
B	Red Hat Linux 6.0	GNU C++
C	Microsoft Windows NT 4.0	Java

Figure 2 - Operating system/language combinations for each channel

As with the Knight and Leveson experiment [KNI86], no single software engineering methodology was imposed on the programmers – each was allowed to develop their program using whatever method they saw fit.

3.   TESTING AND RESULTS

There were only a finite number of possible states in which the simulation could be in and these were specified as scenarios within the requirements document. Due to the real-time nature of the simulation, it was impossible to devise a series of tests that would cover all possible timing criteria, and so tests were formulated based upon these documented situations, consisting of a total of 440 tests per system. In all tests, timing constraints were set to random values.

3.1 The Multi-Version System

Of most concern when testing a multi-version system is the possibility of a common-mode failure that results in a multi-version system processing a task incorrectly; failures that result in the voter being unable to reach a consensus opinion and failures that cause the voter to perform an operation that results in the failure of a system as a whole are less serious, as in either scenario, human operators can be alerted that the system is in a fail state.

The analysis of the three multi-version channels indicated that channel A and channel C suffered from unacceptably high rates of failure, with only channel B dependable enough to pass the acceptance test that was necessary before any channel can be entered into a dependable multi-version system. This is shown in figure 3.

Channel	Probability of Failure
A	25.22%
B	1.59%
C	78.18%

Figure 3 - The probability of failure among the multi-version channels

As can be seen, the vast majority of failures were caused by channel C; this was largely due to the channel's inability to process blanks of non-preserved order, which automatically caused the channel to fail in 75% of all test inputs. Altogether, the 1320 tests performed on the three channels revealed a total of 480 faults. This means that for any given test on a single channel, there was a 36.36% probability of it resulting in a failure.

However, at the conclusion of testing, only two common-mode failures had been discovered. This implies that even though two of the channels are unacceptably undependable, the overall multi-version system would only unknowingly forward an incorrect decision in 0.45% of tested possible situations. Figure 4 shows the overall distributed of faults in all tests.

Figure 4 - The results of all tests performed on the multi-version channels

The enforced diversity of operating system and platform resulted in diverse code; however, as the two common-mode failures suggest, the diversity of code does not necessarily lead to diverse distributions of faults.

It is interesting to note that both common-mode failures were as a result of entirely unrelated faults within two of the channels; these faults resulted in the simulation moving into the same unrecoverable state, but one channel caused the system to fall into an infinite loop, whilst the other channel simply ceased to execute.

3.2 The Single-Version Systems

All three single-version systems exhibited increased levels of dependability over their corresponding multi-version channels, with the number of faults found in each system dropping significantly, as shown in figure 5.

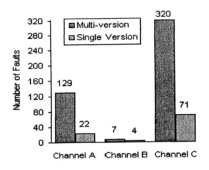

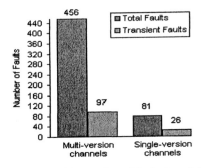

Figure 5 - The number of faults found during testing for each system

Figure 6 - The number of faults found during testing, and the number of them transient

Whilst the failure rates of channel *A* and channel *C* were still unacceptably high, both systems exhibited vastly improved dependability, with failure rates of 5.00% and 16.14% respectively, compared to the failure rates of 25.22% and 78.18% experienced with the multi-version systems on which they were based. Channel *B* also exhibited increased dependability, with its failure rate reduced to 0.91%, although all of the faults found in this channel were transient and so repeated testing may produce different statistics. Interestingly, the proportion of transient faults discovered while testing the systems remained much the same, as is shown in figure 6, and so whilst 55 repeatable faults were discovered among the single versions, the remaining faults appeared to be caused by timing anomalies with the Java simulation, and were therefore difficult to replicate with certainty.

The difficulty in pinpointing the cause of many of the transient faults perhaps underlines the difficulty in debugging real-time applications. One of the greatest areas of interest is that of how many undetected failures occurred in the single-version systems. There are two possible kinds of undetected failure; a blank can be left within the system instead of being extracted, or a blank can be processed through the system incorrectly. The occurrences of these are detailed in figure 7.

	Channel A	Channel B	Channel C
Blank in System	3	0	3
Blank incorrectly processed	3	4	20
Total Undetected failures	6	4	23
Undetected failure rate	1.36%	0.90%	5.23%

Figure 7 - Undetected failures in the single-version systems

As can be seen, *all three* single-version systems had an undetected failure rate that was greater than the 0.45% rate recorded in the multi-version system. Therefore, despite poor quality of components, the multi-version system still theoretically performed more dependably than either of the two poor quality channels in this aspect, and more importantly, would only unknowingly forward an incorrect decision in 0.45% of test inputs. The multi-version system therefore had a higher level of *safety* than the single-version system, although single-version system *B* was more dependable than the multi-version system in the value domain.

A potential problem with the system was its high granularity. In the specification, it was decided that voting would take place before each crane movement; due to the real-time nature of the simulation, this occurred almost constantly, which increased the scope for faults due to the consistent comparison problem. When viewed from the point of view of attempting to produce ultra-dependable software, this leads the experiment to come under the same criticisms as those made of the [KNI86] experiment by [AVI88a] – namely that the lack of rigor in the design paradigm resulted in many of the later weaknesses with the multi-version system.

3.3 The Improved Single-Version System

Although the initial experiment produced some interesting results, there were a number of areas of weakness that needed to be improved. The initial study used the second and third time phases to further test and enhance each individual single-version system; should no multi-version channel have been required, then each programmer would have had much more time to develop a rigorous and thorough specification, and the resulting single-version systems may have been more dependable. As it was, the necessity of completing the multi-version system on time meant that minimal work was applied to design. Related to this was the lack of a pre-written requirements documentation; although assigning the task of writing the requirements documentation in part of the development time was perhaps more realistic, the resulting documentation contained several faults and ambiguities.

In a follow-up study, the authors performed an experiment whereby a single-version controller system was developed independently of any multi-version channels, using an independent programmer, and based on a robust requirements document. The new system was allocated an identical period of development time, and on completion of this, a new series of tests were performed on this single-version system as well as the multi-version system developed in the initial experiment. In order to test the systems more accurately, tighter timing constraints were imposed upon all tests in order to highlight any weaknesses in each system. The results of these tests are shown in figure 8.

Single Version System:

No. of	P x P Failures		NP x NP Failures		P x NP Failures		NP x P Failures		Totals	
blanks	No.	%	No.	%	No.	%	No.	%	No.	%
1	0/64	0	0/64	0	-	-	-	-	0/128	0
2	20/144	13.89	17/144	11.81	13/144	9.03	17/144	11.81	70/576	12.15
									70/704	9.94

Multi-version System Channel A:

No. of	P x P Failures		NP x NP Failures		P x NP Failures		NP x P Failures		Totals	
blanks	No.	%	No.	%	No.	%	No.	%	No.	%
1	0/64	0	38/64	59.38	-	-	-	-	38/128	29.69
2	45/144	31.25	128/144	88.89	115/144	79.86	143/144	99.31	431/576	74.83
									469/704	66.62

Multi-version System Channel B:

No. of	P x P Failures		NP x NP Failures		P x NP Failures		NP x P Failures		Totals	
blanks	No.	%	No.	%	No.	%	No.	%	No.	%
1	0/64	0	2/64	3.13	-	-	-	-	2/128	1.56
2	14/144	9.72	17/144	11.81	19/144	13.19	25/144	17.36	75/576	13.02
									77/704	10.94

Multi-version System Channel C:

No. of	P x P Failures		NP x NP Failures		P x NP Failures		NP x P Failures		Totals	
blanks	No.	%	No.	%	No.	%	No.	%	No.	%
1	0/64	0	0/64	0	-	-	-	-	0/128	0
2	124/144	86.11	144/144	100	131/144	90.97	110/144	76.39	509/576	88.37
									509/704	72.30

Figure 8 – Results of testing the new single version system with multiple blanks (inputs)

As can be seen, the new single-version implementation has an overall failure rate of 9.94%. Although this is unrealistically high for a critical system, it compares favourably with the failure probabilities for each multi-version channel, and at first glance it would appear that the dependability (the reliability in particular) of the single-version system is much greater than that of the multi-version system. However, like the results of the initial experiment, once the safety attribute of dependability is investigated, the picture changes. When each system failure was analysed further, it was found that the new single-version system had an undetected failure rate of 3.27%. When the multi-version system was analyzed with the new test results, *no undetected failure was discovered*. This reinforces the initial experiment's findings that although the multi-version system is less reliable, it is nonetheless safer.

4. CONCLUSIONS AND FUTURE EXPERIMENTS

It appears to be the case that for both our initial experiment and follow-up experiment, the traditional single-version approach produced more *reliable* systems in terms of overall numbers of faults and failures discovered, with the level of granularity and an ambiguous requirements document resulting in a less reliable multi-version system. However, the multi-version system resulted in fewer undetected failures occurring than in a single-version system, despite the poor quality of its individual channels. Most failures in one or two versions of the multi-version system can be detected through result comparison. In these cases, the production cell can stop in a pre-defined safe state. Therefore, although the single-version systems produced fewer faults, the multi-version system could still be seen as being potentially the *safer* of the two approaches. It is evident that regarding the single-version method as a "seem-to-be" safer design decision for safety-critical applications is not generally justifiable, even for a given amount of resources.

Although the size of the software developed is still small compared to real-world applications (but certainly greater than that of [KNI86] and [AVI88b]), to develop more realistic software systems would be extremely difficult without commercial backing, and would be unjustified given that no previous experimental data of its type is available. Once we have gathered sufficient empirical evidence, we intend to seek out sources of data from the safety-critical industry, in order to validate our models further.

5. ACKNOWLEDGEMENTS

This work was partially supported by the EPSRC IBHIS and e-Demand projects.

6. REFERENCES

[AVI77] A. Avizienis and L. Chen, "On the implementation of *N*-version programming for software fault-tolerance during execution," in *Intl. Conf.* Comput. Soft. & Appli., New York, pp.149-155, 1977.

[AVI84] A. Avizienis and J.P.J. Kelly, "Fault tolerance by design diversity: concepts and experiments," *IEEE Computer*, vol. 17, no. 8, pp. 67-80, 1984.

[AVI88a] A. Avizienis and M.R. Lyu, "On the effectiveness of multi-version software in digital avionics," in *AIAA/IEEE 8th Digital Avionics Systems Conference*, San Jose, pp. 422-427, Oct. 1988.

[AVI88b] A. Avizienis et al., "In search of effective diversity: a six-language study of fault-tolerant flight control software," in *18th Int. Symp. Fault-Tolerant Comput.*, pp.15-22, Tokyo, 1988.

[ECK85] D.E. Eckhardt and L.D. Lee, "A theoretical basis for the analysis of multi-version software subject to coincident errors," *IEEE Trans. Soft. Eng.*, vol.SE-11, no.12, pp.1511-1517, 1985.

[HAT97] L. Hatton, "*N*-version design versus one good version," *IEEE Software*, vol. 14, no. 6, pp.71-76, 1997.

[KEL91] J.P.J. Kelly, T.I. McVittie, and W.I. Yamamoto, "Implementing design diversity to achieve fault tolerance," *IEEE Software*, pp.61-71, 1991.

[KNI86] J.C. Knight and N.G. Leveson, "An experimental evaluation of the assumption of independence in multi-version programming," *IEEE Trans. Soft. Eng.*, vol.SE-12, no.1, pp.96-109, 1986.

[KNI90] J.C. Knight and N.G. Leveson, "A reply to the criticisms of the Knight and Leveson experiment," *ACM Software Eng. Notes*, Jan. 1990.

[LAD99] P. Ladkin et al, "Computer-related incidents with commercial aircraft," http://www.rvs.uni-bielefeld.de/publications/Incidents/, 1999.

[LAP95] J.-C. Laprie, "Dependability – its attributes, impairments and means," in *Predictably Dependable Computing Systems*, Springer-Verlag, pp.3-24, 1995.

[LEV95] N.G. Leveson, *Safeware: system safety and computers*. Addison-Wesley-Longman, NY, 1995.

[LOT96] A. Lötzbeyer and R. Mühlfeld, "Task description of a Flexible Production Cell with real time properties," Internal FZI Tech. Report, ftp://ftp.fzi.de/pub/PROST/projects/korsys/task_descr_flex22.ps.gz), 1996.

[RAN95] B. Randell and J.Xu, "The evolution of the recovery block concept," in *Software Fault Tolerance*, Wileys, pp.1-22, 1995.

[SCI00] http://www.scintilla.utwente.nl/shintabi/engels/thema_text.html

[TOW01] P.Townend, J. Xu, and M. Munro, "Building dependable software for critical applications: *N*-version design versus one good version," in *Proc. 6th IEEE WORDS-6*, pp. 105-111, Rome, Jan. 2001.

Fault detection in safety-critical embedded systems

DOMEN VERBER[1], MATJAŽ COLNARIČ[1], AND WOLFGANG A. HALANG[2]

[1]*University of Maribor, Faculty of Electrical Engineering and Computer Science, 2000 Maribor, Slovenia;* [2]*FernUniversität Hagen, Faculty of Electrical Engineering, 58084 Hagen, Germany*

Abstract: In the paper, a proposition for a systematic approach to fault detection in building a dependable and fault-tolerant control system is presented. A network of simple monitoring cells that monitor and evaluate functioning of critical sub-processes of the system is proposed. Further, different approaches for the implementation of the monitoring cells are observed.

Key words: Safety-critical embedded systems, fault-tolerant control systems, fault detection, fault localization and isolation

1.   INTRODUCTION

A typical present day control system consists of physical process components, sensors, actuators, distributed computers with communication networks, and several thousands of lines of code. Examples of these are control systems in industrial plants, nuclear reactors, avionics, etc. The size and the complexity of such systems increase every year and so does the probability of a fault in one of the many components. Each fault in such a system can cause severe material loss or even endanger human lives.

Most of the researchers working on the problem of fault-tolerant computing are only providing partial solutions (e.g. [1,2,3]). However, for appropriate consideration of all problems, a holistic approach is necessary.

The work presented in the paper is a part of the research founded by the Slovenian Ministry of Education, Science and Sport. The primary issue of this research is the study and the development of methods and tools for hierarchically organized fault-tolerant control systems. The proposed model should deal with faults in the environment, in the hardware and in the software of the embedded system. Basic research topics covered with the project are fault detection, fault localization and isolation, graceful degradation of the functionality of the system in a case of minor fault, and controlled and safe shut-down of the system in the case of severe defects.

In the article, a practical proposition of how to deal with fault detection of such systems is given. The basic idea is to use a network of simple monitoring cells that monitor and evaluate functioning of critical sub-processes of the system.

2.   FAULT DETECTION BY MEANS OF MONITORING CELLS

A typical control system can be usually divided into a set of well-defined sub processes or tasks. Each task takes its inputs from sensors and from the results of other processes, and produces results that are used by other tasks, or influence the controlled system through actuators. Tasks are triggered by synchronous or asynchronous events.

There are several causes of faults in such a model. E.g., the components of the controlling process can breakdown due to hardware or software related errors. For the same reasons, values of input and output signals can be out of their predefined ranges or they do not apply to functional specifications of the system. In hard real-time systems, improper temporal behaviour is also considered as a fault. Another not so obvious source of errors can be temporal inconsistencies of the signals; e.g. the dynamics of changing of signals can be too steep, frequencies of event occurrence can be to high, etc.

Failure in the systems can be handled by redundancy and diversity, with reconfiguration etc. [2], but first the failure in the system must be detected. To do this, some sort of a dependable monitoring subsystem must be used that detects abnormalities in the system and triggers appropriate corrective actions. To lower the complexity, safety related issues of the system should be designed, evaluated and implemented independently and in parallel with the functional part. This is also true for fault detection. To achieve this, a set of monitoring components (we named it monitoring cell - MC) is introduced. In early phases of the development of the system each MC is considered as an abstract object. In later phases, the MCs can be implemented as hardware and/or software components. The basic task of the monitoring cell is to monitor the validity of input and output values of the sub process. A monitoring cells are only parts of larger fault detection and fault prevention system.

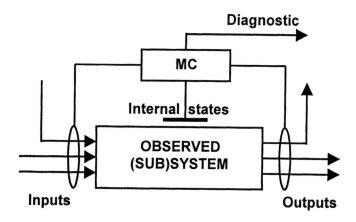

Figure 1. Concept of the Monitoring cell

Monitoring cell should be simple and should produce as little interference with the production environment as possible. It should be built from simple and robust components with low probability of failure. It should work with both custom built and Commercial Off-The-Shelf (COTS) components. It is supposed to be built in such way that it could be formally verified and possibly certified by a certification authority. Even if by this we cannot formally prove that the system will be dependable as a whole, we should prove that the safety-related subsystem is. When MC detects failure in the sub-process it usually does not react on its own. Instead, it signals the source and cause of error to the upper layers in the safety-related subsystem.

The proposed architecture of MC can be divided into four parts: decoder logic, validation logic, state machine and timing logic.

Decoder logic converts observed variables of the system into a form that can be used by monitoring systems. Usually it partitions the definition domain of each input and output value into a set of ranges and assigns to them appropriate discrete values. With this, discrete and continuous values can be mapped into a manageable set of states. Another possibility is that observed values are degraded by means of its accuracy to reduce complexity of the monitoring function (e.g. for A/D conversion of inputs fewer bits are used than that used by observed function). If it is convenient, all relevant internal variables that represent the current context of the task can also be observed in this way.

Decoder logic can also detect if observed values are out of predefined ranges and produce the appropriate diagnostic signals. Further, some physical characteristic of the hardware components can be measured to detect any abnormalities (e.g. measurement of the environment temperature or measurement of electric current consumption). Thus, early correction actions can be taken by the system even before the controlled function is activated.

Decoder logic also latches all relevant values of the inputs to be used when outputs are produced and/or when a validation of dynamic changes is performed.

Validation logic makes sure that the outputs of the system are consistent with the inputs. In the basic case when input and output values are transcribed into small sets of discrete states, a list of all valid combinations can be enumerated and later observed. In more general cases, validation logic can be understood as a pattern-matching algorithm. It tests of a current combination of (mapped) inputs and outputs is valid. In this case validation logic can be represented as a Boolean function of the observed inputs, outputs, internal states and time. In addition to Boolean output of validation logic, other diagnostic signals can be generated that may give the hints as to what is the cause of the failure.

State machine is an optional component that moderates when evaluation logic should perform its evaluation. There are situations where behaviour of the monitored component changes significantly during the application execution (e.g. when the system can operate in several different modes). Also, if the controlled function is performed in several steps, it may be desired to observe and monitor each individual step separately. By this, inconsistencies in process execution can be detected early enough, and some correction measures can be taken. In a simple scenario, state machine logic can be left out because the evaluation is done only twice: first, when input values are evaluated and second when output values and input/output combinations are tested. This can be triggered by data arrival or by additional signals from controlled sub-process.

Timing logic is an optional component that can be used to validate temporal properties of the process. In the most basic scenario, this logic performs a similar function to a simple watchdog timer. When a task starts, the timer is set to the task's deadline. The timer is reset by the production of outputs. If no output is generated in a predetermined time, MC signals to the fault-tolerant subsystem that temporal requirements are violated. In more complex situations, timing logic is coupled with the state machine and additional checkpoints are added into the process. Again, this allows temporal inconsistencies to be detected early enough to react in time.

Other usage of the timing logic is in the monitoring of dynamic behaviour of the system. For example, by comparing two successive signals in a given time interval, it can detect if the changes are too steep or if the frequency of arrival of the signals is to high.

3. IMPLEMENTATION OF MC

There are several possible approaches for the implementation of MCs, and when mapping is simple enough, its implementation can be automated and/or emulated in the early stages of development.

In simple cases software solutions can be applied. With this, each MC can be implemented as a set of monitoring routines that runs together with production software. Simple mapping tables or decision trees can be used by software implementation. These routines can be integrated into the operating system. In this case evaluation routines are divided into two parts. The first set of routines is called after inputs are acquired and before the code of the main function is called. It performs preparation and validation of inputs. After the code of the task is executed and before outputs are produced, another set of routines is called that evaluates outputs and input-output combinations.

The next example shows how these routines can be integrated into the code. Each input, output and other parts of the algorithm are associated with a constant that identifies them.

```
functon PerformTask:
AcquireInputs(i1,i2)
if not MCEvaluateInputInt(INPUT1_ID,i1) then
    HandleException
if not MCEvaluateInputFloat(INPUT2_ID,i2) then
    HandleException
MCSetDeadline(FUNCTION1_ID)
Compute(i1,i2,o1)
if not MCEvaluateOutputInt(OUTPUT1_ID,o1) then
    HandleException
if not MCEvaluateResults(FUNCTION1_ID) then
    HandleException
ProduceOutputs(o1)
```

A higher degree of dependability and agility can be achieved by using dedicated hardware solutions. In most cases they can be implemented with simple discrete logic (i.e. FPGA): decoder logic can be implemented with a collection of comparators, validation logic is implemented by simple logical gates; the state machine and the timing logic are implemented by means of flip-flops and simple registers.

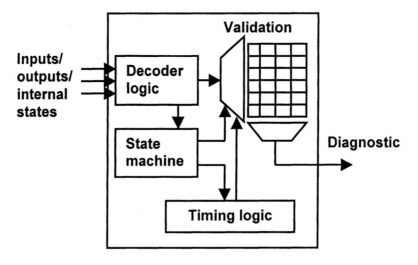

Figure 2. Hardware implementation of the MC

If the requirements are simple enough, automated generation of the VHDL description from the application specification is possible.

If the observed system is very complex or if it behaves in a non-deterministic way, then simple validation logic may not be good enough. In this case more sophisticated methods should be implemented. For example, validation logic can be observed as a pattern classification problem in the neural net paradigm [4], fuzzy functions can be used, etc.

4.   OTHER POSSIBLE USE OF MC

There are some other possible uses of the MCs. When mapping functions are simple enough, MC can be implemented (emulated) before the actual process is built. By this, it can be used either as a surrogate of the process or as an additional test bed for then original task.

MC can also be used as a last resort in the situation of primary process failure. Based on the simplified knowledge of the mapping inputs into outputs, it can be used to generate rough output results. In this case, for each valid input combination, the most appropriate output must be noted.

5. CONCLUSION

The paper represents the work in progress. There are several aspects of the problem of fault detection that are not yet adequately resolved. One of the problems is how are the parameters for the MC gathered from specifications of the system. This can be difficult if fault-tolerant issues are not appropriately considered in the development (e.g. definition of pre- and post- conditions of tasks, physical descriptions of inputs and outputs, temporal requirements, etc.).

Appropriate mapping of inputs and outputs into simple states is also a difficult part of using MCs and is still an open issue. Some kind of learning technique may be used with a learning set gathered from mathematical models or testing runs.

To test different approaches to MC implementation several short-term subprojects are started that cover software implementation, hardware implementation and the use of machine learning techniques (neural networks and fuzzy logic).

In the future, other aspects of the development of the fault-tolerant system will be investigated.

REFERENCES

[1] N. Storey, 'Safety-Critical Computer Systems', Addison-Wesley Pub, august 1996.
[2] D. S. Herrmann, 'Software Safety an Reliability',
[3] J. P. Bowen in M. G. Hinchey, 'High-Integrity System Specification and Design', Springer, April 1999.
[4] L.W. Fausett, 'Fundamentals of Neural Networks', Prentice Hall, 2001.

Dependability Characterization of Middleware Services

Eric Marsden, Nicolas Perrot, Jean-Charles Fabre and Jean Arlat
LAAS-CNRS, Toulouse, France

Abstract: Integrators of CORBA-based dependable systems require information on the robustness of candidate middleware implementations, in order to select the implementation that is best suited to their requirements. We illustrate an approach for characterizing the dependability of middleware service implementations, with respect to corrupt method invocations arriving over the network. Preliminary results from experiments targeting the CORBA Event Service are presented.

Key words: middleware, dependability characterization, fault injection

1.   INTRODUCTION

Middleware architectures such as CORBA offer a uniform distributed software platform, accommodating various executive layers and programming languages, and providing transparent distribution of application objects. Today, as computing architectures become increasingly complex and computing resource constraints less severe, these features are generating interest for an increasing spectrum of applications, including embedded systems. For instance, developing software components for the wide range of configurations deployed in space applications requires middleware platforms that scale across different satellite configurations, from static telecom architectures to open space stations.

The set of offered features is not the only criterion in the choice of a middleware implementation: performance and robustness are equally important characteristics. While the performance characteristics of middleware have been widely studied, there has been little work on dependability characterization, and thus system integrators lack a clear understanding of the behaviour of middleware candidates in the presence of faults (whereas there is a considerable body of work on the characterization of executive software, e.g. [Koopman and DeVale 1999, Arlat *et al* 2002]). We know of no work on field-based studies of the types of failures that occur in middleware-based systems, and there has, to the best of our knowledge, been little work on the evaluation of the robustness of middleware [Pao *et al* 2001].

In this paper, we present a fault injection approach that is suited to the dependability characterization of middleware service implementations. Building on early work targeting the CORBA Name Service [Marsden and Fabre 2001-a], we have extended our experimental campaigns to the CORBA Event Service, targeting a wider range of candidate middleware implementations. The objective of this paper is to describe our experimental approach, and to give examples of the types of results that can be obtained.

The paper is organized as follows: Section 2 summarizes the method that we have defined to characterize middleware-based systems. Section 3 presents the experiment framework that we have used to carry out fault injection campaigns, and gives some preliminary results. Section 4 provides conclusions.

2.   METHOD

Middleware is generally seen as a layer of software that lies between the operating system and the application layer. A high-level view of an ORB is sufficient for most CORBA development. Indeed, the CORBA specifications are implementation-agnostic, and do not mandate any specific representation for CORBA objects, or impose any particular implementation techniques for brokers, or require any particular form of interaction with the underlying operating system. For dependability analysis, however, more detailed knowledge of the architecture of a CORBA-based system is necessary, particularly with respect to the error confinement regions implied by the architecture.

2.1   Dependability characterization of middleware

Several factors must be considered before devising a fault injection campaign:
- The fault model: which classes of faults to apply, where to insert them, and when? The injection may be triggered by the occurrence of an event of interest, or occur after a predetermined time period. The fault may be

transient in nature (*e.g.*, a single bit-flip), or permanent (*e.g.*, a stuck-at fault).

- The workload: what operational profile or simulated system activity should be applied during the experiment? The workload is evidently very dependent on the target system. Different workloads may lead to different results, since they cause different fault activation patterns.
- The oracle: which core assertions can be stated regarding the correctness of the target's behaviour?
- The observations: how to monitor the system's behaviour and classify the failure modes? It is important that all significant events be observed, which may be difficult in a distributed system, particularly when temporal issues are considered.

In the following, we focus our attention on the characterization of the faults that can affect a CORBA-based distributed system. The types of faults that can affect such systems can be classified as shown in Table 1.

Table 1. Classification of faults affecting a CORBA-based system

Fault Types	Description and examples
Physical	Single Events Upsets or soft faults that can affect the hardware level, in particular RAM or the processor's registers
Software	Design or programming errors affecting the various software levels (application, middleware or operating system)
Resource management	"Process aging" leading to such effects as memory leakage, fragmentation effects and even exhaustion of resources, e.g., file descriptors, disk full conditions, etc.
Communication	Message loss, duplication, incorrect sequencing, delay or corruption

The rest of this section lists a number of approaches that we have proposed [Marsden and Fabre 2001-b] for fault injection in a CORBA environment. These fault injection techniques aim to simulate the different fault classes that were identified above:

Corruption of the memory space: this fault model simulates the impact of faults that affect the host's memory subsystem, in regions such as RAM or I/O controllers.

Code mutation techniques: investigate the impact of software faults, by artificially inserting bugs into the source code of the target, and observing the behaviour of the modified candidate (called a *mutant*).

Robustness testing: injecting corrupted data at the interface of the system. A related characterization technique is stress testing, where the performance of the system is assessed under extreme system load.

Syscall interposition techniques: investigate fault propagation from the operating system to the middleware level. Experiments consist of intercepting system calls made by the middleware, and returning various error codes, to see whether the middleware handles these error conditions gracefully.

Communication faults: simulating the loss, duplication, reordering and corruption of messages. The experiments we report on later in this article have used this fault model, investigating the impact of corrupt method invocations arriving over the network.

2.2   Targeting CORBA Services

The first target for our work on robustness benchmarking has been the suite of CORBA services, because their standardized interface makes it easy to compare different implementations. Furthermore, by providing services to all the participants in a distributed system, they constitute a potential error propagation channel for the system. Our previous work involved the CORBA Name Service, which provides a hierarchical directory for object references. The work we report on in this article concerns the CORBA Event Service, which provides a publish/subscribe communications infrastructure for CORBA-based systems. This service supplements CORBA's standard synchronous request/reply interactions between clients and servers, reducing the static dependencies between components and facilitating system evolution and upgrade.

The CORBA Event Service is based on the notion of an Event Channel, which mediates between event producers and event consumers. Producers and consumers are decoupled: a producer does not know the number of consumers or their identities, and consumers have no knowledge of which supplier generated a given event. The role of the event channel is to accept subscriptions from consumers, and to forward incoming events to each consumer (Figure 1).

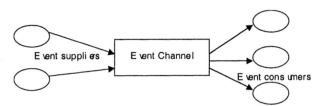

Figure 1. The CORBA event service

Event consumers can either use a pull model (regularly polling for event arrival) or a push model (the event channel sends a message to the consumer as soon as an event arrives), and likewise event producers can choose to push events to the channel, or to allow the channel to pull events by invoking a method implemented by the producer.

The features provided by the Event Service have proven to be insufficient for certain applications, particularly in the telecom domain. The CORBA Notification Service was developed as a more powerful version of the event service, providing a filtering mechanism, and allowing clients to specify Quality of Service attributes on event delivery. Given that the Notification Service is a strict extension of the Event Service, we have included some notification implementations in our experiments (but only test them in compatibility mode, ignoring their extended capabilities).

Our experiments aim to determine how robust the service implementation is, with respect to the corrupted method invocations that we apply. The goal is to investigate the effect of injected faults on the service delivered, for instance on the latency with which events are delivered, and whether event notifications can be lost.

2.3 Injecting Communication Faults

The experiments that we report on in the next target communication faults, specifically the result of corrupted IIOP messages on the event service. This fault model simulates three different classes of faults:

- Transient physical faults in the communication subsystem, resulting for example from faulty memory in routers, or faulty DMA transfers with the network card. This form of corruption, even over reliable transport protocols such as TCP (on which is based IIOP, the most common protocol used in CORBA), is more frequent than is commonly assumed, due to the fact that the TCP checksum is only 16 bits [Stone and Partridge 2000].

- Propagation to the machine or system of a fault that occurred on a remote machine interacting with it. The fault may have affected the remote operating system kernel, its protocol stack implementation, or the remote ORB, leading to the emission of a corrupted request.

- To a limited extent, malicious faults (however, the errors which we simulate are unlikely to be representative of the activities of a malicious user of the system).

The types of errors that we have investigated are single bitflips and the zeroing of two successive bytes in a message. These are among the most common patterns of corruption identified in [Stone and Partridge 2000]. There are several possible means of injecting these faults. We could use dedicated network hardware, but this is cumbersome and expensive. Faults could be injected at the protocol transport layer using software-implemented fault injection (for example by instrumenting the operating system's network stack, as in [Dawson and Jahanian 1995]). However, this form of corruption has a high probability of being detected by the remote host's network stack, and therefore of not being delivered to the middleware level. Consequently, we choose to inject faults at the application level, before encapsulation by the transport layer. In this way we simulate the proportion of corrupt packets that TCP incorrectly delivers as being valid.

3.   TESTBED AND RESULTS

3.1   Experimental Testbed

The experimental testbed that we have used for our experiments consists of a number of components:
–   A workload, which activates the target service's functionality. The workload that we have used consists of an event producer, and two event consumers. The events generated by the producer contain a timestamp and a sequence number. When it receives an event, an event consumer compares the message timestamp to the current time, to determine how much time was taken for the event to be delivered. The consumers also compare the sequence number with a counter that they maintain locally, to determine whether event notifications are being lost.
–   An injector, which sends a corrupted request to the target once the workload has been running for a certain time span. Our fault injector is an event producer, which invokes the push method on the event channel. This message is corrupted using either the bit-flip fault model or the double-zero fault model.
–   Monitors, that observe the behaviour of the target (for instance, CORBA exceptions received by any of the participants, or the crash of a process composing the workload) and log their observations to an SQL database.
–   Offline data analyzers, to identify the various failure modes by examining the data collected by the monitoring components, and produce statistics for an entire campaign.

In our setup, the event service and the various producers and consumers are running on different machines. We use a producer-push, consumer-pull configuration, with untyped events. The workload is able to detect invalid events delivered to it by examining their sequence number. We also monitor the effect of the fault on delivery latencies and on message loss rates.

Each experiment corresponds to a single injected fault. A controller process launches the target service and obtains its object reference (in the implementations which we have targeted, the event service is implemented as a Unix dæmon). It then starts two event consumers, who register with the event channel, and then launches the event producer. After 20 seconds, the fault injector sends a corrupted push request to the target service and waits for the reply. If no reply arrives within 20 seconds, a ServiceHang failure mode is signaled. At the end of the experiment, the monitoring components check for the presence of the different failure modes by trying to launch a command on the target host, checking that the consumer and producer applications are still running, checking for returned exceptions, etc.

Our experiments have been carried out on a rack of x86-based machines running Linux kernel version 2.4.18. For each campaign, the workload components are recompiled using the corresponding vendor's ORB implementation. The machines are connected by a FastEthernet network, and their clocks are synchronized using the NTP algorithm. The results of the campaigns are logged to an SQL database, and analyzed offline.

The failure modes that we monitor are: i) crash of the operating system kernel on the machine hosting the service, ii) crash of the service (attempts to establish a network connection to the service are refused), iii) hang of the service (the service accepts an incoming connection, but does not reply within a given time span), iv) application failure (error propagation to the application level), and v) the raising of a CORBA exception. These failure modes are not exclusive: for instance, a service crash will generally result in clients of the service receiving an exception indicating that a communication error has occurred.

For each targeted implementation, a fault injection campaign involves running an experiment for each bit or octet position in the push request. A campaign lasts around 24 hours per target for the bit-flip fault model.

This fault injection technique is very portable, since the only implementation-specific component in our testbed is the code responsible for launching the target implementation. The technique is also non intrusive, and does not require any instrumentation of the targeted service.

3.2 Preliminary Results

Our fault injection campaigns have targeted a number of candidate implementations of the Event Service:
- The CosEventService for *ORBacus* 4.4.1 for C++, a commercial ORB from IONA;
- The *ORBacus* CosNotification Service, version 2.0;
- The CosEventService from *TAO* version 1.2.1, an open-source ORB developed at Washington University (this implementation has some real-time capabilities, that we did not use in our experiments);
- *OmniNotify* 1.x, a CosNotification implementation for the open-source ORB *omniORB*, developed by AT&T Laboratories Cambridge;
- The CosEventService for *MICO* version 2.3.6, an open-source ORB (www.mico.org).

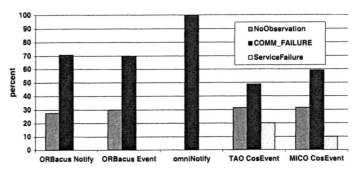

Figure 2. Client-side exceptions for bit-flip experiments.

Figure 2 illustrates some results obtained from experiments where a single bit of the method invocation is corrupted. The graph shows results for every possible bit position in the push request sent to the event service. The ServiceFailure outcome indicates that the service crashed after receiving the corrupt method invocation. The COMM_FAILURE outcome signifies that the client received a CORBA exception informing it that a non-transient communication error occurred. Each experiment is classified according to the most serious failure mode observed; failure of the service is considered more serious than the observation of a communication failure exception received by the fault injector. In these experiments (that are reproducible), each target was subjected to 80 fault injections.

An initial observation is that the *TAO* and *MICO* implementations of the event service crash relatively frequently, whereas the three other implementations do not crash when subjected to the exceptional inputs that we generate. The crashes are unfortunate from a robustness point of view, since they imply that a malicious or corrupted object that is able to send remote method invocations to the service is able to cause denial of service through the loss of event notifications.

A further observation is that the set of experimental outcomes is quite limited: we have not observed any examples of kernel crash or hang, nor any application failure outcomes. Furthermore, the set of exceptions that are observed in these experiments is restricted by the fact that the invoked method does not have a return value. We observed a wider range of exceptions in our experiments targeting the CORBA Name Service [Marsden and Fabre 2001-a], since the method that we corrupted returned information to the client. We can carry out further analysis of an implementation's behaviour by examining the errors detected by the service but not transmitted to the client. Certain implementations can be configured to output messages showing the CORBA exceptions that are detected locally, but not transmitted to the client. For instance, the breakdown of server-side observed exceptions for the *ORBacus Notify* implementation is shown in Figure 3.

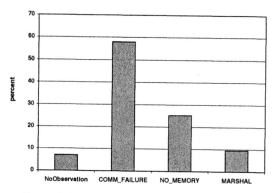

Figure 3. Server-side exceptions for *ORBacus Notify*

We can further analyse the results obtained according to the position in the message where the corruption was inserted. Bit-flips in the first 32 bits of the message are detected by the service as COMM_FAILURE exceptions; this is due to the fact that all CORBA method invocations start with four "magic" octets, so their corruption can easily be detected by the service. The NO_MEMORY exceptions are probably due to the bit-flip having affected a portion of the message that represents a length; the ORB attempts to allocate a buffer of this length, but the allocation fails due to the announced length being greatly increased by the bit-flip. The marshalling exceptions are due to the payload of the push request being corrupted.

We can also try to determine why an implementation crashes when it receives badly formatted messages, by examining a trace of the system calls made by the service. We observe that the *MICO* implementation exits when a memory allocation request fails; it would be preferable from a robustness point of view to return a NO_MEMORY exception to the client, as do the *ORBacus* implementations. The *TAO* implementation attempts to access memory that is not allocated to it (probably accessing a memory address that was calculated with respect to an offset read from the message), and is aborted by the operating system. Figure 4 shows an example trace for the *TAO* implementation, showing that it was aborted after having read an IIOP message from the network.

```
select(19, [7 9 10 11 12 13 14 15 16 17 18], NULL, NULL, {4, 408508}) = 1 (in [18], left {4, 410000})
gettimeofday({1017746631, 433883}, NULL) = 0
read(18, "GIOP\1\2\0\0\270\0\0\0\6\0\0\0003\0\0\0\0\0fo\33\0\0\0"..., 1020) = 196
brk(0x80d7000)             = 0x80d7000
brk(0x80db000)             = 0x80db000
brk(0x80e2000)             = 0x80e2000
brk(0x80e9000)             = 0x80e9000
--- SIGSEGV (Segmentation fault) ---
+++ killed by SIGSEGV +++
```

Figure 4. System call trace for the *TAO* implementation

4.   CONCLUSION

The analysis of failure modes for reliable embedded platforms is mandatory to design the architecture of the system and to select the appropriate dependability mechanisms. These include both wrapping techniques to improve the error detection mechanisms, and fault tolerance techniques to recover from various types of faults. It is worth noting that a clear understanding of middleware failure modes may have a strong impact on the architectural mechanisms used to enhance the system's fault tolerance.

The work reported in this paper aims at providing objective information about the behaviour of a middleware-based systems in the presence of faults. Some results concerning the analysis of real industrial middleware targets are presented. Although very preliminary, these results show the types of insights that can be obtained from fault injection experiments. Our ongoing work is aimed at investigating the effect of injected faults on delivery latency and on the rate of event loss.

Acknowledgement. This work is partially supported by the European Community (project IST-1999-11585: DSoS — Dependable Systems of Systems).

5.   REFERENCES

[Arlat *et al* 2002] J. Arlat, J.-C. Fabre, M. Rodríguez and F. Salles, "Dependability of COTS Microkernel-Based Systems", IEEE Trans. on Computers, vol. 51, no. 2, pp. 138-163, 2002.

[Dawson and Jahanian 1995] S. Dawson and F. Jahanian, "Probing and Fault Injection of Dependable Distributed Protocols", *The Computer Journal*, vol. 38 no. 4, pp. 286-300, 1995.

[Koopman and DeVale, 1999] P. J. Koopman and J. DeVale, "Comparing the Robustness of POSIX Operating Systems", Proc. 29th Int. Symp. on Fault-Tolerant Computing (FTCS-29), pp. 30-37, Madison, WI, USA, 1999. IEEE CS Press.

[Marsden and Fabre 2001-a] E. Marsden and J.-C. Fabre, "Failure Mode Analysis of CORBA Service Implementations", Proc. IFIP/ACM Int. Conf. on Distributed Systems Platforms (Middleware'2001), pp. 216-231, Heidelberg, Germany, 2001. LNCS 2218.

[Marsden and Fabre 2001-b] E. Marsden and J.-C. Fabre, "Failure Analysis of an ORB in Presence of Faults", DSoS Project IST-1999-11585, november 2001, 45 p. (also available from LAAS-CNRS)

[Pan et al 2001] J. Pan, P. J. Koopman, D. P. Siewiorek, Y. Huang, R. Gruber and M. Jiang, "Robustness Testing and Hardening of CORBA ORB Implementations", Proc. IEEE/IFIP 2001 Int. Conf. on Dependable Systems and Networks (DSN'2001), pp. 141-150, Göteborg, Sweden, 2001. IEEE CS Press.

[Stone and Partridge, 2000] J. Stone and C. Partridge. "When the CRC and TCP Checksum Disagree". Proc. 2000 SIGCOMM Conference, pp. 309–319, 2000. ACM Press.

Adaptive Middleware for Ubiquitous Computing Environments

Stephen S. Yau and Fariaz Karim
Computer Science and Engineering Department
Arizona State University
Tempe, AZ 85287, USA

Abstract: Rapid growth in inexpensive, short range, and low-power wireless communication hardware and network standards are now enabling the construction of ubiquitous computing and communication environments. Devices in ubicomp environments form short range and low power mobile ad hoc networks whose topologies are usually dynamic due to arbitrary node mobility. Typical applications in ubicomp environments are context-sensitive, adaptive, and often engage in impromptu, and volatile communication. These properties require both programming and runtime support in the application and system levels. A middleware approach can be very effective to provide these support to reduce the effort required to develop ubicomp software, in addition to providing the commonly known middleware services, such as interoperability, location transparency, naming service, etc. In contrast to middleware architectures for fixed networks, a middleware for ubicomp environments should be adaptive to various contexts, be reconfigurable, and should be of high-performance to facilitate ad hoc communication among objects. In this paper, an adaptive middleware, which is reconfigurable and context sensitive, is presented for applications in ubiquitous computing environments.

Keywords: Ubiquitous computing, adaptive middleware, mobile ad hoc networks, context-sensitive applications, reconfiguration, smart classroom.

1.   INTRODUCTION

The concept of ubiquitous computing (ubicomp) [1,2] focuses on integrating computers with the physical environment, making computing and communication transparent to the users. Devices that operate in these environments are usually embedded with low-power and short-range wireless communication capabilities. In addition, the devices are free to move arbitrarily (e.g. a wearable device moves with a living carrier), usually have bandwidth and energy constraints, and are equipped with multiple sensors. The topologies in ad hoc networks are dynamic, and usually no dedicated network connectivity devices exist. Based on physical environmental conditions and other stimulus, nodes in this environment form numerous webs of ad hoc short-range wireless networks to exchange information, and react in a transparent fashion.

User applications running in ubicomp environments have the following characteristics [3-5]:

- Context and resource sensitivity: Applications use various data about the surrounding environment to adapt their behavior and interactions.
- Impromptu and volatile distributed interaction: Communication channels among applications tend to be instantaneously established and terminated due to changing contexts and node mobility.
- Intelligent human computer interaction: Applications provide richer and natural interfaces to support common forms of human expression, such as speech, gesture, etc.

Based on the above characteristics, it is necessary to provide system support for the development and runtime support for applications that are adaptive in response to different contexts. In this respect, middleware can be very effective due its basic services, such as interoperability, naming, location-transparency, etc. Hence, a middleware for ubicomp environments should have the following capabilities:

- **Support for adaptive and context-sensitive application development:** This capability enables a middleware to facilitate the development phase of adaptive and context-sensitive applications. To address context-sensitive applications, such a middleware should have an interface definition language to associate various object methods with desirable contexts. In addition, a middleware should also be able to use the interface specification to generate application-specific context-detectors and analyzers to further ease the development phase. On the other hand, to address applications that are adaptive in response to various contexts, a middleware for ubicomp environment should provide the runtime services for coordinating the adaptation triggering and context-analysis capabilities. Although the nature of specific adaptation is application-specific, a middleware, in summary, should provide a flexible framework for effectively developing and deploying adaptive and context-sensitive application software. In summary, this capability allows an application developer to focus on the application development rather than diverting much effort to context detection, analysis, and adaptation triggering mechanisms.

- **Runtime support ad hoc communication among applications:** Devices in ubicomp environments usually form mobile ad hoc networks [6] that enable impromptu and volatile interactions among the applications resident in these devices. To directly address the nature of ad hoc interaction, the communication support in a middleware for ubicomp environment must be adaptive to various network events, such as arrival of new nodes, departure of existing nodes, and route changes (for multihop ad hoc networks). Since communication is more expensive than computation in wireless environments, a middleware should utilize its communication and service discovery services intelligently based on the contexts and actual need of the application software. In summary, the second capability allows the devices to interact autonomously using various types of application-specific context as the conditions for managing the communication.

- **Application-specific adaptive services:** In addition to the basic capabilities, a middleware should provide various application-specific services in adaptive fashion. Some examples of these services are as follows:

a) **Security:** Due to the open interactions in ubicomp environments, various security capabilities, such as key exchange, encryption, authentication, intrusion detection and assessment, must be incorporated into a middleware. In addition, these services should be adaptive in response to the changes in the environments and application requirements.

b) **Group management:** To support collaborative computing among devices, devices should be able to form ephemeral groups based on specific contexts or situations [7]. The management of these groups should be efficient and adaptive since dynamic changes in the group membership and topology is a norm rather than an exception in ubicomp environments.

- **Interoperability with middleware for other domains:** To allow a greater degree of interoperability, a middleware for ubicomp environments should provide interoperability support such that an enterprise application can communicate with an ubicomp application without significant effort on the developers' parts. This requires that a middleware should provide runtime services for exchanging service information and application data with different types of middleware. In summary, this capability will allow plug-and-play of various types of middleware across multiple domains, such as mobile ad hoc, infrastructure-based mobile, and enterprise networks.

A middleware for ubicomp environments should also be reconfigurable, provide the support for constructing additional middleware services (e.g. group communication, authentication), and be interoperable with other types of middleware to enable a broader level of application interoperability. Enterprise middleware specifications, such as CORBA [8], and middleware for mobile networks, such as ALICE [9], LIME [10], iMAQ [11], Bluedrekar [12], and XMIDDLE [13] do not completely address the fundamental issues related to providing adaptive support for applications in ubicomp environments. In this paper, we will present an adaptive middleware, based on Reconfigurable Context-Sensitive Middleware (RCSM) [5, 14-16], for ubicomp environments.

2.   OUR APPROACH

Our approach to developing the adaptive middleware is based on the Reconfigurable Context-Sensitive Middleware (RCSM), which has the following properties:

- Facilities for application-specific adaptation by providing mechanism for context-sensitive object interface definition and application-specific context detector generation.
- Facilities for autonomous and symmetric communication channel establishment and object activation based on application-specific context.
- Context-sensitive service discovery and distribution among devices in ubicomp environments.
- Group communication and information dissemination services.

In addition, the architecture of RCSM has the following features:

- Co-designed in software and reconfigurable Field Programmable Gate Arrays (FPGA) to achieve both software-hardware reconfiguration and high performance. Software is used for application-specific services, and the FPGA is used for providing core RCSM services.
- Architecture is modeled after CORBA Object Management Architecture (OMA) to allow interoperability with middleware for fixed networks.

In the rest of this paper, we will give an overview of RCSM and discuss its principal support for applications in ubicomp environments. A smart classroom is being developed as a test bed for evaluating RCSM in practical setting.

3. APPLICATION DEVELOPMENT AND AD HOC INTERACTION SUPPORT IN RCSM

Most ubicomp application software can be characterized as context-sensitive. *Context-sensitive applications* are characterized by their use of context to drive their operations and/or adaptation mechanisms. Examples of context-sensitive applications can be found in [17-19]. RCSM provides both development time and runtime support for these applications as follows:

- A context-aware interface definition language for context-sensitive object interface specification and application-specific context detector generation.
- A context-sensitive communication mechanism to enable ad hoc service discovery and communication among the devices.

The first capability allows an application developer to focus on the application development rather than spending effort on the generation of context-detection and analysis. The second capability allows the devices to interact autonomously using various types of application-specific context as the conditions for managing the communications.

RCSM facilitates context-sensitive application development as follows:

1. RCSM provides context-aware interface definition language (CA-IDL) to specify context variables and expressions in an IDL file. Context variables and expressions are programming constructs used in CA-IDL to use the current values of different types of contexts.
2. After identifying the object interface, and the object developer identifies the methods that need to be context-sensitive.

3. The methods identified in Step 2 are associated with a context variable or context expression using two simple rules described in [14].
4. The IDL file is then processed by the CA-IDL compiler to generate an Adaptive Object Container (ADC), which include the following objects: a context reflector, a base object, and a dispatcher.
5. The base object is then extended to implement the actual object along with the definitions of its methods.

We are currently extending CA-IDL and its compiler to support situation-awareness [6] in applications. Now, we describe how RCSM facilitates ad hoc interactions of context-sensitive applications in the devices.

Ad hoc interaction refers to the impromptu and decentralized interaction among a set of devices. Evolving standards, such as Bluetooth [20], IrDA [21], IEEE 802.15 [22] provides both radio and transport layer capabilities for ad hoc networking. However, to directly support the ad hoc interaction in the application level, RCSM provides the necessary facilities as follows:

a) RCSM provides an adaptive runtime support for ad hoc networking through context-triggered communication channels. *Context-triggered* communication is a type of communication model where a communication channel is established between a pair of devices A and B whenever the following conditions are true:
– Each device has at least one application object, which has previously specified its interest to be activated in a particular context, which is currently true. Lets refer to these objects as OA and OB for Devices A and B respectively.
– OA and OB are suitable to exchange data with each other. By suitability, we mean matching of the object interface signatures, including number of parameters and parameter types, radio frequency identifiers, etc.

b) R-ORB, which is the Object Request Broker (ORB) of RCSM, is responsible for managing context-triggered communication channels as follows:

– R-ORB uses the notion of proximity and application-specific context to establish a handshaking channel with another device.
– A context-sensitive service discovery/distribution procedure is performed by both R-ORBs to identify if each device has any suitable object to engage in information exchange. Suitability is defined as matching of the object interface signatures, including number of parameters and parameter types, radio frequency identifiers, etc.

– R-ORB establishes a symmetric communication [14] channel with the remote device.

4.   ADAPTIVE OBJECT ACTIVATION IN RCSM

Context-sensitive object activation is the process of invoking a context-sensitive object whenever its specified context is true. RCSM performs this activity using object-specific Adaptive Object Container (ADC):

1. An application object becomes context-sensitive by associating at least one of its methods with a context variable or a context expression (as mentioned in Section 1). This is accomplished by using Context-Aware Interface Definition Language (CA-IDL) [5].
2. The CA-IDL compiler generates a customized Adaptable Object Container (ADC), which periodically receives different context data. Using these context data and based on the CA-IDL specification, ADC decides if the current context matches the desired context of the application object. If it does, ADC generates a context-match event.
3. The context-match event is then passed to context-sensitive ORB. In this phase, the ORB performs service discovery operation, and if the identity-match event occurs, establishes a context-triggered communication channel with the other device.
4. After the communication channel is established, the ORB notifies the appropriate ADC, which in turn activates the object and invokes the appropriate method.

5.   ADDITIONAL FEATURES OF RCSM

5.1   Reconfigurable Architecture of RCSM

The core services of a middleware, such as the R-ORB functionality, must be highly efficient to address different degree of scalability. However, these operations are usually repeated instructions and often need not be changed. In contrast, application-specific services of a middleware, such as an ADC, needs to be generated anew whenever an interface is changed. Often times sophisticated scalability improvement techniques are not economical in embedded devices due to different constraints. It is shown that reconfigurable processors are useful in computations that are regular [23]. As such, R-ORB is based on a software-hardware co-design approach to achieving both reconfigurability and performance desired for applications in ubicomp environments. FPGAs are a type of reconfigurable hardware components that can be reprogrammed after fabrication to achieve flexibility and customizability. This property lead us to choose FPGAs for R-ORB implementation since most ORB-specific operations, such as data marshalling, context-processing connection management, and R-GIOP protocol processing are also regular and require high performance to increase its sensitivity of the overall RCSM services. In addition, reconfigurability is also useful in R-ORB, since it is expected that different configurations of R-ORB may be necessary to fit the sensors (which are in fact peripherals of a device) and constraints of embedded devices.

5.2   RCSM-CORBA Interoperability

To provide interoperability with middleware for another domain, RCSM is also being designed to provide RCSM-CORBA protocol primitives. The following are the main features of this aspect:

- CORBA Object Support in RCSM: RCSM's CA-IDL is partially based on the syntax and semantics of CORBA IDL, version 2.3. As such, it is possible define CORBA object in RCSM. In this case, the context of the object is not specified, and as such it can be invoked any time following a service discovery operation between a pair of devices.
- CORBA Object-Context-Sensitive Object Interaction: To support the interaction between a pair of CORBA and a context-sensitive object, RCSM's R-GIOP protocol interacts as a CORBA GIOP protocol whenever a valid CORBA request is received. To facilitate this, the service discovery mechanism of RCSM is also extended to discover CORBA objects in other nodes, such as PCs and workstations.

In addition, RCSM is currently extended with ephemeral group management and information dissemination services.

6.   TEST BED DEVELOPMENT

To evaluate RCSM, we are currently implementing a smart classroom test bed to facilitate teaching and collaborative learning among college level students. The test bed will facilitate different activities leading to efficient teaching and collaboration in a classroom. For example:
- Automated synchronization and selection of lecture slides between the instructor's PDA and PC.

- Instructor assigns students into groups to collaboratively solve a particular problem. The PDAs of the students in the same group forms an ad hoc network. Using the ad hoc network, the PDAs aid the students to exchange their ideas to solve the assigned problem.

7. DISCUSSION

In this paper, we have presented how an adaptive middleware, such as RCSM, can be effectively used to support applications in ubicomp environments. Specifically, we have presented RCSM's support for context-sensitive interface specification and adaptive mechanisms for establishing context-triggered communication channels. We are validating the functionality of the RCSM using a software-hardware co-design approach for various embedded devices in ubicomp environments. We are also currently constructing a *Smart Classroom* test bed to evaluate RCSM in a real-life setting. Our test bed nodes are being constructed using PDAs, various sensors, FPGAs, and short-range radio modules. Future research includes additional services for RCSM, such as various security features and reconfiguration. On the architecture aspect, RCSM will be improved to use reflection and context cooperatively. Moreover, the interoperability of RCSM with middleware for other types of environments will be explored.

ACKNOWLEDGEMENT

This work is partially supported by National Science Foundation under grant no. ANI-0123980. Microsoft and Tektronix contributed part of the equipment for the construction of the test bed. Our project web site is http://www.eas.asu.edu/~rcsm.

REFERENCES

[1] M. Weiser, "The Computer for the Twenty-First Century", *Scientific American,* pp. 94-10, September 1991.
[2] M. Weiser, "Some Computer Science Problems in Ubiquitous Computing", *Communications of the ACM,* Vol. 36, No. 7, July 1993, pp. 75-84.
[3] G. Abowd and E. D. Mynatt, "Charting Past, Present, and Future Research in Ubiquitous Computing", *ACM Trans. Computer Human Interaction,* Vol. 7, No.1, pp. 29-58, March 2000.
[4] MIT Laboratory for Computer Science, The Oxygen Project, http://www.oxygen.lcs.mit.edu/.

[5] S. S. Yau and F. Karim, "Reconfigurable Context-Sensitive Middleware for ADS Applications in Mobile Ad Hoc Network Environments", *Proc. 5th IEEE Int'l Symp. Autonomous Decentralized Systems (ISADS 2001)*, pp. 319-326, March 2001.

[6] Internet Engineering Task Force, *Mobile Ad Hoc Networks Charter*, http://www.ietf.org/html.charters/manet-charter.html, 2001.

[7] S. S. Yau, Y. Wang, and F. Karim, "Situation-Awareness in Application Software for Ubiquitous Computing Environments", submitted for publication in the *proceedings of the 26th IEEE Int'l Computer Software and Applications Conference (COMPSAC 2002)*, Oxford, UK.

[8] Object Management Group, *CORBA 2.5 Specification*, http://www.omg.org.

[9] M. Haahr, R. Cunningham and V. Cahill, "Supporting CORBA Applications in a Mobile Environment", *Proc. 5th ACM/IEEE Int'l Conf. Mobile Computing and Networking (MobiCom 99)*, August 1999, pp. 36-47.

[10] A. Murphy, G. Picco, and G.-C. Roman, "LIME: A Middleware for Physical and Logical Mobility", Proc. 21st Int'l Conf. Distributed Computing Systems (ICDCS 2001), April 2001, http://www.cs.rochester.edu/u/www/u/murphy/.

[11] K. Chen, S. H. Shah, K. Nahrstedt, "Cross-Layer Design for Data Accessibility in Mobile Ad Hoc Networks", to appear in *Journal of Wireless Personal Communications*, 2002, http://cairo.cs.uiuc.edu/adhoc/index.html.

[12] IBM Research, Bluedrekar Project, http://www.research.ibm.com/BlueDrekar/.

[13] C. Mascolo, L. Capra, S. Zachariadis, and W. Emmerich, "XMIDDLE: A Data-Sharing Middleware for Mobile Computing", *Int'l Journal on Wireless Personal Communications*. Paper location: http://www.cs.ucl.ac.uk/staff/W.Emmerich/publications/index.html.

[14] S. S. Yau and F. Karim, "Context-Sensitive Middleware for Real-Time Software in Ubiquitous Computing Environments", *Proc. 4th Int'l Symp. Object Oriented Real-Time Distributed Computing (ISORC 2001)*, Magdeburg, Germany, pp. 163-170, May 2001.

[15] S. S. Yau and F. Karim, "Context-Sensitive Distributed Software Development for Ubiquitous Computing Environments", *Proc. 25th Int'l Computer Software and Applications Conference (COMPSAC 2001)*, USA, October 2001, pp. 263-268.

[16] S. S. Yau and F. Karim, "Context-Sensitive Object Request Broker for Ubiquitous Computing Environments", *8th IEEE Workshop on Future Trends of Distributed Computing Systems (FTDCS 01)*, Italy, October 2001, pp. 34-40.

[17] G. Chen and D. Kotz, "A Survey of Context-Aware Mobile Computing Research", *ACM Operating Systems Review*, 35(1), January, 2001, http://www.cs.dartmouth.edu/reports/authors/Kotz,David.html.

[18] N. Marmasse and C. Schmandt, "Location-aware Information Delivery with comMotion", *Proc. 2nd Int'l Symp. Handheld and Ubiquitous Computing (HUC 2K)*, http://www.media.mit.edu/~nmarmas/cmHUC2k.pdf.

[19] J. Pascoe, "Adding Generic Contextual Capabilities to Wearable Computers", *Proc. 2nd IEEE Int'l Symp. On Wearable Computers*, October 1998, pp. 92-99, http://www.cs.ukc.ac.uk/pubs/1998/676/.

[20] *Specification of the Bluetooth System*. Core, version 1.0 B. Specification location: http://www.bluetooth.com/.

[21] *IrDA Protocol Standards*. Specification location: http://www.irda.org/standards/standards.asp.

[22] *Working Group for Wireless Personal Area Networks*. Group location: http://grouper.ieee.org/groups/802/15/.

[23] A. DeHon, "The Density Advantage Configurable Computing, *Computer*, Vol. 33, No. 4, April 2000, pp. 41-49.

Finegrained Application Specific Customization of Embedded Software[1]
Some Considerations

Danilo Beuche, Olaf Spinczyk, Wolfgang Schröder-Preikschat
Otto-von-Guericke-Universität Magdeburg

Abstract: The paper describes techniques, which have been developed to simplify the customization of the PURE operating system family for embedded systems and can be applied to almost any embedded software intended for reuse. The approach is based on feature modeling and the use of aspect-oriented programming and supported by a complete tool chain.

Key words: embedded systems, configuration, feature modelling, aspect oriented programming

1.   INTRODUCTION

Software engineers who are not familiar with the problems of embedded systems often wonder why so little of their nice ideas about how software should be designed make it into embedded software. This is especially true for deeply embedded systems. Object-oriented programming with 8 and 16 bit microcontroller is an exception of the rule. C and assembly are the predominant languages in this field.

Reuse of software is very limited. One could say — and many do believe — , that this is caused by the fact, that most of the programmers are engineers or physicists not computer scientists.

But this is only one half of the story. The question to ask is: Could a computer scientist program nice, reusable software for the same problem in the same time which fits into the microcontroller? This is the heart of the

---

[1] This work has been partially supported by the Deutsche Forschungsgemeinschaft (DFG), grant no. SCHR 603/1, and SCHR 603/2, and the Bundesministerium für Bildung und Forschung (BMBF) grant no. 1IS903E5.

problem: Most of the concepts for reuse developed for workstation or pc class software are not feasible for programming small microcontrollers with limited processing power and memory in the low kilobytes. The trade-off for reusable software is its runtime efficiency and/or the required memory space.

The PURE operating system family [1] is targeted at deeply embedded systems and it is implemented using the object-oriented language C++. Several publications have shown that PURE is able to meet the requirements of deeply embedded systems. This is mainly due to the capability of PURE of being very fine-grain configurable. However this capability also was one of the most serious problems during the development of PURE: namely, to make users able to deal with the vast number of configuration decisions. Pure allows the user to control the provided functionality on a very detailed level because only by excluding every unneeded PURE functionality it is possible to make applications fit into a small microcontroller.

This problems lead to the development of additional techniques which made the PURE system easier to use and eventually opened previously impossible ways of doing things.

Using a small example throughout the paper it will be shown that it is possible to provide programmers with reusable abstractions suitable for embedded use. The next section introduces the example and explains the relevant properties of the implementation. The following section introduces the feature-based modeling for software used to hide the reusable implementation from a deployer of a reusable abstraction. The fourth section provides ideas on the use of aspect-oriented programming in embedded contexts. The concluding section summarizes the work and presents some ideas for future work.

2.   THERE IS NO RIGHT WAY

The problem of reuse is quite simple: if an optimal solution for a problem under a given set of constraints is available, it is not necessarily the optimal solution for the same problem under a different set of constraints.

To illustrate this problem three different applications of the cosine function are introduced:

Application 1	Application 2	Application 3
A high precision value is required, real-time execution is not required but the available memory to store constant data is limited.	The second application requires a high precision of the returned cosine value, the angle might be any value but the calculation has to be finished fast and within a deterministic time frame	A sensor measures the angle only in 16 discrete values, the application has tight real-time requirements and very limited code space available.

While it is easy to provide a common cosine implementation for all 3 applications using the standard iterative algorithm shown in figure 1, which returns correct values for every input value, this algorithm is not able to meet the additional constraints of applications 2 and 3. Its timing is hard to predict and it requires a large amount of code for its floating point operations[2]

```
#include "cosine.h"
const double DEG2RAD = 0.01745329251994 /* (PI/180) */
double cosine(const int degree)
{
    const double rad = (double)degree * DEG2RAD;
    double res_last, sign = fac_value = power = res = 1.0;
    double faculty = 0.0;
    double square = rad * rad;
    do
    {
        res_last = res;
        sign=(sign==1.0)?-1.0:1.0;
        fac_value *= ++faculty;
        fac_value *= ++faculty;
        power *= square;
        res = res_last + sign * (power/fac_value);
    } while (res != res_last);
    return res;
}
```

Figure 1: Sourcecode for iterative cosine calculation

A different solution (see figure 2), which provides deterministic runtimes is based on a table of known cosine values and interpolation to calculate the result for arbitrary values. The trade-off here is that depending on the number of the known values the accuracy of the result differs. Using more values consumes more data memory to store the table.

While this implementation is appropriate for many applications, for some an even more simplistic solution is possible. Because only a limited number of discrete angle values with equal distances are possible, it is very easy to implement a purely table based cosine function (see figure 3). No calculation is required, especially no floating point operation at all occurs.

The code sizes for the different implementations are very different. Table 1 shows code and data space requirements for a number of different platforms ranging from 8bit controllers to 32bit processors. The application consisted of a single call to the cosine function in main. The void application is just an empty main function.

---

[2] It is assumed that the processor does not have a floating point unit.

Table 1: Code and data sizes (bytes) for sample cosine applications

Processor	App. 1	App. 2	App. 3	void App.
M68HC12 (16bit, w/o FPU)	821+233	11287+1078	13204+1448	77+50
PowerPC (32bit, w/o FPU)	152+104	4408+284	5044+84	32
PowerPC (32bit, w/ FPU)	88+96	184+240	252+40	8

```
#include "cosine.h"
#define POINTS 24
double cosine_table[POINTS+1] = { 1.0, 0.965925, 0.866025,
0.707106, 0.5, 0.25881, 0.0}; // remaining table values omitted
const double pointdistance = (360.0 / (double)POINTS);

double cosine(const int degree)
{
    double div_degree = ((double)degree / pointdistance);
    double p1 = cosine_table[(int)div_degree];
    double diffdegree = div_degree - (int)div_degree;
    double p2 = cosine_table[(int)(diff) + 1];
    return p1 + (p2 - p1)*div_degree;
}
```

Figure 2: Sourcecode for cosine calculation with interpolation

```
#define INTERVAL 15
double cosine_table[24] = { 1.0, 0.965925, 0.866025,
0.707106, 0.5, 0.25881, 0.0}; // remaining table values omitted

double cosine(const int degree)
{
    return cosine_table[degree / INTERVAL];
}
```

Figure 3: Sourcecode for cosine calculation with table

Taking the requirements of the applications into account, a good embedded programmer would choose to use implementation 1 for the first application, because it provides the best accuracy and consumes no valuable data memory (beside the used stack space). Implementation 2 goes with the application 2 as it provides the required real-time characteristics. For application 3 obviously the implementation 3 is best suited without discussion.

Three times cosine, three different implementations. This is the crux of embedded programming: in most cases there is not just one right way to do something. Reuse concepts for embedded systems have to take this into account.

3. PUTTING THE PUZZLE TOGETHER

The simplest solution to the reuse problem is to provide a library with all three implementations (or more). But here the problems already start:

1. How to choose the right implementation from the library?
2. How to use more than one implementation in the same system?

Using an informal description of library function properties for each function is only feasible for a small number of functions. Larger libraries designed for reuse should provide more support for the user of the library in her or his search for an appropriate implementation.

The remainder of the section describes the approach used to make the PURE operating system family easier to (re-)use. As a demonstration example the cosine problem will be used.

3.1   Step 1 —Analysing and Modeling of the Problem Domain

The first problem is that on one side there is a user who needs a function with a set of properties. On the other side there are a number of implementations, which fit more or less to the needs of the user. To bring both sides together it is necessary to establish a common language to describe the requirements and properties of software components (functions, classes, modules, ...).

The approach chosen for PURE was feature modeling. Feature modeling is a relatively simple approach for modeling the capabilities of a software system introduced by Kang et al. [4]. A feature model represents the commonalities and variabilities of the domain. A feature in FODA [3] is defined as an *end-user visible characteristic of a system*. Features are organized in form of *feature models*. A feature model of a domain consists of the following items:

- **feature description**

Each feature description in turn consists of a feature definition and a rationale. The definition explains which characteristic of the domain is described by the feature, so that an end-user is able to understand what this feature is about. This definition may be given as informal text only or in a defined structure with predefined fields and values for some information like the binding of the feature, i.e. the time a feature is introduced in the system (configuration time, compile time, . . .).

The rationale gives an explanation when or when not to choose a feature.

---

[3] Feature-oriented Domain Analysis

- **feature value**

Each feature can have an attached type/value pair. This allows to describe non-boolean features more easily[4].

- **feature relations**

The feature relations define valid selections of features from a domain. The main representation of these relations is the *feature diagram*.

Such a diagram is a directed acyclic graph, where the nodes are features and the connections between features indicate whether they are optional, alternative or mandatory. Table 2 gives an explanation on these terms and shows its representation in feature diagrams.

Table 2: Explanation of feature diagram elements

Feature Type	Description	Graphical Representation
Mandatory	Mandatory feature B has to be included if its parent feature A is selected	A ↓ B
Optional	Optional feature B may be included if its parent feature A is selected	A ○ B
Alternative	Alternative features are organized in alternative groups. Exactly one feature of such the group B,C,D has to be selected if the groups parent feature A is selected	A B C D

From characteristics of the problem a domain analyst derives the features relevant for the problem domain. For the cosine example a feature model should contain a feature, that allows to specify the precision required for the results (`Precision`) 4, a feature, that represents whether discrete angle values are used (`ValueDistribution`), a feature to express that fixed calculation time (`FixedTime`) is required and so on. The complete feature model is shown in figure 4.

The feature model of a problem domain (in our case the cosine world) can be presented to an application engineer and she or he should be able to select the feature the application requires. If necessary feature values have to be set.

---

[4] Typed features with values are not part of the original feature model proposal. However, this extension is required to describe many domains and has been proven to be very useful.

The CONSUL[5] environment developed in our group allows to check the selection interactively and shows whether there are errors in the selection (invalid feature combinations) or open selections (i.e. open alternative feature groups). The evaluation of feature models and associated rules are done with help of a Prolog interference engine.

3.2   Step 2 - Mapping the Features to Implementations

Once the feature selection is finished it must be mapped to an implementation. The number of valid feature combinations is in most cases too high to provide specific implementations for each possible selection.[6]

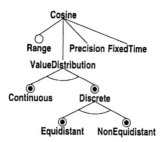

Figure 4. Feature model of cosine domain

In the given example only three different implementations are available. Implementation 1 should only be used if FixedTime is not selected. If the input angle values are equidistant implementation 3 seems to fit best. But even with equidistant values when the number of input values gets very high (e.g. >360) implementation 2 or 1 could be used to save memory. If values are not equidistant implementation 2 can be used if FixedTime is selected and implementation 1 otherwise. Further enhancements could be done when more information about the target system is available. For instance, if it would be possible to detect whether the platform has a hardware floating-point unit, the cosine function of the floating point unit should be called directly in every case.

The question is how to describe these dependencies. The description must be easy to use and expressive enough to allow complex dependency rules. Acknowledging the fact, that embedded programming requires the use of different languages like assembly, C, C++ and others, it has to be a language independent way.

The CONSUL component description language allows to attach such

---

[5] COnfiguration SUpport Library

[6] The names in parentheses are the feature names used in the resulting feature model, see figure 4.

dependency rules to any construction element of a software system (component, class, function, makefile, object, file etc.). Like the feature model the component description is evaluated using Prolog and the result is a description of the software system to be generated. In turn a generator interprets this description to build the actual system from it. Figure 5 shows a simplified[7] component description for the example.

3.3   Step 3 - Taking Benefit from Aspect-Oriented Programming

Looking at the given implementations, it is obvious that the feature Range is not implemented by any of the alternatives. It shouldn't do any harm, because each implementation is able to cope with any angle. But if a check of the angle is required e.g. for security reasons an additional optional subfeature CheckedRange of Range could be introduced.

The implementation of this feature is quiet easy, a simple comparison will do. But it has to be introduced in all implementations only if the corresponding feature is selected. The common solution for this scenario in C/C++ programs is to use a preprocessor macro here, which inserts the required code if a preprocessor variable is set. Using the CONSUL component description it would be easy to do it this way.

But closer examination reveals, that this approach is quite problematic: each implementation has to be changed and the implementation itself gets more complicated. Help comes from a relatively new programming concept, aspect-oriented programming (AOP). AOP was introduced by Kiczales [6] and is about separation of concerns. An *aspect* allows to implement a feature of a software system in a modular way that crosscuts different parts or, in our case, different configurations.

In the cosine example the range check feature is obviously independent from the rest of the cosine implementations, but the implementation effects all three versions of the function.

---

[7] To save space more complex configuration rules have been omitted. Nevertheless it is a complete description.

```
Component("Cosine")
{
    Description("Efficient cosine implementations")
    Parts {
    function("Cosine") {
      Sources {
        file("include", "cosine.h",def)
        file("src", "cosine_1.cc",impl) {
          Restrictions{

Prolog("not(has_feature('FixedTime',_NT))")}}
        file("src", "cosine_2.cc",impl) {
          Restrictions {
            Prolog("has_feature('FixedTime',_NT),
                    has_feature('NonEquidistant',_NT")}}
          file("src", "cosine_3.cc",impl) {
            Restrictions {
              Prolog("has_feature('FixedTime',_NT),
                      has_feature('Equidistant',_NT")}}
      }
    }
}
Restrictions { Prolog("has_feature('Cosine',_NT)") }
}
```

Figure 5: (Simplified) component description for cosine component

The AspectC++ language [7] developed in our group enriches the language C++ with the aspect concept. Figure 6 illustrates how an aspect can be used in our example to implement the range check feature throughout all versions of the cosine function. By adding this aspect to the component description (figure 5) it can be directly enabled and disabled by selecting the CheckedRange feature.

It is not necessary to change the three cosine function implementations because the AspectC++ language guarantees that the code following the keyword advice is always run before cosinus is executed. This is achieved by binding the advice code to the pointcut cosfct. A pointcut describes the points in the program code were an aspect can interfere. The pointcut arguments can be used to expose context information from these points[8].

```
aspect CosRange {
    pointcut cosfct (const int arg) = args (arg) &&
    execution ("double cosinus(...)");

    public:
```

---

[8] Interested readers should visit www.aspectc.org

```
    advice cosfct (arg) : void before (const int arg)
{
    // ARGMIN and ARGMAX are ''feature values''
    if (arg < ARGMIN || arg > ARGMAX)
      appropriate_action ();
  }
};
```

Figure 6: Sourcecode for the `CosRange` aspect

4.   RELATED WORK

Software engineering techniques like feature modeling are getting more and more interest from the embedded community. Kang who was one of the developers of the FODA methodology presented with FORM [5] an approach to use feature model based techniques for distributed, component based command and control systems. FODAcom [8] applies feature modeling to the telecom domain. All these approaches lack a complete tool chain for the developers which allows to generate systems from a feature model. They use feature models mainly to organize the design and implementation work.

The FAST method of Weiss and Lai [9] describes the process to develop and deploy customizable software families and requires the implementation of generators. However the[9] modeling approach is not based on feature models.

5.   CURRENT STATE AND FUTURE DEVELOPMENT

The feature modeling and aspect-oriented programming techniques described in the previous sections have been implemented in our group in prototypical form [3],[2]. The resulting tools have been used to build an interactive configuration enviroment for the PURE operating system family. The resulting feature model consists of about 220 features which are used to configure the 57 components consisting of some 350 classes.

Although these tools made the configuration of PURE much easier, there are still a number of unresolved issues. Reuse of parts of a feature model across problem domains is not yet possible. To be able to reuse feature models in different domains it should be possible to merge feature models

[9] Feature-Oriented Reuse Method

but no currently available feature modeling approach allows this.

The AspectC++ environment is still in its early stages but has already been used successfully with PURE, however many C and C++ constructs are not yet fully supported.

REFERENCES

[1] D. Beuche, A. Guerrouat, H. Papajewski, W. Schröder-Preikschat, O. Spinczyk, and U. Spinczyk. The Pure Family of Object-Oriented Operating Systems for Deeply Embedded Systems. In *IEEE Proceedings ISORC'99*, 1999.

[2] D. Beuche, W. Schröder-Preikschat, O. Spinczyk, and U. Spinczyk. Streamlining Object-Oriented Software for Deeply Embedded Applications. In *Proceedings of the TOOLS Europe 2000*, pages 33–44, Mont Saint-Michel, Saint Malo, France, June 5–8, 2000.

[3] A. Gal, W. Schröder-Preikschat, and O. Spinczyk. AspectC++: Language Proposal and Prototype Implementation. In *OOPSLA 2001 Workshop on Advanced Separation of Concerns in Object-Oriented Systems*, Tampa, Florida, Oct. 2001.

[4] K. Kang, S. Cohen, J. Hess, W. Nowak, and S. Peterson. Feature Oriented Domain Analysis (FODA) Feasibility Study. Technical Report CMU/SEI-90-TR-21, Software Engineering Institute, Carnegie Mellon University, Pittsburgh, PA, USA, Nov. 1990.

[5] K. C. Kang, K. Lee, J. Lee, and S. Kim. Feature Oriented Product Lines SoftwareEngineering Principles. In *Domain Oriented Systems Development — Practices and Perspectives*, UK, 2002. Gordon Breach Sience Publishers. to appear.

[6] G. Kiczales, J. Lamping, A. Mendhekar, C. Maeda, C. Lopes, J.-M. Loingtier, and J. Irwin. Aspect-Oriented Programming. In M. Aksit and S. Matsuoka, editors, *Proceedings of the 11th European Conference on Object-Oriented Programming (ECOOP '97)*, volume 1241 of *Lecture Notes in Computer Science*, pages 220–242. Springer-Verlag, June 1997.

[7] O. Spinczyk, A. Gal, and W. Schröder-Preikschat. AspectC++: An Aspect-Oriented Extension to C++. In J. Noble and J. Potter, editors, *Proceeding of the 40th International Conference on Technology of Object-Oriented Languages and Systems (TOOLS Pacific 2002)*, Sydney, Australia, Feb. 2002.

[8] A. D. Vici and N. Argentinieri. FODAcom: An Experience with Domain Analysis in the Italian Telecom Industry. In *Proc. of the 5th International Conference on Software Reuse*, pages 166–175, Victoria, Canada, June 1998.

[9] D. M. Weiss and C. T. R. Lai. *Software Product-Line Engineering: A Family-Based Software Development Approach*. Addison-Wesley, 1999. ISBN 0-201-69438-7.

Checking the Temporal Behaviour of Distributed and Parallel Embedded Systems

Wolfgang A. Halang
Fernuniversität
Fachbereich Elektrotechnik und Informationstechnik
58084 Hagen, Germany
wolfgang.halang@fernuni-hagen.de

Nihal Kececi
Université du Québec à Montréal
Département d'informatique
Montréal, Québec H3C 3P8, Canada
nkececi@lrgl.uqam.ca

Grace Tsai
Fairleigh Dickinson University
Department of Computer Science
Teaneck, NJ 07666, U.S.A.
tsai@alpha.fdu.edu

Abstract An independent test facility is described, which simulates the environments of distributed and parallel embedded real time systems with special emphasis on the exact modeling of the prevailing time conditions. Its main application areas are software verification and safety licensing. Following the black box approach, just by providing worst case oriented input patterns to integrated hardware/software systems and monitoring the corresponding outputs, the time behaviour of such systems can precisely be determined. High accuracy time information is provided by employing a hardware supported timer synchronised with legal time, viz., Universal Time Co-ordinated, as received via GPS satellites.

Keywords: Black box testing, software verification, simulation, safety licensing, high precision timing, GPS.

1.   INTRODUCTION

The problems encountered in establishing proper real time behaviour of distributed or parallel embedded systems are difficult and manifold, and, hence, not satifactorily solved, yet. They are exacerbated by the need to prove that the timing behaviour of integrated hardware/software systems meets given specifications. This holds, in particular, for systems working in safety related environments, which must be approved by licensing authorities in a fully independent manner.

The main requirement real time embedded systems must fulfill is that their operation keeps pace with external processes, i.e., the acquisition and evaluation of process data, as well as appropriate reactions, must be carried through on time in synchrony with the events occurring in these embedding processes. It is a difficult design issue to guarantee punctuality of real time systems, because the response times depend on the computers' actual workload and the operating system overhead, and may differ from one external request to the next.

Only in trivial cases and when not using operating systems it may be possible to predict time behaviour by analysing program code. The common testing practice of instrumenting programs with output statements to obtain information on intermediate programs states is not applicable to timing analysis, because it is intrusive and, thus, alters the time behaviour. Furthermore, tests in actual application environments are often either too expensive, too dangerous, or simply impossible for other reasons. Hence, such environments must be simulated, and the black box approach has to be taken in examining embedded systems, i.e., they may not be modified under any circumstances, and any internal details are disregarded. It is only observed whether instants and values of outputs generated conform to the given requirements. Thus, maximum objectivity in quality assurance and safety licensing is guaranteed.

In this paper it is shown that an examined distributed or parallel embedded system's environment can effectively be simulated, and its operation in the time dimension be supervised and monitored using standard real time computers extended by a number of hardware and software features. The software implemented in the embedded system under examination is checked by one or more test plans prescribing external stimuli and their respective timing. These test plans are totally independent on the examined software, and are executed on different machines. Hence, this software verification method appears to be a candidate for recognition as an official safety licensing procedure.

2. FUNCTIONALITY OF THE TEST FACILITY

In contrast to the conventional white box testing, which requires information about the testees' implementation, black box testing allows tests solely on the basis of specifications (cf. [1] for an introduction). Since

- the hardware and software for generating and evaluating test data is totally independent of testee implementation, thus allowing their development by other people — even at the same time as the implementation, and as

- the tests start at the external (standard) interfaces settled in the specifications suggesting the use of universal test environments,

the here pursued approach seems especially suitable for safety licensing.

Nevertheless, some of the "ingredients" necessary for this were applied for similar purposes already rather early. Thus, for a long time it is quite customary to use simulators for testing process control computer systems (leaving aside the classical testing of VLSI hardware being inconceivable without simulation) in some specialised industrial domains; for examples see [8, 3, 4, 6, 5].

Furthermore, the use of monitoring systems to observe the behaviour of computer systems was advocated for in the scientific literature, especially for error detection in distributed systems (see [7] for an overview). Though, the interactivity of this search process makes it almost indispensable to provide mechanisms for re-runs (see, e.g., [14]). Especially in the domain of real time systems, even pure monitoring is feasible (see [9]), particularly to verify the observance of logical and, above all, timing conditions.

Though, there are only few publications (such as [12, 11]) about integrated test environments with monitoring and simulation components. The mentioned contributions are tailored towards special architectures and mainly designed for white box testing. A good survey of this — established 1980 in [2] and still existing — "lost world" of industrial software testing practices in the real time domain can be found in [13].

According to the application conditions mentioned in the introduction, a testing environment useful to support safety licensing of integrated hardware/software systems operating under real time conditions needs to provide the following services:

- simulation of the environment, in which an examined embedded system is working, by generating *reproducible* input patterns oriented at typical and worst case conditions,

- surveillance if the outputs produced by the examined system are correct and appear within given time limits,

- no interference with the examined system, particularly no lengthening of its program code and execution time,

- interfacing to the examined system with the same hardware connectors as in the actual operating environment,

- access to the *legal time*, i.e., Universal Time Co-ordinated (UTC), for correct time stamping of events, correct timing of simulated external events, and to allow for putting distributedly acquired monitoring data into correct relation, which are obtained when examining distributed or parallel systems,

- free and easy programming (or configuration) of arbitrary test plans, and

- providing easily readable, concise reports on the test results.

3. HARDWARE ARCHITECTURE OF THE TEST FACILITY

A prototype of a simulation unit meeting the requirements compiled in the preceding section was built. For an overview on the hardware structure of the unit we refer to Figure 1.

Grouped along the internal I/O bus of a standard microprocessor, there is a video terminal to operate the unit, a printer for the reports, and a mass storage device. The latter may hold larger data sets to be provided as inputs to the embedded system examined, besides the files needed internally. In accordance with the system's interconnection pattern to its environment, the simulation unit is equipped with process peripherals such as digital interfaces, analogue converters, and IEC 488 attachments as well as with various serial line interfaces. Since the number and type of these connections varies with different systems examined, there is the possibility to insert corresponding peripherals into I/O slots of the unit. All external lines are brought to appropriate plugs, to enable easy connection to various systems.

In contrast to this, the further attachments mentioned now are always present. A bidirectional interface to the examined system's I/O data bus allows to simulate other peripheral devices. Their addresses are freely selectable. A number of registers is provided that work independently and in parallel, into which the microcomputer can store such addresses. Each register's output and the I/O address bus lines of the system on

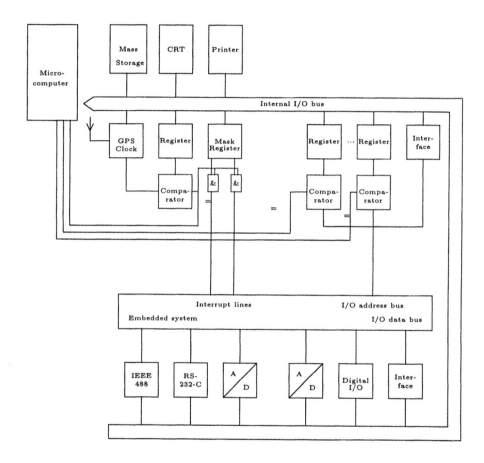

Figure 1.   Hardware architecture of a testing facility (handling one node each of a distributed or parallel embedded system)

test are fed into corresponding hardware comparators which send signals to the microprocessor when they detect matches of their inputs.

A similar feature is combined with the system clock in order to generate, as specified in test plans, exactly timed signals, to be supplied to the interrupt input lines of the examined system. The microprocessor always loads the next of these interrupt times into the comparison register. Upon equality with the clock, the comparator raises a signal that is transmitted to the microprocessor, where it initiates an associated routine, and to all interrupt lines whose corresponding bits in the mask register are set. This interrupt generation feature with exact timing is indispensable for a software verification device, because the environment of an examined system must be modeled as closely as possible, and because time signals delayed by randomly distributed durations may lead to erroneous test results. The feature is not only employed to feed interrupt signals into an examined system, but also to initiate data inputs synchronised with a time pattern.

4.   SOFTWARE COMPONENTS OF THE TEST FACILITY

The environment simulator is furnished with a real time multitasking operating system, and a programming environment containing, as the main component, a high level process control language, extended by a few features that support the special hardware. In this language, test plans are written which formally specify the requirements embedded systems have to fulfill. For each interrupt source to be simulated, a test plan contains a time schedule that generates periodic or randomly distributed interrupts according to worst case conditions. The identifications and the occurrence times of these interrupts are recorded for later usage in performance reports. According to the temporal patterns of interrupts, the test plan processor writes appropriate data to the different outputs that are fed into an examined system. Analogously, the test plan specifies those events, coming from an examined system, that are to be awaited, and the reactions to be carried out upon their occurrence.

With the help of the I/O address comparison features the inputs of the environment simulator are supervised to determine a tested system's reaction times, and whether it provides correct output values. Together with their sources and their arrival times these data are also recorded to be used in the final reports. Since only the external reactions to a given workload are considered, the simulation method takes the operating system overhead into account, too. By the possible interconnection of the I/O busses of the testing and the tested device, any kind of peripherals, including DMA units, can be simulated. To carry this through, a test plan only needs to specify a suitable data source or sink, and an appropriate transfer rate. Further useful functions, that can be invoked in test plans, are I/O bus traces and the logging of I/O port activities with time specifications, to be provided in appropriate buffer areas of the simulation unit.

5. TIMING OF HIGHEST ACCURACY

An important aspect for the assessment of distributed and parallel real time embedded systems is the observability of the environment, i.e., it must be possible to observe every event of interest generated by the external (the embedding) process, and to determine their correct timing as well as temporal and causal order. This holds in particular for simultaneously occurring events in distributed systems whose simultaneity will, of course, only be recognised at a later stage when they will be (sequentially) processed. Also, this is a prerequisite for correctly processing avalanches of asynchronous interrupts. To enable observability and to establish information consistency between internal real time data bases and the environment, distributed and parallel real time embedded systems — and corresponding testing facilities — require a common time base to measure the absolute time of event occurrences.

For the correctly timed generation of outgoing stimuli and the time stamping of all monitored process events the environment simulator employs a high precision timer and interrupt controller as depicted in Figure 2, whose original design was described in [15]. It uses the correct time information broadcast via the Global Positioning System (GPS).

Alarm jobs, i.e., time instants coded in 32 bits with a resolution of 100 μsec including seconds, minutes, and hour of the day, and unique alarm numbers identifying associated activities, are submitted to the timing controller using an 8 bits wide data bus. Submissions may arrive at any time. A novel *S*mallest *I*nput *F*irst *O*ut (*SIFO*) memory is used to keep a sorted list of alarm jobs. Its function is similar to the one of the well-known FIFO with the exception that it is not just a buffer but automatically sorts the incoming data, too. In this application, the SIFO also has to assemble the incoming 8 bits wide data stream to alarm job descriptors of 40 bits each. This assembling and the sorting need some time and, therefore, an additional input FIFO is used to ensure zero delay data input. The last SIFO location holds the alarm job descriptor with the next due date. If the timer receives an alarm job due even earlier, then this one will replace the former. However, the contents of the last SIFO location is always presented at the data output. If the

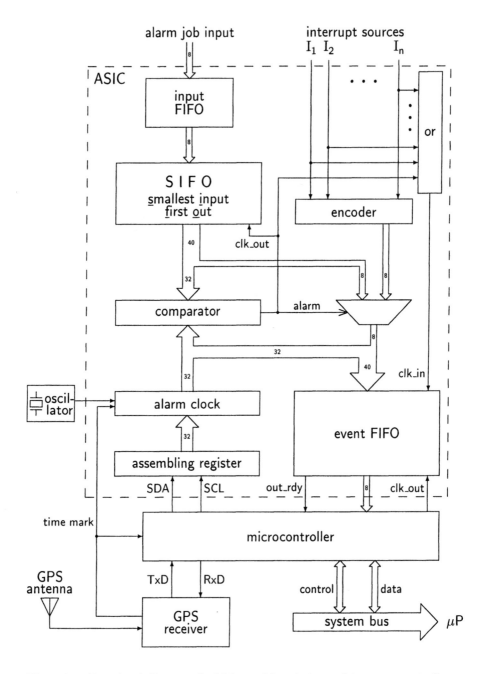

Figure 2. Functional diagram of a high precision timing and interrupt controller

due time of the alarm job at the SIFO output is (smaller or) equal to the actual time as given by the alarm clock, then the comparator generates an alarm signal, which triggers the output (event) FIFO to read the actual time and the corresponding alarm number from the SIFO. To prevent delays, the SIFO immediately forwards the next alarm job descriptor to its output.

For time stamping all monitored process events, the high precision time processor was now extended by an interrupt receptacle. When an interrupt signal occurs at one of the newly provided input lines $I_1 \ldots I_n$, a corresponding time stamp is formed by the interrupt's arrival time and the encoded interrupt line number. The time stamp descriptor is latched into the event FIFO. Until they will be read out by the microcontroller, the event FIFO buffers the alarm job and interrupt descriptors.

As shown in Figure 2, this high precision timer and interrupt controller consists of an application specific integrated circuit (ASIC) implementing an alarm job handler and a time stamping unit for arriving interrupts, a GPS receiver with attached antenna, and a microcontroller interfacing the GPS receiver to the ASIC. The information obtained by the GPS receiver includes, among others, UTC time and date, position and GPS status. It is transmitted via a serial data interface to the microcontroller, which sends commands to the receiver for configuration purposes and requests specific data. At system set-up and every midnight the time information is transferred into the alarm clock inside the ASIC using a synchronous serial link. To this end, first single bytes of information are assembled in a corresponding register and, then, transferred to the alarm clock. Thus, the alarm clock keeps track with leap seconds and the beginning of months. Our alarm clock prototype has a resolution of 100 μsec. It is driven by a free running oscillator and synchronised with UTC every second using the time mark signal as provided by the GPS receiver, which has an accuracy of ± 1 μsec. The microcontroller monitors the time mark signal. The controller is also used to read out the event FIFO as soon as it contains data. It keeps a list of all time and event driven activities sorted according to increasing deadlines.

6. CONCLUSION AND OUTLOOK

A very important subject of future reserach activities will be the automatical generation of test plans from specifications, i.e.,

- (automatical) generation of test plans and test data for all standardisable testing options, and

- (automatical) checking of the test results

for non-trivial specifications, requiring to join formal and experimental verification. Naturally, the idea of creating appropriate test plans for any kind of testees and test options to be investigated with the help of expert systems is unavoidable. Such expert systems will be similar to those ones already used for the detection of hardware malfunctions.

REFERENCES

[1] R.A. DeMillo, W.M. McCracken, R.J. Martin and J.F. Passafiume: *Software Testing and Evaluation*. Benjamin Cummings Publ., 1987.

[2] R.L. Glass: Real-Time: The "Lost World" of Software Debugging and Testing. *Comm. ACM*, 23, 5, 264–271, 1980.

[3] G. Hauser: Test von Steuerungssoftware mit Hilfe der Realzeitsimulation. In F. Breitenecker and W. Kleinert (Eds.), *Informatik-Fachberichte* 85, pp. 495–499, Springer-Verlag, 1984.

[4] K. Hellmold: Multiprozessorsystem für die parallele Simulation von zeitdiskreten Systemen. In M. Goller (Ed.), *Informatik-Fachberichte* 56, pp. 227–233, Springer-Verlag, 1982.

[5] H.B. Keller: Verteilte/modulare Echtzeitsimulation komplexer Systeme. In W. Ameling (Ed.), *Informatik-Fachberichte* 179, pp. 73–83, Springer-Verlag, 1988.

[6] R. Kodweiß: Software-Konzept für Echtzeit-Simulation. In D. Möller (Ed.), *Informatik-Fachberichte* 109, pp. 251–253, Springer-Verlag, 1985.

[7] C.E. McDowell and D.P. Helmbold: Debugging Concurrent Programs. *ACM Computing Surveys*, 21, 4, 593–622, 1989.

[8] J.M. Mohan and M. Geller: An Environmental Simulator for the FDNY Computer-Aided Dispatch System. In R.L. Glass (Ed.), *Real-Time Software*, pp. 75–90, Prentice-Hall, 1983.

[9] U. Schmid: Monitoring Distributed Real-Time Systems. *Real-Time Systems*, 7, 33–56, 1994.

[10] U. Schmid: Synchronized Universal Time Coordinated for Distributed Real-Time Systems. *IFAC Control Engineering Practice*, 1995.

[11] E. Schoitsch, E. Dittrich, S. Grasegger, D. Kropfitsch, A. Erb, P. Fritz and H. Kopp: The ELEKTRA Testbed: Architecture of a Real-Time Test Environment for High Safety and Reliability Requirements. Proc. *IFAC SAFECOMP '90*, Gatwick, pp. 59–65, 1990.

[12] W. Schütz: A Test Strategy for the Distributed Real-Time System MARS. Proc. *IEEE CompEuro'90*, Tel Aviv, pp. 20–27, 1990.

[13] W. Schütz: *The Testability of Distributed Real-Time Systems*. Ph.D. Thesis, Technical University of Vienna, 1992.

[14] J.P. Tsai, K.-Y. Fang, H.-Y. Chen and Y.-D. Bi: A Noninterfering Monitoring and Replay Mechanism for Real-Time Software Testing and Debugging. *IEEE Transactions on Software Engineering*, SE-16, 8, 897–916, 1990.

[15] W.A. Halang, M. Wannemacher, P.A. Laplante and A.D. Stoyen: High-Precision Temporal Synchronization in Multimedia Systems. In B. Furht (Ed.), *Handbook of Multimedia Computing*, CRC Press, 1998.

Transforming Execution-Time Boundable Code into Temporally Predictable Code

Peter Puschner
Institut für Technische Informatik, Technische Universität Wien, Austria

Abstract: Traditional Worst-Case Execution-Time (WCET) analysis is very complex. It has to deal with path analysis, to identify and describe the possible execution paths through the code to be analyzed, and it has to model the worst-case timing of the possible paths on the target hardware. The latter is again non-trivial due to interference of modern hardware features like instruction pipelines, caches, and parallel instruction-execution units on the processor.

To simplify WCET analysis we have proposed a new programming paradigm, single-path programming. Every program following this paradigm has only a single possible execution path, which makes path analysis and thus WCET analysis almost trivial. In this work we show how any real-time program code that is WCET-analyzable can be transformed into single-path code. This demonstrates that the single-path paradigm provides a universal solution to simplify WCET analysis.

Key words: real-time systems, programming paradigms, worst-case execution time, computer architectures

1. INTRODUCTION

Knowing the worst-case execution time (WCET) of tasks is crucial for building real-time systems. Only if safe WCET bounds for all time-critical tasks of a real-time system have been established can the correct timely operation of the whole real-time computer system be verified. During the last decade many research groups have undertaken research on (static)

WCET analysis of real-time tasks and many sub-problems of WCET analysis have been solved, see (Puschner and Burns, 2000).

Despite the numerous efforts and results in WCET-analysis research there are still three significant obstacles to a safe and exact WCET analysis:

1. *Limits of automatic path analysis*: To compute a tight WCET bound, WCET analysis needs exact knowledge about the possible execution paths through the analyzed code. Deriving this information automatically is, in general, not possible: First, the control flow of a program typically depends on the input data of the program. Thus a WCET bound cannot be predicted purely from code analysis but needs additional information about possible input data or about the effects the possible input data have on the control flow. Second, the fully automatic program analysis would be in conflict to the halting problem. In order to allow for a WCET analysis despite these fundamental limits, current WCET tools rely on the user to provide the lacking path information (Colin and Puaut, 2000; Engblom and Ermedahl, 2000). Deriving this path information is an intellectually difficult, time-consuming, and error-prone task.

2. *Lack of hardware-timing data*: Modern processors use speed-up mechanisms like caches, instruction pipelines, parallel execution units, and branch-prediction to enhance execution performance. These mechanisms are complex in their implementation and have mutual interferences in their timing. Besides , the mechanisms and their timing are generally scarcely documented to protect the manufacturer's intellectual property (Petters and Färber, 1999). These facts taken together make it difficult if not impossible to build reliable tools for static WCET analysis of modern processors.

3. *Complexity of analysis*: It has been shown that the number of paths to be analyzed for an exact WCET analysis grows exponentially with the number of consecutive branches in the analyzed code when this code is to be executed on modern processors. Except for very simple programs this high complexity makes the full path enumeration needed for an exact WCET analysis intractable (Lundqvist and Stenström, 1999). WCET analysis therefore has to do with pessimistic approximations. These approximations, however, over-estimate WCET and make a certain waste of resources at runtime unavoidable.

In a previous paper (Puschner and Burns, 2002) we presented the single-path paradigm, a radical programming paradigm that avoids the problems of WCET analysis. Using this paradigm, programmers write programs whose behaviour is independent of input data. These programs only have a single execution path that is executed in each program execution. The execution time of programs written in the praradigm is therefore exactly predictable.

The fact that programs only have a single execution path makes WCET analysis trivial: First, path analysis is superfluous – observing the execution path of a code execution with any input data yields the singleton execution path. Second, there is no need for static WCET analysis. If programs only have a single path, as proposed, this singleton path is necessarily the worst-case path. Thus, obtaining the WCET by "exhaustive" measurements (either on the target or on a cycle-accurate hardware simulator) is possible. There is no need to build highly sophisticated tools for static analysis as this is the case for traditional code where the high number of input-data dependent test cases makes measurement-based WCET analysis infeasible.

Another property of the single-path approach is that the execution time of single-path code is free of jitter. Thus it is not necessary to introduce delay constructs into the code if a constant execution time of the code is required. Also, the timing analysis of multiple tasks with communication or synchronization constraints gets less complex if the execution times of the code between communication and synchronization points is fixed as opposed to the case when code execution times are variable.

An approach that only permits programs with a single execution path may seem to allow programmers to write only very simple programs. In this paper we demonstrate that the proposed approach is not at all that restrictive. In fact, we show how any piece of code that is WCET-analyzable can be translated into single-path code. The translation builds on if-conversion (Allen et al., 1983) to produce code that keeps input-data dependent alternatives local to single conditional operations with data-independent execution times. While if-conversion only translates branching code within innermost loops, the here-presented conversion also converts loops – all loops with input-data dependent termination conditions are translated into loops with constant iteration counts.

The paper is structured as follows: Section 2 explains the terms and assumptions used throughout the paper. Section 3 introduces the main concepts of the single-path approach. Section 4 explains the translation rules that are needed to translate WCET-analyzable programs into programs with a single execution path. Section 5 provides a program example and shows its conversion into single-path code. Section 6 gives a summary and conclusion.

2. TERMS AND ASSUMPTIONS

We view a program as a piece of code that defines the transformation of an initial store (assignment of values to all program variables) into a new, final store. The valid set of initial stores for an application is assumed to be known. The program itself consists of actions whose deterministic semantics define the single operations (assignment, expression evaluation, condition evaluation, etc.) and the control flow of actions in this transformation. The control-flow semantics describe the starting point and the end points of the program as well as the transitions and the transition conditions between actions. The control flow semantics of an action define zero, one, or two alternative successors of the action. We call actions with one successor sequential actions and actions with two alternative successors branches. Actions with no successors mark program end points.

The programs considered in this work are purely computational. They are free of any communication, synchronization, or other blocking during their execution, see the *simple-task* model described in (Kopetz, 1997). Instead we assume that inputs to a program are available before its execution starts (as part of the initial store) and results are written to memory locations that are read by the I/O subsystem when the execution has completed. Also, the values of variables only change as the result of the operations performed by the program execution. There are no volatile or shared variables that change their values asynchronously to program execution.

We define an *execution path* as a sequence of actions that starts with a valid initial store at the starting point, obeys the semantics of the actions, and terminates at an end point of the program. The program code and the possible initial stores characterize the feasible execution paths of a program.

For each pair of different execution paths there is a maximal sequence of actions that is a prefix of both paths. By definition the last operation of such a prefix is a branch. As all operations are assumed to be deterministic and the actions preceding the branch are identical for both paths, the choice of different successors has to be due to differences in the initial store (i.e., input variables) of the executions. We therefore call such a branch an *input-data dependent branch*. There are also branches that are not input-data dependent. The latter do not occur as the last operations of a maximum common prefix of any two execution paths.

Each action of an execution path has an *execution time*, a positive integral number (e.g., number of processor cycles). We assume that the execution time of an action depends on the semantics of the operation it performs and the sequence of actions preceding the action on the execution path. The execution times of actions on a path are considered to be unaffected by actions that are not local to the path (e.g., the actions performed prior or in parallel to that path). The execution time of an action is further assumed to be independent of the store on which the action is performed, i.e., the durations of operations are assumed to be independent of the actual values of their operands and memory access times are assumed to be homogeneous for all variables. The *execution time of an execution path* is the sum of the execution times of the actions of the path.

3.   THE SINGLE-PATH APPROACH

As mentioned before, WCET analysis is in general complex because programs behave differently for different input data, i.e., different input data cause the code to execute on different execution paths with differing execution times. The single-path approach avoids this complexity by ensuring that the code has only a single execution path. This approach uses code transformations to transform input-data dependent loops and branches. It transforms loops with input-data dependent termination conditions into loops with invariable iteration counts. Input-data dependent branches with the semantics of *if* or *case* statements and their alternatives are transformed into strictly sequential code. To be precise, the code resulting from the transformation of branches avoids data dependencies in execution times by keeping input-data dependent branching local to single operations with data-independent execution times.

The sequential code generated by the above-mentioned transformation includes so-called predicated operations, i.e., operations that realize branches within single machine instructions and have a constant, data-independent execution time. The predicated instruction used is the *conditional move instruction*. It is implemented on a number of modern processors (e.g., Motorola M-Core, Alpha, Pentium P6) and has the following general form:

```
movCC destination, source
```

The conditional move compares the condition code *CC* with the condition code register. If the result is *true* the processor copies the contents of the *source* register to the *destination* register. If the condition evaluates to *false*, the value of *destination* remains unchanged.

In the next section we show how the conditional move instruction and program transformations are used to create code whose execution time is constant and therefore fully predictable.

4.   CONVERTING WCET-ANALYZABLE CODE INTO SINGLE-PATH CODE

Every well structured and WCET-analyzable piece of program code can be translated into code with a single execution path. (By WCET-analyzable code we understand code for which the maximum number of loop iterations for every loop is known. A WCET bound is thus computable.) The translation replaces all input-data dependent alternative statements and loops by deterministic code, i.e., code that restricts all input-data dependencies to conditional move instructions.

In the following we show how input-data dependent conditional statements and loops are translated. We use *if* statements with two alternatives to illustrate the translation of conditionals. The translation of conditionals with more than two alternatives is very similar and therefore not specifically described. Further, *goto* and *exit* statements are not considered in this paper. Any functionality can also be implemented without the latter.

4.1   Translation of Conditionals

Conditional branching statements conditionally change the values of one or more variables. The translation of conditional branches is straightforward. It generates sequential code with conditional move assignments for each of the conditionally changed variables. This conversion from control dependencies into data dependencies is called if-conversion (Allen et al., 1983, Park and Schlansker, 1991) and is traditionally only used to translate the bodies of innermost loops into non-branching code, see Figure 1.

if *cond* **then** *result* := *expr1;* **else** *result* := *expr2;*	*tmp1* := *expr1;* *tmp2* := *expr2;* **test** *cond;* **movt** *result, tmp1;* **movf** *result, tmp2;*

Figure 1. Branching statement and corresponding sequential code generated by if-conversion.

When translating assignments in nested conditional branches that are input-data dependent, the conditions of all nested branches have to combined in the conditions of the generated conditional assignments.

To describe the translation of conditionals more formally, we assume that each branch uses the input variables $v_1',...,v_m'$ to compute the values for variables $v_1,...,v_n$. Thus, using if-conversion an *if* statement is translated into sequential code as shown in Figure 2.

if *cond* **then** $(v_1,...,v_n) := F1(v_1',...,v_m')$ **else** $(v_1,...,v_n) := F2(v_1',...,v_m')$	$(h_1,...,h_n) := F1(v_1',...,v_m')$ $(h_1',...,h_n') := F2(v_1',...,v_m')$ *cond*: $(v_1,...,v_n) := (h_1,...,h_n)$ **not** *cond*: $(v_1,...,v_n) := (h_1',...,h_n')$

Figure 2. General form of if-conversion.

The last two lines of the code on the right side of Figure 2 are guarded assignments with the guards being the condition of the *if* statement and its negation, respectively. We use these guarded assignments of tupels to represent a number of conditional move operations. The guard represents the condition of the respective conditional moves (see also Figure 1).

Figure 3 shows how nested *if* statements are translated. First, the condition of the current *if* and the enclosing conditions are combined. This new conditional is then translated into sequential code using if-conversion.

-- conditions so far: *cond-old* **if** *cond-new* **then** ... **else** ...	**if** *cond-old* **and** *cond-new* **then** ... **else** ...

Figure 3. First step of the translation of a nested *if* statement.

4.2   Translation of Loops

Loops with input-data dependent termination conditions are translated in two steps. First, the loop is changed into a simple counting loop with a constant iteration count. The iteration count of the new loop is set to the maximum iteration count of the original loop. The old termination condition is used to build a new branching statement inside the new loop. This new conditional statement is placed around the body of the original loop and simulates the data dependent termination of the original loop in the newly generated counting loop.

Second, the new conditional statement, that has been generated from the old loop condition, is transformed into a constant-time conditional assignment. As a result the entire loop executes in constant time.

Figure 4 illustrates the first step of the loop transformation. In the translated version (right), the variable *finished$_x$* has been introduced to store the information if the original loop would have executed the current iteration or would already have terminated.

-- conditions so far: *cond-old*
while *cond-new* **do** max *expr* times
    stmts;
	finished$_x$:= **false**;
	for i_x := 1 **to** *expr* **do**
	begin
	    if not *cond-new*
	    then *finished$_x$* := **true**;
	    if *cond-old* **and not** *finished$_x$*
	    then *stmts*;
	end

Figure 4. Translation of a loop.

Applying the described transformation to existing real-time code may yield temporal predictability at very high cost, i.e., execution time. Thus we consider the illustration of the transformation as a demonstration of the general feasibility of our approach, rather than proposing to use the transformation for generating temporally predictable code from arbitrary real-time code. In order to produce code that is both temporally predictable and well performing the programmer needs to use adequate algorithms, i.e., algorithms with no or minimal input-data dependent branching.

5. AN EXAMPLE

The example illustrates the described transformation. It shows an implementation of *bubble sort* and the corresponding single-path code.

On its left side Figure 5 lists a typical traditional implementation *of bubble sort*. The function has one parameter, the array *a* to be sorted. The function uses two nested loops to transport elements to their correct positions. In each iteration of the inner loop two neighbouring array elements are compared. If the comparison evaluates to true the two elements are swapped, otherwise no operation is performed.

```
static void bubble1(int a[])           static void bubble2(int a[])
{                                      {
  int i, j, t;                           int i, j, s, t;
  for(i=SIZE-1; i>0; i--)                for(i=SIZE-1; i>0; i--)
  {                                      {
    for(j=1; j<=i; j++)                    for(j=1; j<=i; j++)
    {                                      {
      if (a[j-1] > a[j])                     s = a[j-1];
      {                                      t = a[j];
        t = a[j];                            s <= t: a[j-1] = s;
        a[j] = a[j-1];                       s > t:  a[j-1] = t;
        a[j-1] = t;                          s <= t: a[j] = t;
      }                                      s > t:  a[j] = s;
    }                                      }
  }                                      }
}                                      }
```

Figure 5. Traditional (left) and single-path (right) version of *bubble sort*.

Note that the branching statement causes an execution-time variability in the inner-loop body. Depending on the result of the branching condition the duration of each iteration of the inner loop is either long or very short. As the body of the inner loop executes *SIZE(SIZE-1)/2* times when sorting an array of *SIZE* elements, one immediately concludes that *bubble1* has at least *SIZE(SIZE-1)/2+1* possible execution times. If branch prediction hardware is used the number of possible execution times is in fact much higher.

On its right side Figure 5 shows the *bubble sort* code after the transformation of input-data dependent branches. The *if* statement in the inner loop has been replaced by four conditional move instructions.

To compare the execution characteristics of the two implementations we generated executable programs for both versions. The *bubble1* version was directly compiled and linked for the Motorola M-Core processor (Motorola, 1997). As our compiler does not translate the guarded assignments we produced the code for *bubble2* by editing the machine code of *bubble1* – we replaced the conditional branch of the *if* statement by sequential code, including conditional move instructions. Both versions were then tested on a cycle-accurate M-Core simulator. The results are summarized in Table 1. For the experiment an array size of 10 was assumed.

Table 1. Number of execution paths, minimum and worst-case execution time of *bubble sort* variants for array size 10.

Implementation	# Paths	min. Exec. Time	WCET
Traditional	3628800	675	810
Single Path	1	972	972

The traditional version of *bubble sort* has a big variability of execution times (675-810 CPU cycles). As expected, the single-path version has a single execution time for all inputs (972 cycles). The WCET of the single-path implementation is about 20% greater than that of the conventional implementation. This seems to be a reasonable price given the fact that finding this execution time is trivial – there is only one path to evaluate. The traditional solution has more than 3.6 million paths (a huge number given that simple piece of code). While identifying the worst-case path is not too difficult for this simple, one can immediately think of more complex code with a much greater number of paths that are not so easy to analyze. In that case the advantage of having a single path is obvious. As path analysis is unnecessary the problems of path analysis, i.e., potential flaws and pessimism, are non-existent.

6. CONCLUSION

In an earlier paper we presented the single-path programming paradigm. This programming paradigm makes it possible to write programs that can be easily analyzed for their WCET. The key element of this programming paradigm is to keep input-data dependent branching local to single machine instructions with invariable execution times. The conditional move instruction is the most important of those instructions.

In this paper we showed how every piece of code that is WCET-analyzable (i.e., the maximum number of iterations can be bounded for all loops) can be transformed into single-path code. This is done by converting all input-data dependent conditional statements and loop statements and by using if-conversion to translate all remaining input-data dependent branches into sequential code with conditional moves. WCET analysis for the single-path code is trivial: The WCET is obtained by executing the code with any valid input data on a hardware simulator or even the target hardware and measuring the execution time of the single execution path.

Although we demonstrated how input-data dependent code is transformed we do not consider this transformation as an adequate method for producing single-path code from any piece of code – Relying purely on the transformation will, in general, leave the programmer with very inefficient code. To get code that cannot only easily be analyzed for its WCET but also has a good performance, developing or selecting algorithms where execution paths do only marginally or not at all depend on input data is important. Identifying and developing algorithms that are well-suited for our approach will be a central focus of our further research.

REFERENCES

Allen, J., Kennedy, K., Porterfield, C., and Warren, J. 1983. Conversion of Control
   Dependence to Data Dependence. *Proceedings of the 10th ACM Symposium on Principles
   of Programming Languages*: 177-189.
Colin, A., and Puaut, I. 2000. Worst Case Execution Time Analysis for a Processor with
   Branch Prediction. *Real-Time Systems*, 18(2/3):249-274.
Engblom, J., and Ermedahl, A. 2000. Modeling Complex Flows for Worst-Case Execution
   Time Analysis. *Proceedings of the 21st IEEE Real-Time Systems Symposium*: 163-174.
Kopetz, H. 1997. *Real-Time Systems*. Kluwer Academic Publishers.
Lundqvist, T., and Stenström, P. 1999. Timing Anomalies in Dynamically Scheduled
   Microprocessors. *Proceedings of the 20th IEEE Real-Time Systems Symposium*: 12-21.
Motorola Inc. 1997. *M-Core Reference Manual*.
Park, J., and Schlansker, M. 1991. On Predicated Execution. *Technical Report HPL-91-58*,
   Hewlett Packard Software and Systems Laboratory, Palo Alto, CA, USA.
Petters, S., and Färber, G. 1999. Making Worst Case Execution Time Analysis for Hard Real-
   Time Tasks on State of the Art Processors Feasible. *Proceedings of the 6th IEEE
   International Conference on Real-Time Computer Systems and Applications*: 442-449.
Puschner, P., and Burns, A. 2000. Guest Editorial: A Review of Worst-Case Execution-Time
   Analysis. *Real-Time Systems*, 18(2/3):115-127.
Puschner, P., and Burns, A. 2002. Writing Temporally Predictable Code. *Proceedings of the
   7th IEEE International Workshop on Object-Oriented Real-Time Dependable Systems*.

BOTTOM-UP PERFORMANCE ANALYSIS OF HW/SW PLATFORMS

Kai Richter, Dirk Ziegenbein, Marek Jersak, Rolf Ernst
Institute of Computer and Communication Network Engineering
Technical University of Braunschweig
D-38106 Braunschweig / Germany
{richter|ziegenbein|jersak|ernst}@ida.ing.tu-bs.de

Abstract   Today's complex embedded systems integrate multiple hardware and software components, many of them provided as IP from different vendors. Performance analysis is crucial for such heterogeneous systems. There already exists a variety of formal timing analysis techniques for small sub-problems, e. g. task performance, scheduling strategies, etc.. In this paper, we analyze these individual approaches in the context of performance analysis of heterogeneous platforms at different levels of abstraction, and present a three-level bottom-up analysis procedure.

Keywords: Timing Verification, Scheduling Analysis, Platform-Based Design

1.   INTRODUCTION

The advances in silicon technology enable the integration of more and more functionality in a single system. (Future) platform-based systems-on-chip (SoC) integrate multiple programmable micro-controllers and DSPs with specialized memories and dedicated or weakly programmable hardware accelerators, which are connected using complex on-chip networks. Examples are multimedia-processors as found in set-top boxes and entertainment systems. A similar development can be observed for physically distributed systems.

The design of such systems is driven by conflicting objectives and constraints such as cost, timing, power, and reliability. The increasing heterogeneity of such systems with respect to architecture components, design tools, specification languages, etc., adds to the overall design complexity. As a result, the design can only be managed with enormous increase in design productivity in order to meet time-to-market requirements. In response, industry shifted to platform-based design. Reusing existing hardware components, often provided as IP, drastically reduces design time. Operating systems and device drivers supplement the hardware components, and well defined APIs allow fast, mainly software-based platform customization.

The emerging limits of todays platform integration methodologies are verification and optimization of system timing and memory. Verification is currently limited to simulation approaches, such as in VCC [3], Seamless CVE [16], CoWare [4], or CoCentric [22]. In addition to the long-term simulation runs, simulation approaches provide only marginal optimization support, since the influence of the individual design decisions on the simulation results is unclear. Other known limitations of simulation such as incomplete coverage and corner case identification are aggravated since many of the design errors only result from system integration requiring detailed knowledge which is often not available to the integrator.

Formal analysis techniques represent a promising alternative for timing and memory constraint verification. In contrast to simulation, formal analysis ensures complete corner case coverage by nature. With a carefully selected level of system and component abstraction, the results are conservative, i. e. they are guaranteed under all circumstances. Formal analysis approaches capture the component and system properties using parameterized mathematical models. Such models account for instruction execution, critical program paths, scheduling influence, and component interaction in order to derive conservative bounds on system function timing or required memory size.

In this paper, we discuss and evaluate several basic ideas underlying formal analysis approaches in the context of HW/SW platform integration. We investigate a representative subset of existing individual analysis approaches in order to find a reasonable level of detail at which platform performance analysis can be currently performed. We propose a three-step bottom-up approach. While much effort has been put into timing analysis at the task and the single resource level, approaches to global timing analysis of complex heterogeneous HW/SW platforms are comparatively rare. Therefore, the component interaction is discussed more thoroughly.

The paper is organized as follows. The next section presents out three level analysis hierarchy. Section 3 reviews analysis techniques for single tasks. The influence of operating systems on single architecture components is considered in Section 4. The analysis of multi-component platforms is captured in Section 5. We conclude the paper with an evaluation of the current analysis possibilities.

2.   THE THREE-LEVEL APPROACH

The analysis of target system timing can be divided into three parts:

1. analysis of a single task executed on a target system component in absence of resource sharing techniques (task level)

2. analysis of resource sharing effects on a single resource component (resource level)

3. analysis of component interaction in multi-component systems (system level)

At the task level, timing analysis is performed separately for each task. Upper and lower bounds on task execution times are obtained. Since these times may depend on the target architecture (i. e. the processor the task will be executed on), the implementation has to be considered in this step. The sources of intervals can be input data dependent task behavior (due to input data dependent control structures) or limited analyzability of the target architecture (due to features like pipelining, caches etc.). There are many recent contributions combining implicit or explicit program path analysis and cycle-true processor modeling, such as [13, 6, 25, 9]. In addition, task communication can be determined to analyze communication channel load and timing [25]. Such parameters are then captured using a reasonable, abstract intermediate representation (abstract task model), e. g. SPI [5].

At the resource level, there is a huge amount of work, e. g. [14, 12, 24] and many more, mainly in the domain of real-time operating systems to calculate task response times. Again, these response times abstract from the actual implementation. All of these approaches assume certain event models, e. g. periodic or burst. From the IP perspective, these can be used to specify operation conditions for which the response times are guaranteed.

For single-component systems, the resource level already is the system level. There also exist many techniques for homogeneous multi-processors [20]. However, this does not hold for heterogeneous multi-component systems.

The system-level analysis for heterogeneous HW/SW platforms has been neglected for a long time. In a recent publication, Pop et. al. [17] extended the existing scheduling analysis to specialized classes of multi-component platforms. In [18], we proposed to couple the existing approaches rather than finding solutions with only limited applicability. We identified the lack of compatibilities between event models as being the key obstacle for this analysis coupling process, and proposed to use event model interfaces within an iterative event model interfacing technique.

Each analysis technique focuses on only one of the three mentioned steps: task, resource, or system level analysis. As a result, a sound and complete analysis of the whole system requires several individual approaches to be combined bottom-up, i. e. starting at the task-level and ending up with complete system level performance information. Furthermore, all approaches make certain assumptions on the system's tasks and resources. Otherwise, the techniques can not be reasonably applied to a given problem. Here, two important issues have to be considered. First, it is a prerequisite that the lower levels within this analysis hierarchy provide the information that is required by the more high-level approaches. In other words, the information is propagated through the analysis bottom-up. Secondly, the information provided should not be overly detailed. Otherwise, these details can neither be utilized by a subsequent analysis step, nor can analysts benefit from the efficiency of less detailed approaches. In general, the performance parameters that are propagated should be consistent at all levels of the analysis hierarchy. The following sections introduce analysis techniques at each of the mentioned steps (task, resource, system).

3.   TASK-LEVEL ANALYSIS

This section briefly summarizes timing analysis approaches for individual tasks in absence of operating systems. Typically, such analysis is based on basic blocks, i. e. blocks of code with a single control flow. The latency time model in [13] is established as a standard model for static approaches, which is also called the *sum-of-basic-blocks* model. Here, the overall task execution time is the sum of all basic block execution times multiplied by the corresponding execution count for each of the basic blocks. Evidently, the execution time of a basic block depends on the target architecture whereas the execution count is architecture independent. Both values, time and count, are intervals representing the worst case and best case bounds. As a result, the overall execution time is an interval, too.

It is assumed that all executions of one basic block have the same time interval. However, data dependent instruction execution and pipelined architectures as well as unpredictable cache behavior and register allocation lead to a widely varying basic block execution time. This effect is referred to as overlapping basic block execution. Many other approaches to task execution time analysis are also based on the analysis granularity of basic blocks or single basic block transitions [8] or require complex modifications to execution time determination [15]. Very few approaches like [9] also consider more fine-grain influences of complex processor architectures, e. g. pipelines and super-scalar machines. The major drawback of such detailed approaches is state-space explosion.

The SYMTA (SYMbolic Timing Analysis) tool suite [25] extends the sum-of-basic-blocks approach by raising the analysis granularity from basic blocks to task segments which are sequences of basic blocks having a single input data independent control flow across basic block boundaries. Due to the raised granularity, the number of points where worst case assumptions (e. g., empty pipeline) have to be made is reduced leading to a higher analysis accuracy.

Additionally, SYMTA allows to specify task execution contexts which provide information on the input data in order to predict input data dependent control structures. This way, execution paths are selected and task segments can be merged even further. As a result, not only a single task execution time interval but also a set of comparatively narrow execution time intervals, one for each context, can be given.

4.   RESOURCE-LEVEL ANALYSIS

In this section, the influence of resource sharing is investigated, based on the core execution times from the previous section.

In the area of real-time operating systems, there are several substantially different resource sharing (scheduling) strategies. Preemptive scheduling based on static priorities (e. g. rate-monotonic), dynamic priorities (e. g. earliest deadline first), and time-slicing (e. g. time division multiple access and round robin) are among the most important strategies. For each of the mentioned strategies, a set of analysis approaches exist. The approaches take the scheduling strategy and the core execution times (from the previous section) as input to a self-contained mathematical description in order to calculate conservative bounds on the response times of tasks.

In the early 70's, Liu and Layland proposed a preemptive priority-driven scheduling to guarantee deadlines for periodic hard real-time tasks [14]. They considered a static (Rate Monotonic) and a dynamic (Earliest Deadline First) priority assignment and provided a formal analysis framework for both. In [10], Kopetz and Gruensteindl proposed TTP (time triggered protocol) for communication scheduling in distributed systems and presented an analysis. TTP implements the TDMA (time division multiple access) scheduling strategy. Both contributions assume a periodic activation of tasks. Recent extensions of the mentioned work allow periodic activation with jitter, e. g. [20], and arbitrary deadlines [12]. Sprunt et. al. [21] analyze the influence of sporadic task preemption. Tindell presents an approach for task bursts [24].

Gresser [7] and Thiele et. al. [23] use more general activation models. They introduce a vector of sequential time intervals rather than a few parameters (period, jitter, etc.) only, in order to calculate performance quanta for each task. Gresser uses this model for analysis of dynamic priority (EDF) scheduling. Thiele et. al. analyze a mixture of hard and soft real-time tasks in network processors with a specialized scheduling algorithm.

The above mentioned approaches are only concerned with the coarse-grain influences of scheduling, i. e. task preemption or –in the case of non-preemptive scheduling– delay. However, the operating system that implements the scheduling strategy also needs to be considered. Most importantly, the context switching overhead has to be considered, as well as the OS drivers to control busses or other peripherals. If possible, these are usually included in the task execution time, e. g. communication primitives. The context switch overhead can be added to the overall execution time. House keeping functions can be treated as extra tasks without any specific functionality.

In contrast to the scheduler and the housekeeping functions, the OS drivers require special attention. Many drivers manage and modify static data structures, e. g. communication buffers and other queues, which are shared among several tasks. In other words, the driver function is called by more than one task. Clearly, such driver functions must not be preempted by calls to the same driver, since this would result in an unknown state of the shared data. This is usually solved using OS semaphores and/or monitors. As a result, a task may experience an additional delay to resolve such conflicts. Extensions to the basic scheduling analysis approaches can be found in [2, 20, 24]. Although such conflicts can not be seen before tasks are integrated for resource sharing, the information about the actual blocking times needs to be obtained at the individual task level. The approach in [25] can be used.

Other fine-grain influences, e. g. in the presence of caches and pipelines, are more complex to include in the performance models. Ferdinant et al. [6] account for the cache state during task performance analysis. This way, they compute worst-case delays resulting from cache misses which result from preemption. This problem is also addressed in [11]. Clearly, such influences can neither be completely captured at the task level, nor at the resource sharing level, since the actual task performance results from a combination of both. In contrast to semaphore blocking, most of the current scheduling analysis approaches do not include parameters representing fine-grain influences like caches, etc. These are usually conservatively estimated based on experience.

5.   SYSTEM-LEVEL ANALYSIS

While there exist a huge amount of work in the area of task and resource level analysis, there is only little work on system level analysis, i. e. the analysis of multiple connected and interacting resource components.

One reason for this lack of global models are incompatibilities of the input event models, e. g. periodic or burst. An input event model describes the frequency and type of input events that lead to task or communication execution. In effect, the input events determine the system workload. Resource sharing analysis techniques, therefore, typically assume certain input event models, as mentioned in Section 4.

The importance of transitions between different event models has been widely neglected in literature. In general, global heterogeneous system analysis is currently limited to special classes of problems. Pop et. al [17] extended the idea of self-contained mathematical equations as presented in Section 4 to capture distributed interacting tasks. Their approach is limited to static priority task scheduling combined with a TDMA bus protocol. However, it is doubtful that a general approach to a self-contained solution for arbitrarily complex platform architectures can be found, mainly because of the highly complex dependencies in such systems. Other approaches like [1] require a completely homogeneous system in terms of input description, scheduling algorithms and architecture structure. Then, the analysis problem is solved by finding critical paths in the system level description. Such approaches are neither applicable to strongly heterogeneous systems, nor do all of them account for the influence of scheduling.

In a recent publication [18], we have presented a more general approach. The basic idea is to re-use the existing work mentioned in Section 4 (and possibly the work in [17], too) for the individual components. At the system level, we couple the individual analysis to obtain a global platform performance model. This is not trivial due to the mentioned event model incompatibilities. However, we developed an event interface model to overcome the limitations of the individual scheduling analysis approaches. But before we present our event interface model, we will give a brief overview about event models in the context of scheduling analysis.

5.1.   Event Models

In the literature on real-time analysis, there are four event models of major importance. A simple and efficient assumption is a stream of *periodic* input events. Here, the arrival of events can be captured by a single parameter, the period T. Often, periodic events are allowed to deviate with respect to their period. This adds another parameter to the periodic model, the *jitter* (J). Other models capture *bursts* of events. A burst is characterized by a number of events (burst length b) within a given time interval (the outer period T). This outer period may also jitter (J). If known, a minimum time distance (the inter-arrival time t) between two successive events within a burst can be specified. *Sporadic* events are captured by the minimum inter-arrival time t, only.

The models of Gresser and Thiele are closest to a general event model trying to capture rather complex event stream patterns. Both models target general event stream modeling at the cost of model complexity that excludes direct application of most of the analysis techniques mentioned above.

5.2.   Event Model Coupling

In this section, we present the actual coupling of event models. We first discuss compatibility issues between the four event models introduced in the preceeding section, and derive event model interfaces (*EMIF*s) to transform the parameters of one event model into those of another model. In those cases, where no simple interface can be derived, we introduce the interposition of event adaptation functions (*EAF*s) like buffers and timers in order to couple initially incompatible event models. This step incorporates buffer sizing and event delay determination due to the additional system functions.

We introduce the basic idea of event model coupling using a simple example. Consider a (sub)system consisting of two tasks $\mathcal{P}_1$ and $\mathcal{P}_2$ which exchange data via event stream *ES*. Let us assume the two tasks are mapped to two different resources. Other tasks are implemented on both resources, too. Each resource implements a different resource sharing strategy (*RSST*). Let us furthermore assume, that the output of $\mathcal{P}_1$ is produced with jitter, while the analysis of $\mathcal{P}_2$ requires a sporadic event model. Clearly, the two local analysis approaches for $\mathcal{P}_1$ and $\mathcal{P}_2$ can not be coupled directly since the two event models (jitter and sporadic) are basically incompatible. However, we are able to *derive the required* parameter values of the sporadic event model *from the known* values of the jitter event model: The minimum temporal separation of two successive events with jitter is the period minus the maximum jitter: $t_2 = T_1 - J_1$. In the following, we generalize this idea.

5.2.1   Event Model Interfaces.

The intended use of event model interfaces (*EMIF*s) is shown in Figure 1. $\mathcal{P}_1$'s output event model X results from the selected technique to analyze the $\mathcal{P}_1$'s execution behavior with respect to the resource sharing strategy $RSST_1$.

Table 1. EMIFs for simple model transformations

$EMIF_{X \to Y}$	Y=periodic	Y=jitter	Y=burst	Y=sporadic	
X=periodic	$T_Y = T_X$ (identity)	$T_Y = T_X, J_Y = 0$	$T_Y = T_X, b_Y = 1, t_Y = T_X$	$t_Y = T_X$	(lossy)
X=jitter	—	$T_Y = T_X, J_Y = J_X$ (identity)	—	$t_Y = T_X - J_X$	(lossy)
X=burst	—	—	$T_Y = T_X, b_Y = b_X, t_Y = t_X$ (identity)	$t_Y = t_X$	(lossy)
X=sporadic	—	—	—	$t_Y = t_X$	(identity)

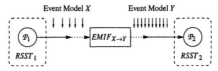

Figure 1. An event model interface (*EMIF*)

Similarly, the required input event model Y of $\mathcal{P}_2$ is determined by the selected analysis technique for $RSST_2$. Now, it is the $EMIF_{X \to Y}$'s task to translate the event stream's properties from event model X into an instance of event model Y. Such interfaces are generally uni-directional $(X \to Y)$. They can only transform instances of X into instances of Y, not vice versa.

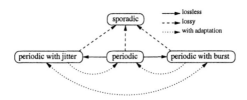

Figure 2. Possible event model interfaces

Figure 2 depicts the possible transformations $(X \to Y)$ for which such an *EMIF* can be found. The solid lines indicate that the interface losslessly (i. e. with the same modeling accuracy) transforms the information of model X into model Y, while the dashed lines indicate a loss of information during the transformation process. The dotted lines indicate that the transformation requires additional adaptation of the input event stream.

In the beginning of this section, we already solved this interfacing for the transformation (jitter→sporadic). The *EMIF*s of the other feasible transformations are given in Table 1. In case when $X = Y$, no event model interface is actually needed, since the parameter values are identical. As can be seen in the table, for only 5 out of 12 (not considering $X = Y$) possible event model transformations an *EMIF* can be given. For the other seven transformations like (jitter→periodic) no *EMIF* can be found. Which model combinations are interfaceable can be determined by formally analyzing the corresponding event models: we need to show that the behavior of every instance of event model X is contained in the set of all possible instances of model Y. In other words, we have to bound the given event stream X using the parameters of the event model Y. We have to find upper and lower bounds representing the maximum and minimum load arrival, respectively. Proofs can be found in [18].

5.2.2 Event Adaptation Functions.

As already mentioned, periodic event streams with jitter can not be captured by purely periodic event models. However, in digital signal processing systems, internal events are often assumed periodic since the system's overall input is purely periodic. But due to resource sharing and/or data-dependent task execution times, internal events most likely experience a jitter. To keep up with periodic models, buffers and timers are widely used to re-synchronize such events according to the initial period. This shows that it is generally possible to couple initially incompatible event models for analysis at the cost of additional system functions. We refer these functions to as event adaptation functions (*EAF*s). An example for the use of *EAF*s is given in Figure 3.

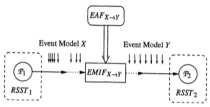

Figure 3. An *EMIF* with event adaptation function (*EAF*)

The actual functionality of these *EAF*s has to be derived from the two event models. For the above mentioned very simple case (X=jitter→Y=periodic), the *EAF* can be found straightforward. A buffer of size 1 and an output issue period of T_Y is needed. Now, we can derive an *EMIF* for this situation by simply setting T_Y to the value of T_X. In general, the parameters of the timed buffers need to be formally derived from the model transformations. Again, we refer to [18] for formal details.

5.3. Output Event Interfaces

The actual coupling of the individual analysis techniques from Section 4 is an iterative procedure of selecting analysis approaches and adapting the input event models depending on the analysis assumptions until all event models converge. This can be complex, since in many situations, the analyst has more than one option. Balancing between analysis efficiency (as in completely periodic events) and behavioral freedom (as in strongly bursty event streams) is a nontrivial task. Additionally, output event models have to be derived in order to find the required *EMIF*s and *EAF*s.

The basic idea of deriving output event models is simply based on abstract event propagation through architecture components. An input event activates a dedicated function inside the component. A corresponding output event will occur after the function is completed, i.e. after the corresponding response time. When having a constant response time, each event experiences the same propagation delay. Thus, the output model is identical to the input model. However, in complex software systems only upper and lower bounds for the response time will be given, e. g. due to data dependent task execution times or a varying number of preemptions by other tasks. For a periodic input model, the output is not purely periodic anymore, but will experience a jitter that equals the difference between the upper (t_{resp}^{+}) and the lower (t_{resp}^{-})response time bounds. An overview of how output event models can be derived from the analysis characteristics (input event model and response time) is provided in [19].

6.   CONCLUSIONS

In this paper, we presented a three-level bottom-up approach to formal timing analysis of complex heterogeneous HW/SW platforms. We started with analyzing single task execution on the target processors. Subsequently, we analyzed the influence of resource sharing strategies for single architecture components. Both areas have been investigated in the past. However, this does not apply to the analysis of the complex interactions in heterogeneous multi-component platforms. We introduced an event interface model in order to couple the approaches to resource sharing analysis for single resources (step 2) to obtain a system-level performance model.

In summary, a sound and complete analysis of the whole system currently requires several individual approaches to be combined. Other approaches to gather platform performance at once are either not practical due to algorithm inefficiencies, or too restrictive to analyze real-world heterogeneous platforms.

The interface model enables the integration of analysis techniques in the same way components and simulators have been coupled in the past. Designers of complex platforms can for the first time benefit from the large amount of work in the area of formal timing analysis. However, existing component simulators can be integrated, since the formal nature of our methodology provides excellent corner case identification support. By carefully selecting the level of detail/abstraction, designers can balance between analysis efficiency and data accuracy.

REFERENCES

[1] Rajeev Alur and David L. Dill. A theory of timed automata. *Theoretical Computer Science*, 126(2):183–235, 1994.

[2] N. C. Audsley, A. Burns, M. F. Richardson, K. Tindell, and A. J. Wellings. Applying new scheduling theory to static priority preemptive scheduling. *Journal of Real-Time Systems*, 8(5):284–292, 1993.

[3] Cadence. *Cierto VCC Environment.* http://www.cadence.com/products/vcc.html.

[4] CoWare. *CoWare N2C.* http://www.coware.com/cowareN2C.html.

[5] R. Ernst, D. Ziegenbein, K. Richter, L. Thiele, and J. Teich. Hardware/software codesign of embedded systems - The SPI Workbench. In *Proceedings IEEE Workshop on VLSI*, Orlando, USA, June 1999.

[6] Christian Ferdinand and Reinhard Wilhelm. On predicting data cache behavior for real-time systems. In *Proceedings of International Conference on Languages, Compilers, and Tools for Embedded Systems (LCTES)*, pages 16–30, 1998.

[7] K. Gresser. An event model for deadline verification of hard real-time systems. In *Proceedings 5th Euromicro Workshop on Real-Time Systems*, pages 118–123, Oulu, Finland, 1993.

[8] C. Healy, R. Arnold, F. Mueller, D. Whalley, and M. Harmon. Bounding pipeline and instruction cache performance. *IEEE Transactions on Computers*, pages 53–70, January 1999.

[9] A. Hergenhan and W. Rosenstiel. Static timing analysis of embedded software on advanced processor architectures. In *Proceedings of Design, Automation and Test in Europe (DATE '00)*, pages 552–559, Paris, March 2000.

[10] H. Kopetz and G. Gruensteidl. TTP - a time-triggered protocol for fault-tolerant computing. In *Proceedings 23rd International Symposium on Fault-Tolerant Computing*, pages 524–532, 1993.

[11] C.-G. Lee, J. Hahn, Y.-M. Seo, S. L. Min, R. Ha, S. Hong, C. Y. Park, M. Lee, and C. S. Kim. Analysis of cache-related preemption delay in fixed-priority preemptive scheduling. In *IEEE Transactions on Computers*, pages 700–713, 1998.

[12] J. Lehoczky. Fixed priority scheduling of periodic task sets with arbitrary deadlines. In *Proceedings Real-Time Systems Symposiom*, pages 201–209, 1990.

[13] Yau-Tsun Steven Li and Sharad Malik. *Performance Analysis of Real-Time Embedded Software*. Kluwer Academic Publishers, 1999.

[14] C. L. Liu and J. W. Layland. Scheduling algorithms for multiprogramming in a hard-real-time environment. *Journal of the ACM*, 20(1):46–61, 1973.

[15] T. Lundquist and P. Stenström. Integrating path and timing analysis using instruction level simulation techniques. In *Proceedings of the ACM SIGPLAN Workshop on Languages, Compilers and Tools for Embedded Systems*, Montreal, Canada, June 1998.

[16] Mentor Graphics. Seamless Co-Verification Environment. http://www.mentorg.com/seamless/.

[17] P. Pop, P. Eles, and Z. Peng. Bus access optimization for distributed embedded systems based on schedulability analysis. In *Proc. Design, Automation and Test in Europe (DATE 2000)*, Paris, France, 2000.

[18] K. Richter and R. Ernst. Event model interfaces for heterogeneous system analysis. In *Proc. of Design, Automation and Test in Europe Conference (DATE'02)*, Paris, France, March 2002.

[19] K. Richter, D. Ziegenbein, R. Ernst, L. Thiele, and J. Teich. Model composition for scheduling analysis in platform design. In *submitted to Proceeding 39th Design Automation Conference*, New Orleans, USA, June 2002.

[20] L. Sha, R. Rajkumar, and S. S. Sathaye. Generalized rate-monotonic scheduling theory: A framework for developing real-time systems. *Proceedings of the IEEE*, 82(1):68–82, January 1994.

[21] B. Sprunt, L. Sha, and J. Lehoczky. Aperiodic task scheduling for hard real-time systems. *Journal of Real-Time Systems*, 1(1):27–60, 1989.

[22] Synopsys. *CoCentric System Studio*. http://www.synopsys.com/products/cocentric_studio/.

[23] L. Thiele, s. Chakraborty, M. Gries, A. Maxiaguine, and J. Greutert. Embedded software in network processors - models and algorithms. In *Proc. 1st Workshop on Embedded Software (EMSOFT)*, Lake Tahoe (CA), USA, October 2001.

[24] K. W. Tindell. An extendible approach for analysing fixed priority hard real-time systems. *Journal of Real-Time Systems*, 6(2):133–152, Mar 1994.

[25] F. Wolf and R. Ernst. Execution Cost Interval Refinement in Static Software Analysis. *The EUROMICRO Journal, Special Issue on Modern Methods and Tools in Digital System Design*, 47(3-4):339–356, April 2001.

TEMPORAL PARTITIONING AND SEQUENCING OF DATAFLOW GRAPHS ON RECONFIGURABLE SYSTEMS

Christophe Bobda

Heinz Nixdorf Institute/Paderborn University

Fuerstenallee 11, D-33102 Paderborn, Germany

bobda@upb.de

Abstract   FPGAs(Field Programmable Gate Arrays) are often used as reconfigurable device. Because the functions to be implemented in FPGAs are often too big to fit in one device, they are divided into several *partitions or configurations* which can fit in the device. According to dependencies given in the function a Schedule is calculated. The partitions are successively downloaded in the device in accordance with the schedule until the complete function is computed. Often the time needed for reconfiguration is too high compared to the computation time [1, 11]. This paper presents a novel method for the reduction of the total reconfiguration time of a function by the generation of a minimal number of configurations. We present the framework that we developed for the fast and easy generation of configurations from a function modeled as DFG (dataflow graph).

Keywords: Reconfigurable Computing, Temporal Partitioning, Fast Synthesis

1.   INTRODUCTION

Combining the dataflow aspect and the inherent parallelism which characterizes some classes of functions, FPGAs can be used to implement those functions more efficiently than CPUs and more flexible than ASICs. FPGAs have successfully been used to provide fast computation in many application areas including text and image processing and floating point computation.
Reconfiguration is used to implement functions of any size in FPGAs with small capacity. This is done by dividing the functions in partitions which fits in the FPGAs. The partitions are implemented as configurations or bitstreams which are successively downloaded into FPGAs to compute the desire functions. This process is usually called *temporal partitioning* or *temporal placement*. Most of the works done on temporal partitioning assume the FPGAs to be either partially reconfigurable or time multiplexed. That means many configurations

are stored on the chip and can be quickly (in nano seconds) downloaded in the
FPGAs when needed. But the reality is different. Most of commercials FPGAs
are neither time multiplexed nor really partial reconfigurable. For this purpose,
many solutions proposed are not easily applicable. In practice high level tools
are used to capture and solve problems which are geometrically based. The
consequence is an inefficient use of the FPGA capabilities like the regularity
structure. This paper examines the use of non-partial reconfigurable FPGAs to
implement large functions. The goal is to minimize the reconfiguration overhead which is always too high compare to the computation time of function in
FPGAs. We have developed a framework for the capture, the temporal partitioning and the generation of configurations from a given function in form of
a DFG. Our framework is based on the JBits[6] API. We reduce the temporal
placement problem to the placement of a small amount of modules in different
configurations by dealing with cores. The rest of the paper is organized as
follows: Section 2 presents the main work which has been carried in the temporal placement and temporal partitioning. In section 3 the formulation of the
temporal placement problem based on the definitions already given in [12, 14]
is given. The realization of overlapping between cores is shown in section
4. Section 5 presents the list scheduling based temporal partitioning method.
To illustrate the concept of section 5, the partitioning method is applied on a
real life problem in section 8. Section 9 concludes the paper and gives some
directions for future work.

2.   RELATED WORK

The most used and perhaps the simplest approach to solve the temporal partitioning problem is the (enhance)list scheduling [11, 3, 10, 4, 13]. This method
first places all the nodes of a DFG representing the problem to be solved in a
list. Partitions(configurations) are built stepwise by removing nodes without
predecessor in the list and allocate them to a partition until the size of the partition reached a limit(the size of the FPGA). Integer linear programming(ILP)
[10, 5, 8] can be applied to solve some optimization constrains like timing.
Other methods like network flow [9] and genetic algorithm [15] are also applied to find temporal partitions and optimize parameters like communication
cost and configuration latency.

In order to reduce the reconfiguration overhead, Pandey et al[11] suggested
the reduction of number of partitions with resource sharing. For a new partition,
a minimal resource set is chosen and a partition is built upon this resource
set. Trimberger[13] proposed a time multiplexed FPGA architecture in which
configurations can be stored directly on the chip. Reconfiguration is done in
micro cycle. In a micro cycle a new configuration is downloaded from the
on-chip memory. The CLBs(configurable logic block) contain micro-registers

to temporally hold results of previous computation step when switching from one configuration to another.

The geometrical view of the partial reconfiguration is considered in some extent in [12, 14]. The space and temporal placement of computational nodes of a DFG representing the problem to be computed in the FPGA is mapped, for example, to a packing problem[12]. Problems with high reconfiguration time(which are the focus of this paper) have been defined as a matter of future work. In practice high level description languages and tools are used to specify and solve a problem with important geometrical aspects. This leads to a non efficient use of the regularity structure of FPGAs[2] as well as waste of resource. We present an approach for the minimization of reconfiguration. For the Xilinx Virtex FPGA family that we use as RPU(reconfigurable processing unit), cores can be generated in the JBits environment. This java-based interface provides some basic functions like adders, comparators, subtracters, multipliers, multiplexers which can directly be placed on different locations on the FPGA and routed together to build complex functions.

3.   PROBLEM FORMULATION

This section deals with definition and formulation of the problem to be solved. Since the definitions provided in [12, 14] are the most adapted for the temporal placement, we choose to adopt it and adjust them to fetch our considerations.

Definition 1 (Dataflow Graph) *Given a set of tasks* $T = \{T_1, ..., T_k\}$ *a dataflow graph is a directed acyclic graph* $G = (V, E)$, *where* $V = T$. *An edge* $e = (T_i, T_j) \in E$ *is defined through the (data)dependence between task* T_i *and task* T_j.

Each node T in the DFG is equivalent to a core C which can be placed on the RPU H with length h_x and width h_y.

Definition 2 (Temporal placement) *Given a DFG* $G = (V, E)$ *and a RPU* H *with the size* (h_x, h_y), *a temporal placement is a three dimensional vector function* $p = (p_x, p_y, p_t) : \Omega \to N^3$, *where the values* $p_x(C), p_y(C)$ *denote the coordinates of the lower left position of the core* C *associate to a task* $T \in V$ *on the RPU. The core* C *occupied the space* $[p_x(C), .., p_x(C) + w_x(C)]$ *in the x direction,* $[p_y(C), .., p_y(C) + w_y(C)]$ *in the y direction and* $[p_t(T), .., p_t(T) + w_t(C)]$ *in the time dimension.*

Figure 1 illustrate a temporal placement of a problem graph with three cores(+),(*) and (>) representing tasks T_1, T_2 and T_3) with dependencies ($T_1 \to T_2$) and ($T_1 \to T_3$) on a partial reconfigurable FPGA.

In our formulation of the temporal partitioning, modules are allowed to overlap in space and time. Reconfiguration happens in today's FPGAs by the complete replacement of configuration, a process which is too costly compare to the

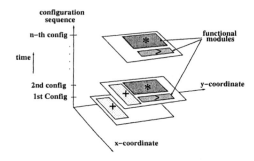

Figure 1.   A temporal Placement

computation time[11, 1]. To avoid such overhead, we exploit the free resources of modules already selected to run in the FPGA in a time interval to implement the modules for other computation. This process require no additional overhead, because only free resource are use.

In fig.2, all the modules could not be placed simultaneously on the device if overlapping was not allowed.

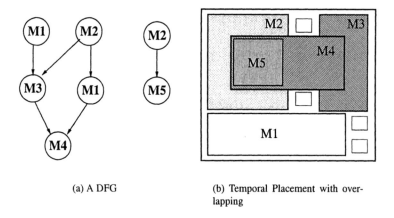

(a) A DFG   (b) Temporal Placement with over-
                                       lapping

Figure 2.   A DFG and the corresponding temporal placement with ressource sharing

4.   IMPLEMENTATION OF OVERLAPPING CORES AND RESSOURCE SHARING

If two cores C_1 and C_2 share the same resource C_0 and if the free resource in core C_0 are enough to implement the functionality of C_0, then C_0 can be shared by C_1 and C_2 without additional resource. For example, a Virtex register implemented in the JBits use only the F_1 and G_1 inputs of the slice 0 or 1 of a

```
ALGORITHM I: generate_partitions(DFG G, DEVICE dev)
1  BEGIN;
2  list_nodes := generate_nodes_list_with_priority(G);
3  WHILE (!list_node.empty()) DO
4    allocated_list.reset();
5    FOR(i := 1; i < list_nodes.size();i++)
6      chosen_node := node_list[i];
7      best_node := get_best_overlapping_node();
8      IF (best_node = NULL)
9        IF (allocated_list.size + chosen_node.size < dev.size)
10         allocated_list.insert(chosen_node);
11         list_node.remove(chosen_node);
12       ELSE
13         implement_overlap(chosen_node, best_node);
14   list_partition.insert(allocated_list);
15 END;
```

Figure 3.   The temporal partitioning algorithm

CLB(Configurable logic Block). Its outputs are the X_q and Y_q outputs of the corresponding slice. The resource $F_2, .., G_4, F_2, .., G_3, cin, X, X_B, Y_B$ as well as the remaining X_q and Y_q are free in the two slices of the CLBs allocated to the register core. They can be used o implement another register in the same core.

If the core C_0 has no additional resource, I/O Multiplexing is commonly used to allocate the common resource C_0 either to C_1 or to C_2 depending on a predefined schedule. For two inputs I_1 and I_2 and a condition C, I/O multiplexing is implemented as follow: If $C = 1$ then $Z = I_1$, else $Z = I_2$. This is equivalent to the boolean equation $Z = C.I_1 + notZ = C.I_2$ which can easily be implemented in a 3-inputs LUT.

As we can see in this example, sharing resource in FPGA without additional overhead is possible, since the cores provided in the JBits environment use only a fraction of the resource allocated to them.

5.   THE TEMPORAL PARTITIONING ALGORITHM

This section provides the description of our partitioning algorithm. The method *generate_partitions* (ALGORITHM I) is a list scheduling like method which takes as inputs a DFG G and a device type dev and return a list of all partitions *list_partition*.

At the begin all the nodes of the DFG are inserted in *list_nodes* in order of decreasing priority (line 2). In order to make a maximum use of overlapping capability, the priority is high in function of the non inclusion of the core in other cores, the non precedence by other cores in the list and the size of the core. At each step of the partitioning, a node *chosen_node* with maximum priority is removed from $list\_nodes$ and inserted in $allocated\_list$(lines 6, 10 - 11, 14 - 16), which is the list of all elements of the current partition. It represents the resource running in the FPGA in a time interval. In order to make an efficient use of those resource for the next time interval, we first check for intersection between $chosen\_node$ and the nodes currently assigned to $allocated\_list$. The function $get\_best\_overlapping\_node$ will return the node which has a maximum overlapping core with $chosen\_node$. If no such node exists, $chosen\_node$ will be added to the current partition $allocated\_list$, if the resulting partition fits in the device (lines 7 - 11). In the case where a best overlapping node exists, the overlapping concept as shown in section 4(lines 12 - 13) will be implemented. The current partition $allocated\_list$ is inserted in the list of all partitions when all the nodes in $list\_nodes$ have been processed (line 14). If the list of nodes $list\_nodes$ is not empty, a new partition is created and the processing continues (lines 3 - 14).

6. PLACEMENT OF MODULES IN CONFIGURATIONS

Having the list of all partitions, we use an enhanced *eigenvector based placement* to arrange the cores of each partition on the surface of the device and the resource inside the merged cores. This method has the advantage of placing Inputs and Outputs (I/O) elements at the boundary of the cores and the device, which makes pipelining easier. The method is based on the two dimensional spectral embedding of the nodes of the DFG using eigenvectors. Having a spectral embedding of the nodes in the plane, a post-processing method is used to successively remove the nodes not in the actual partition and fit the rest in the device area. The computation of the positions of modules on the device surface happen as follow: Given a DFG $G = (V, E)$ representing the modules and their interconnexion, the **connection matrix, degree matrix** and **laplacian** are first computed.

- The **connection matrix** of G is the symetric matrix $C = (c_{i,j})$ with $(1 \leq i, j \leq |V|)$ and $c_{i,j} = 1 \iff (v_i, v_j) \in E$.

- The **degree matrix** of G is the diagonal matrix $D = (d_{i,j})$, $(1 \leq i, j \leq |V|)$ with $i \neq j \rightarrow d_{i,j} = 0$ and $d_{i,i} = \sum_{j=1}^{|V|} c_{i,j}$.

- The **laplacian matrix** of G is the matrix $B = D - C$.

In [7] Hall proved that the r eigenvectors of the laplacian matrix related to the r smallest non zero eigenvalues of B define the coordinates of the $|V|$ modules of G in an r-dimensional vector space, such that the sum of the distances between the modules is minimal. We first compute the r smallest eigenvalues, then we use a post-processing step to generate the definitive position of each core in the corresponding bitstream.

The algorithm described here is implemented in a framework that we developed.

7. CONFIGURATION SEQUENCING

Given a DFG, our tool compute a **configuration graph**(fig.4) in which nodes represents configurations. Configurations communicate via **inter configuration registers**(fig.4), which are automatically inserted in bitstreams when an arc of the DFG connects two components in different configurations. The inter configuration registers are mapped in the CPU address room and are used for the communication between nodes in different configurations. The nodes of the configuration graph, that means the configurations are successively downloaded in the FPGA until the computation of the original DFG completes.

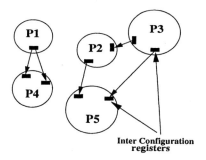

Figure 4. A Configuration Graph

8. CASE STUDY: NUMERICAL SOLUTION OF A DIFFERENTIAL EQUATION

To illustrate and show the efficiency of the method described in this paper, a numerical method for solving a differential equation as described in [12] is considered.

Fig 5 shows the DFG for solving a differential equation of the form $y\prime\prime + 3xy\prime + 3y = 0$ in the interval $[x_0, a]$ with step size d_x and initial values $y(x_0) = y_0$, $y\prime(x_0) = u_0$, using Euler's method as presented in [12]. We consider the worst case, where no additional resource is left in the available cores to implement the core overlapping. I/O multiplexing have to be considered in this case. The size of the different modules for the Xilinx Virtex architecture is given in table 1. As we can see, the size of a 2 inputs 1 output 16 Bit-Multiplexer is less than (10×1). Since the size of a 16 Bit-multiplier is more than (5×20), merging two cores sharing a multiplier module will have a reduction of the

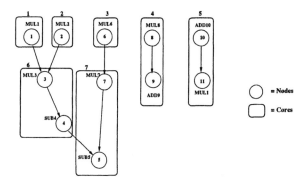

Figure 5.   DFG For the DE-Integrator

Table 1.   Cores Size(in CLB) for the Xilinx Virtex Architecture

Cores	X_Size	Y_Size
16-Bit Add	8	1
16-Bit Sub	8	1
16-Bit Comp	8	1
2 In/1-Out 16-Bit Mux	10	1
16-Bit Mul	5	20

size of a multiplier (5×20) and an augmentation of 3 times the size of a multiplexer($3 \times (9 \times 1)$) on the size of the resulting core. The net gain we have is about 70 CLBs. With this observation the method described in 5 is suited to implement the DFG in a Virtex device. When targeting any of the Virtex above the Virtex 300 with a minimum area of (32×48), the design will completely fit in it. Only one partition will be generated and reconfiguration is not needed.

When targeting the Virtex 100 with size (20×30), the device can not hold more than 4 multipliers simultaneously. Another temporal partitioning algorithm will produce a minimum of two partitions in order to implement the DFG. For 1000 iterations of the DFG computations, the device will be configured 1000 times. With a reconfiguration time of $2s$ the time needed only for reconfiguration will be $2000s$. This solution is not applicable. The algorithm provided in this paper will generate only one partition for the same device. This means the reconfiguration time is reduced to zero.

The device will contain 3 multipliers, 2 substracters one adder one comparator and 9 multiplexers in the worst case. The total number of CLBs needed is 464. The design easily fits in the target device (Virtex 100). Table 2 gives an overview over the sharing of modules among cores in the device.

Table 2.   Resource sharing for the problem of section 8

	(1)	(2)	(3)	(4)	(5)	(6)	(7)
Add1	-	-	-	-	X	-	-
Sub1	-	-	-	-	-	X	-
Sub2	-	-	-	-	-	-	X
Comp1	-	-	-	-	X	-	-
Mul1	-	-	-	X	-	X	-
Mul2	X	-	-	-	-	-	X
Mul3	-	X	X	-	-	-	-

9.   CONCLUSION

This paper has presented a novel approach for the temporal placement of DFG on a reconfigurable platform. The paper shows that allowing overlapping of cores in the space and time can lead to a reduction in the number of partitions. Sharing modules in FPGAs and switching from one core to another can increase the latency of the partitions. Because the latency of a bitstream varies from nanoseconds to microseconds, while the reconfiguration time of an FPGA is more than a second, the overall performance of functions depends more on the reconfiguration time than the computation time.

References

[1] C. Bobda and N. Steenbock. Singular value decomposition on distributed reconfigurable systems. In *12th IEEE International Workshop On Rapid System Prototyping(RSP'01), Monterey California*. IEEE Computer Society, 2001.

[2] T. J. Callahan, P. Chong, A. Dehon, and J. Wawrzynek. Fast module mapping and placement for datapaths in fpgas. In *International Symposium on Field Programmable Gate Arrays(FPGA 98)*, pages 123 – 132, Monterey, California, 1998. ACM/SIGDA.

[3] J. M. P. Cardoso and H. C. Neto. An enhance static-list scheduling algorithm for temporal partitioning onto rpus. In *IFIP TC10 WG10.5 10 Int. Conf. on Very Large Scale Integration(VLSI'99)*, pages 485 – 496, Lisboa, Portugal, 1999. IFIP.

[4] D. Chang and M. Marek-Sadowska. Partitioning sequential circuits on dynamicaly reconfigurable fpgas. In *International Symposium on Field Programmable Gate Arrays(FPGA 98)*, pages 161 – 167, Monterey, California, 1998. ACM/SIGDA.

[5] Ejnioui and N. Ranganathan. Circuit scheduling on time-multiplexed fpgas.

[6] S. Guccione, D. Levi, and P. Sundararajan. Jbits: A java-based interface for reconfigurable computing, 1999.

[7] K. Hall. dimensional quadratic placement algorithm, 1970.

[8] M. Kaul, R. Vemuri, S. Govindarajan, and I. Ouaiss. An automated temporal partitioning tool for a class of dsp applications, 1998.

[9]   H. Liu and D. F. Wong. Circuit partitioning for dynamicaly reconfigurable fpgas. In *International Symposium on Field Programmable Gate Arrays(FPGA 98)*, pages 187 – 194, Monterey, California, 1999. ACM/SIGDA.

[10] I. Ouaiss, S. Govindarajan, V. Srinivasan, M. Kaul, and R. Vemuri. An integrated partitioning and synthesis system for dynamically reconfigurable multi-FPGA architectures. In *IPPS/SPDP Workshops*, pages 31–36, 1998.

[11] A. Pandey and R. Vemuri. Combined temporal partitioning and scheduling for reconfigurable architectures. In J. Schewel, P. M. Athanas, S. A. Guccione, S. Ludwig, and J. T. McHenry, editors, *Reconfigurable Technology: FPGAs for Computing and Applications, Proc. SPIE 3844*, pages 93–103, Bellingham, WA, 1999. SPIE – The International Society for Optical Engineering.

[12] J. Teich, S. P. Fekete, and J. Schepers. Optimizing dynamic hardware reconfiguration. Technical Report 97.228, Angewante Mathematik Und Informatik Universität zu Köln, 1998.

[13] S. Trimberger. Circuit partitioning for dynamicaly reconfigurable fpgas. In *International Symposium on Field Programmable Gate Arrays(FPGA 98)*, pages 153 – 160, Monterey, California, 1999. ACM/SIGDA.

[14] M. Vasilko. Dynasty: A temporal floorplanning based cad framework for dynamicaly reconfigurable logic systems. In P. Lysaght and J. Irvine, editors, *Field Programmable Logic and Aplications FPL 1999*, pages 124–133, Glasgow, UK, 1999. Springer.

[15] M. Vasilko and G. Benyon-Tinker. Automatic temporal floorplanning with guaranteed solution feasibility. In R. Hartenstein and H. Grünbacher, editors, *Field Programmable Logic and Aplications FPL 2000*, pages 656–664, Villach, Austria, 2000. Springer.

Integration of Low Power Analysis into High-Level Synthesis

Achim Rettberg, Bernd Kleinjohann, Franz J. Rammig
University of Paderborn/C-LAB,
Fuerstenallee 11, D-33102 Paderborn,Germany
Tel:. +49 5251 606110, Fax: + 49 5251 606065,
Email: achim.rettberg@c-lab.de

Abstract: This paper describes a new method to integrate low power analysis into high-level synthesis. We addressed especially a specific analysis technique within the scheduling task of high-level synthesis. The analysis technique allows the determination of dedicated turn-on and turn-off mechanism. Therefore, the optimisation of power consumption is simultaneously improved with the design delay.

Key words: high-level synthesis, low power analysis, scheduling, activation interval

1.   INTRODUCTION

Today highly integrated circuits and components entered all design areas. Especially consumer electronic devices, such as mobile-phones and PDA's belong to those integrated circuits. This battery driven devices don't have the ability to recharge the batteries at any time. For this reason, the usage of low power components plays a major role to receive longer operation time of these devices. The primary objective of such developments is the minimization of power consumption. To receive this objective, some methods are used to optimise the devices operation by adjusted cycle frequencies or deactivation of external devices and displays. Other methods optimise the power consumption of devices without modifying the functionality. Usually in this area it is expected to save power consumption. For example, at a laptop 52 % power is needed for the motherboard. The display consumes only 8 % [2]. Methodological investigation shows that there exists in particular asynchronous architectures methods to estimate power consumption [3], [4], [5], [6]. The power consumption is often lower by two sequenced signals with the same value in opposite to signal switch with different values. Sequenced signals with the same value occurred often, because in synchronous designs each rising and falling edge generates an output value. Different estimation methods based on these techniques are developed [7], [8]. If we embed this methods in the methodological design of digital systems [1], a bottom-up approach will be recognizable. Optimisations referred to elementary cells of the final implementation and the data encoding are presented in [9], [10] and [11]. In generally power can be saved on register-transfer level by consideration of different architecture variants [8]. Furthermore it is possible to introduce parallelism and pipelining on architectural level to decrease power consumption. Another possibility offers the usage of guarded evaluation. The integration of registers on the primary inputs of a logical block avoid the switching of it. These registers store the values if the logical block is not used. The insertion of so called gated clocks allows the turning off of non-active design parts [7], [12]. Especially techniques like operand isolation and pre-computation decreases the power consumption enormously. "Operand isolation" means that the operands are computed only once. The splitting of a calculation in pre- and main calculation is called pre-computation. But the integration of those techniques into the synthesis process is very complex and requires a substantial effort.

The selection of the design paradigm (synchronous, asynchronous) influences on one side the power consumption and on the other side the implementation. Furthermore, the methods used for the optimisation are described in [13], [14]. Asynchronous architectures are good for low power designs, because hereby exists no clock-signal within the design. The asynchronous components are self-synchronising by a handshake-mechanism [15]. Thus only active parts of an asynchronous design consumes power. The introduction of parallelism into the asynchronous architecture leads not to a increasing power consumption. The realization of the handshake-mechanism is a design effort. That mean, we need more wires for the implementation. This has to be considered with respect to the asynchronous architecture in opposite to a synchronous implementation.

In this paper we present a method, that discussed the optimisation of the power consumption on the architecture level. The method starts from a data-flow graph. We take into account the analysis method for asynchronous bit-serial architecture that is presented in [16]. In the described method, that is integrated in the high-level synthesis, we develop an analysis method of architectures based on a data-flow level for bit-serial and bit-parallel architectures. The determined algorithms are filter-algorithms, which are used for signal pre-processing.

2. RELATED WORK

In the past several algorithms for high-level synthesis are developed. The major objective for all these algorithms was the minimization of the used resources to save chip area and the optimisation of the systems delay time. An interesting approach for the integration of low power techniques into the high-level synthesis is presented in [17]. The approach focuses on the minimization of resources per cycle whereby power is saved. This could be achieved by mapping the same operation types to a real resource.

Another interesting approach, that performs a power estimation for behavioural level is presented in [18], [19]. The behavioural models are implemented in VHDL. Furthermore, parallelism and pipelining can be used on architectural level to decrease the power consumption.

3. METHODOLOGY AND ANALYSIS

The design of a digital system bases on a high-level specification. The specification is transformed into an algorithmic description, like C or behavioural VHDL source code. During the high-level synthesis the behavioural description of the algorithm is compiled into a structural description. Within the high-level synthesis several method are performed to realize the synthesis process. The methods are namely scheduling, allocation and binding. The scheduling process organizes the operation according the timing information. The mapping of the temporally organized operations and memory elements to real resources is done in the allocation and binding processes. In past approaches, these methods optimises only the delay time and the used area of the digital system. In this context the minimization of the power consumption isn't considered. In our approach, the minimization of the power consumption is the main objective. Therefore, the results of the activation interval analysis [16] based on a special asynchronous architecture [13], [14] should be integrated into the high-level synthesis. The advantages of bit-serial architectures are the elimination of size overhead on logic level for each operation and that parallelism kept upright by using pipelining design style. During the high-level synthesis the algorithmic description is transformed into an internal format, called data-flow graph. The nodes in the data-flow graph correspond to the operations of the algorithmic description.

The edges indicate the data dependencies between the operations. The following definition gives a formal description of the data-flow graph.

Definition 1: Given a directed data-flow graph $G = (V, E)$ with the set $V = \{v_1, ..., v_n\}$ of operations within the graph and the set $E = \{e_1, ...,e_m\}$ for the data dependencies.

Complex operations within the data-flow graph, such as trigonometric functions are replaced by the corresponding algorithm. Each node in the graph is annotated with some characteristics, as power consumption, number of control signal and timing information. The timing information consisted of the delay and throughput. Along the edges we can observe the activation of the specific operations [16]. In our bit-serial asynchronous architecture, during the analysis phase, each operation-node corresponds to a real resource. Therefore, for the asynchronous architecture it is not necessary to perform optimisation on the data-flow graph. But, if we want to analyse bit-parallel architectures an optimisation of the operations within the data-flow graph is important and necessary. This means, we map the data-flow graph to a set of real resources $M = \{m_1, ..., m_k\}$. This will be carried out by the already mentioned high-level synthesis. A formal definition of a valid implementation after the synthesis process is given in definition 2.

Definition 2: Given a graph according to definition 1 and a set $M = \{m_1, ..., m_k\}$ of real resources. For each resource m_i the timing t_i is known. Furthermore a latency-bound L is given. A valid implementation that consists of scheduling, allocation and binding has to fulfill the following terms:

- The latency-bound must be strictly adhered, that mean the delay time of the system is below L.
- The number of nodes running simultaneously on instances of a resource type is lower than the number of allocated instances of the type.

This definition shows the main tasks of the high-level synthesis. Obviously, an analysis of the power consumption could be integrated during the scheduling process. As mentioned before, the main objectives of the high-level synthesis are the minimization of run-time and chip area of the system. An integration of the power consumption optimisation process based on execution interval analysis is described in the next chapter.

4. SCHEDULING UNDER LOW POWER CONSTRAINTS

Without loss of generality we assume that the power consumption p_i is known for each node v_i within the data-flow graph. From this follows:

Definition 3: (limited scheduling respectively to power consumption) Find a schedule that fulfill the following formula:

$$Power_s = \sum_{i=1}^{n} p_i * m_{is} * D_{is} + g_s.$$

Whereas m_{is} is a number of real resources of a certain type in a schedule s, power consumption p_i of a real resource and duration D_i of node i within a schedule s. Furthermore, g_s represents the additional cost for switch-on/off mechanism for a schedule s.

Therefore, the value α defines a bound for the scheduling algorithm. The activation interval analysis described in [16] calculated three different partitions for the data-flow graph depicted in Figure 1, which contains 10 operators. Each partition can explicitly controlled, that mean it can switched on and off. The first partition contain only the operation A. The second one consists of B, C, E, H and J. The last and third partition consists of D, F and G.

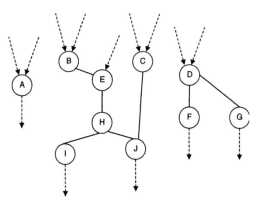

Figure 1. Example of a data-flow graph

Regarding node C in the second partition of the example data-flow graph, it is obvious that it is not necessary to activate this node for the entire running time. The calculation of the so called mobility, which describes the execution timing interval of a node, can be done by a computation of a

ASAP[1] and ALAP[2] scheduling [20]. These scheduling methods are arranges the operations according to the earliest respectively to the latest point of time. The mobility can be computed by the execution timing interval [$asap_v$, $alap_v$] for each node v of the data-flow graph. The formal definition is:

$$Mobil_v = alap_v - asap_v + 1$$

It is possible to compute both schedules in linear time. The ASAP schedule is depicted in Figure 2 for the example data-flow graph. Figure 3 shows the ALAP schedule of the example.

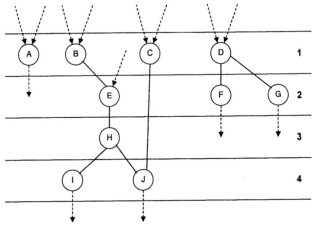

Figure 2. Data-flow graph according to the ASAP schedule

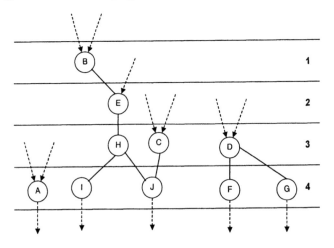

Figure 3. Data-flow graph with ALAP schedule

---

[1] ASAP = as soon as possible
[2] ALAP = as late as possible

A graphical representation of the execution timing intervals for the full design is depicted in Figure 4. Therefore, the mobility for each node is:

- $Mobil_A = 4$
- $Mobil_B = Mobil_E = Mobil_H = Mobil_I = Mobil_J = 1$
- $Mobil_C = Mobil_D = Mobil_F = Mobil_G = 3$

The operations with mobility equal 1 are fixed for exactly one time frame in which they are executed. Operations with a mobility grater than 1 could be executed in different time frames. Especially, those operations are relevant for the minimization of the power consumption. That means, they can explicitly accessed by a switching on and off mechanism. Therefore, they contribute to a low power design. Besides this, those operations can be combined with others to maintain a guarded partition, but it is necessary to take into consideration the delay, power consumption, area for each resource and the data dependencies. This is reasonable for bit-serial architectures with a high data bit-width, because real resources could be saved. Power are saved by the minimization of real resources, but the mapping of operations to the same real resource increases the communication effort. For this reason, it is necessary to include registers and multiplexers in your design, but such components consumes additional power. In the following, we assume not to save real resource, but to integrate activation and deactivation mechanism like gated clocks and guarded evaluation [12].

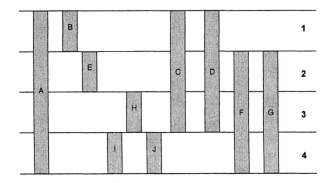

*Figure 4.*Execution intervals of the operators from the data-flow graph

If we summarized the information about the data dependencies and the mobility it is observable that operation A is completely independent of all others. Moreover operation A can be executed at any of the 4 cycles. Additionally, these operation could form an own partition, which can be explicitly activated or deactivated, but the aim is to combine operations that are active/passive in the same time frame to a guarded partition. In accordance with the previous discussion, operations D, F and G can be executed within 3 cycles. As mentioned before, operations B, E, H, I and J have the mobility 1 and will not be considered for the analysis, but those operations build another partition. At this point we received with this method the same results as from the activation interval analysis [16]. Obviously operation C isn't assigned to a partition. The mobility of operation C is 3. For this reason, it is necessary to execute C before the computation of operation J is started. This has to be done within the first 3 cycles. Therefore, operation C can be deactivated for 2 cycles. Basically, this contributes to the minimization of power consumption which could not be identified with an activation interval analysis. One possible partition of the complete data-flow graph is depicted in Figure 5. Each partition can be activated or deactivated with gated clocks or guarded evaluation. If gated clock are used the additional costs based on four AND gates (one for each partition). As mentioned before the target architecture for the high-level synthesis is a bit-serial design. Therefore, the size of a real resource is in most cases smaller than multiplexer and register that are used by mapping of operations to a real resource.

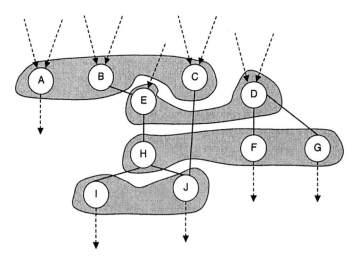

Figure 5. Partitioned data-flow graph

This method depends on the recognition of the data dependencies of the operations from the data-flow graph. Afterwards the ASAP and ALAP schedules are computed to calculate the execution intervals and the mobility. In combination with the mobility and the data dependencies the activation and deactivation partition are calculated. First results of different small filter algorithms for compression shows, that it is possible to received up to 20 %

minimization of the power consumption, see Figure 6. For the standard high-level synthesis benchmark "differential equalizer" it is possible to save up to 10 % of the power consumption by using the low power high-level synthesis for a bit-serial design compared to regular bit-serial implementation.

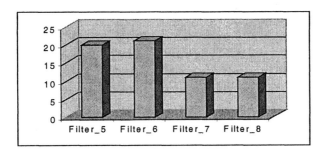

Figure 6. Power savings in percentage for different filter algorithms

5. CONCLUSION AND FUTURE WORK

This paper describes an analysis method based on a data-flow graph that allows the integration of control mechanism for low power designs into the high-level synthesis. Especially, the scheduling which is part of the high-level synthesis is used to activate only active operations.

Furthermore, it is planned to include the allocation and binding processes in the low power analysis. In addition to this, the implementation of a comprehensive design space exploration toolkit focuses on the aspects of power consumption so that timing behaviour is planned.

REFERENCES

[1]   Franz J. Rammig. *"Systematischer Entwurf digitaler Systeme"*. B. G. Teubner, Stuttgart, 1989

[2]   M. J. Irvine, *"Low Power Tutorial"*, in Proceedings ASIC/SOC, Washington D.C., 1999

[3]   M. Laurent, M. Briet, *"Low Power Design Flow and Libraries"*, in NATO ASI Series "Low Power Design in Deep Submicron Electronics", Kluwer Academic Publishers, 1997

[4]   P. Kudva, V. Akella, *"A technique for estimating power in self-timed asynchronous circuits"*, In Proc. International Symposium on Advanced Research in Asynchronous Circuits and Systems November, 1994

[5]   J. Tierno, R. Manohar, M. Martin, *"Energy and entropy measures for low power design"*. In Proc. International Symposium on Advanced Research in Asynchronous Circuits and Systems, IEEE Computer Society Press, März, 1996

[6]   P.A. Beerel, C.-T. Hsieh, S. Wadekar, "Estimation of energy consumption in speed-independet control circuits". In International Symposium on Low Power Design, 1995

[7]   S. Devadas, S. Malik, "A Survey of Optimization Techniques Targeting Low Power VLSI Circuits". In Proc. of the 32nd Design Automation Conference, San Francisco, CA, Juni, 1995

[8]   C. Piguet, *"Circuit and Logic Level Design"*, in NATO ASI Series "Low Power Design in Deep Submicron Electronics", Kluwer Academic Publishers, 1997

[9]   J. Monteiro, S. Devadas, B. Li, *"A methodology for efficient estimation of switching activity in sequential circuits"*. In Proc. of the 31st Design Automation Conference, San Diego, CA, 1994

[10]   M. Stan, W. P. Burleson, *"Bus-Invert Coding for Low Power I/O"*, IEEE Transactions on VLSI Systems, 1995

[11]   Koegst,M.; Franke,G.; Rülke St.; Feske, K., *"A Strategy for Low Power FSM-Design by Reducing Switching Activity"*, PATMOS `97, Sept. 8-10, 1997, Louvain-la-Neuve, Belgium

[12]   L. Benini, G. De Micheli, "Transformation and Synthesis of FSMs for low-power gated-clock implementation". IEEE Transactions on Computer-Aided Design , 1996

[13]   W. Hardt, B. Kleinjohann, "Flysig: Towards High Performance Special Purpose Architectures by Joining Paradigms", in Proceedings of 7th NASA Symposium on VLSI Design, Albuquerque, New Mexico, Oct. 1998

[14]   W. Hardt, B. Kleinjohann, A. Rettberg, L. Kleinjohann, *"A New Configurable and Scalable Architecture for Rapid Prototyping of Asynchronous Designs for Signal Processing"*, in Proceedings of the 12th Annual IEEE International ASIC/SOC Conference, Washington, DC, USA, September 1999

[15]   P.B. Endecott, *"SCALP: A Superscalar Asynchronous Low-Power Processor"*, Dissertation, University of Manchester, 1995

[16]   A. Rettberg, B. Kleinjohann, W. *Hardt "Using Activation Interval Analysis for Low Power"*. In Proc. of the 9th NASA Symposium on VLSI Design, Albuquerque, New Mexico, November, 2000

[17]   J. Monteiro, et. al., *"Scheduling Techniques to Enable Power Management"*, DAC-33, ACM/IEEE Design Automation Conference, 1996

[18]   Kruse, L.; Schmidt, E.; Jochens, G.; Nebel, W., *"Low Power Binding Heuristics"*, PATMOS 1999, pp. 41-50, Kos, Greece, 1999

[19]   Kruse, L.; Schmidt, E.; Jochens, G.; Stammermann, A.; Nebel, W. *"Lower Bounds on the Power Consumption in Scheduled Data Flow Graphs with Resource constraints"*, In Proc. of the Design and Test Conference in Europe (DATE 2000), Paris, France, 2000

[20]   H. Krämer, W.; W. Rosenstiel, *"System Synthesis Using Behavioral Descriptions"*, European Design Automation Conference (EDAC), pages 227-282, 1990

This work has partly been funded by Deutsche Forschungsgemeinschaft (DFG), project RA 612/5-3 (Grundlagen und Verfahren verlustleistungsarmer Informationsverarbeitung: Entwurf verlustarmer Architekturvarianten).

Going Beyond Deadline-Driven Low-level Scheduling in Distributed Real-Time Computing Systems

K.H. (Kane) Kim   and   Juqiang Liu
Department of *Electrical and Computer Engineering*
University of California,
Irvine, CA, 92697, U.S.A
{kane, jqliu} @ ece.uci.edu

Abstract: In real-time computing systems, timing-requirement specifications coming from the application designer are the obvious primary driver for resource allocation. Deadline-driven scheduling of computation-segments has been studied as an advanced mode of scheduling devised to meet the timing requirement specifications. However, it does not reflect additional concerns of the application designer, the damaging impacts of various timing violations on the application. The notion of *risk-incursion function* (RIF) as a framework for specification of such damaging impacts has been established by the first co-author. In this paper, a concrete implementation approach of the RIF-driven resource allocation scheme is discussed first. Then two RIF-based scheduling algorithms are discussed. The results of the experiment conducted to compare the performance of RIF-based scheduling algorithms against that of deadline-driven scheduling algorithms are also provided.

Key words: Real-time, RIF, Risk Incursion Function, RIPF, Risk Incursion Potential Function, Resource Allocation, scheduling, deadline.

1.   INTRODUCTION

As the real-time (RT) computing field continues to grow, calls for significant advances in the technology for resource allocation are increasingly heard in industry. Much of the technology practiced in industry for scheduling of RT computations in the past 35 years has been at the level of assigning priorities to processes.

It has been known for long that the deadline-driven scheduling is a step forward from the fixed-priority scheduling in terms of reflecting the application requirements closely [Fin67, Kop97, Liu73, Ser72]. However, deadline-driven scheduling has not been practiced much. Guiding and helping application designers to specify deadlines have been a challenge for a long time.

In recent years, research produced a programming approach such as the *time-triggered message-triggered object* (TMO) programming scheme [Kim97, Kim00] with which programmers can specify start time-windows and completion deadlines of RT computation-segments in convenient manners. The practice of deadline-driven scheduling is bound to increase.

After all, it is natural for RT application programmers to think about start time-windows and completion deadlines rather than priority numbers. The argument that low priorities can be given to unimportant computation-segments is a peripheral argument for using priority-based scheduling approaches. If such treatment occurs in absence of computing resource failures, such computation-segments are trivial ones which could have been omitted to begin with. If computing resource failures occur and the resulting resource shortage dictates sacrificing the abilities to meet all timing requirements of all computation-segments, then less important computation-segments can be sacrificed. If such a decision is represented by assignment of low priorities to the victimized computation-segments, then the priority is really a number representing criticality or importance rather than a timing requirement. Reflecting criticality is an issue orthogonal to that of reflecting timing requirements. Reflecting criticality can be combined with approaches to reflecting timing requirements, including deadline-driven scheduling.

Therefore, reflecting the start time-window specifications and the completion deadline specifications supplied by application designers in low-level (short-term) scheduling is expected to be the direction increasingly adopted in industry during this decade. To go a step further in reflecting application designers' concerns, the scheduler must be designed to reflect not only timing specifications associated with various RT computation-segments but also specifications of damaging impacts of various timing violations to the application. Typically the impacts of violating the completion deadlines of different output actions vary. The violations of some output deadlines may lead to the failure of the entire application, while the application may continue with lowered application service goals when the violations of some other deadlines occur.

We have taken the position that specifying the damaging impacts of various timing violations to the application is at the core of specifying the quality-of-service (QoS) requirements imposed on the application system. The first co-author established the notion of *risk-incursion function* (RIF) as a framework for specification of such damaging impacts [Kim01]. Basically, the damaging impact potentials incurred by timing violations are called the *risks*. In this paper, we discuss two specific low-level scheduling algorithms devised to reflect RIF specifications. These algorithms function essentially as deadline-driven scheduling algorithms when sufficient computing resources are available for handling the given application. In the situations of computing resource shortage, these algorithms behave toward minimizing the risks to the application. Therefore, these algorithms are advances over deadline-driven scheduling algorithms.

The capabilities of the two algorithms have recently been validated through experiments. The experiment setup and the measurement results are also reported in this paper.

We consider the application software which is constructed in the form of a TMO network. The effectiveness of the TMO programming scheme in easy-to-understand and easy-to-analyze RT distributed programs has been demonstrated in quite a few contexts [Kim97, additional references in http://dream.eng.uci.edu/tmo/tmo.htm]. Execution of TMOs can be facilitated by building an execution engine as middleware running on well-established commercial software / hardware platforms. A middleware model named the *TMO support middleware* (TMOSM) architecture has been established and several prototype implementations on different hardware+OS platforms have been developed [Kim99, Kim02].

Three basic practical types of RIFs are then discussed in Section 2 and a design example is also given to illustrate the application of the RIF scheme. Two RIF-based scheduling algorithms are discussed in Section 3 and the results of the experiment conducted to compare the performance of RIF-based scheduling algorithms against that of deadline-driven scheduling algorithms are also provided.

2. THREE BASIC TYPES OF RIFS AND AN EXAMPLE APPLICATION

An RIF is associated with each output function of the system and indicates the amount of risk incurred when the value carried in and the timing of an execution of the output function deviates from the specified range. Using the RIFs as guides, risk incursion potential functions (RIPFs) associated with outputs from various program units, rather than application system outputs going to application environments, are derived, possibly with the aid of tools. Note that assigning an RIPF to an output action is almost the same as assigning an RIPF to the completion event of the computation-segment that leads to the output.

For short-term resource allocation, e.g., allocation of CPU timeslices, method-segments may be treated as basic resource users.   However, assignment of effective RIPFs for such fine-grain computation units may often be very difficult and costly.   Therefore, an approach considered to be cost-effective in many cases is to associate RIPFs with TMO method completions and each output actions but not with the completions of any smaller computation units.

Here we consider three basic RIF types depicted in Figure 1, which we believe are among the most practical and useful types of RIFs.   In the diagrams, the y axis shows the risk incurred, and the x axis shows the output action time.

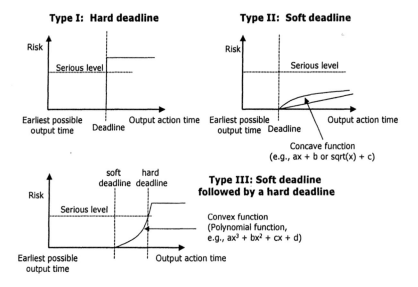

Figure 1. Three basic types of RIF

Type I: For output with a hard deadline.   The risk immediately jumps from zero and exceeds the serious level after the deadline is violated.

Type II: For output with a soft deadline.   The risk starts increasing from zero in a concave fashion after the deadline is violated.   Also, in a certain situation the risk incurred by an inaccurate output may be "erased" after some time interval called the *validity duration* of the risk, e.g., due to a system recovery or the compensating nature of subsequent correctly executed output actions.   In this type of RIF, the risk increases so slowly that it may not exceed the serious level within the lifetime of the application or for the validity duration of the risk.

Type III: For output with a soft deadline followed by a hard deadline.   The risk starts increasing from zero in a convex fashion after the soft deadline is violated. Some time after the soft deadline, the risk exceeds the serious level, and that time instant is the hard deadline for this output.

In generating the characteristic descriptions of the resource requests of various computation-segments, i.e., RIPFs, by reflecting the QoS requirements, an easily understandable and yet rigorous representation of the system being developed and its application environment is of innumerable value to the system engineers. One such representation approach is the TMO structuring scheme. Here we will briefly present an example of the RIF-based system design procedure in the context of TMO-structured top-down design.

CAMIN (Coordinated Anti-Missile Interceptor Network) is a model of a defense command-and-control network which has been used in the authors' laboratory as an example of an advanced RT distributed computing application. For more detailed description of the functionality of CAMIN, readers are referred to [Kim97]. The application environment in CAMIN is a sky, land, and sea segment (together called *Theater*) – in which moving items are taken seriously. The moving items include at least one valuable target to be defended (that is assumed to be the command ship in the sea here) and flying items, both hostile and non-threatening. The high-level requirements are:

Each flying object should be intercepted if it is considered dangerous;

The valuable target (the command ship) can move around to avoid the dangers posed by flying items.

In the first step, the system engineer describes the application as two TMO's, the Theater TMO and the Alien TMO. Alien has one system output, Alien.SysOut1, which sends missiles and non-threatening flying objects (NTFOs) to Theater. Theater also has one system output going to Alien, Theater.SysOut1, which sends information about the current status of the missiles and commercial airplanes leaving from Theater to the outside. In a sense, Alien determines the workload for Theater.

In the next step, the Theater TMO can be further delineated and decomposed into three TMO's, Army's Command Post TMO (CP), Command Ship TMO (CS), and Theater-Remainder TMO (TR), as shown in Figure 2. The system outputs are:

CP.SysOut1: Send an intercept order to TR.
CP.SysOut2: Send a radar spot-check plan to TR.
CP.SysOut3: Hand-over of data on dangerous items to CS.
CS.SysOut1: Send an intercept order to TR.
CS.SysOut2: Send a radar spot-check plan to TR.
TR.SysOut2: Send radar data (both from a scan and a spot-check) to CP.
TR.SysOut3: Send radar data (both from a scan and a spot-check) to CS.

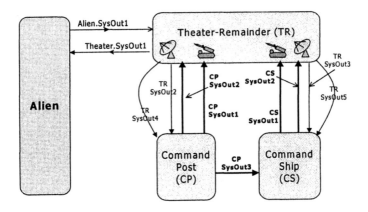

Figure 2. The decomposition of the Theater TMO

Assume that when Alien throws enemy missiles into Theater, it always puts them in the territory covered by the Army's CP and lets them move toward CS.   After receiving the radar data from TR, CP must send CP.SysOut2 in time to require more detailed radar data, the spot-check data, to track the enemy missiles. After some tracking, CP must send CP.SysOut1 in time, which is the interception order, because otherwise the interception will be a failure. Since the radar in the command ship (CS TMO) is a short-range radar, CP also needs to send some warning data about dangerous surviving enemy missiles to the CS in advance. Otherwise, CS might not have enough time to intercept the missiles once CP misses them. Therefore, CP uses CP.SysOut3 to send the warnings with historical data on dangerous items to CS. Given these functionalities, a hard deadline may be imposed on CP.SysOut1, and a soft deadline on CP.SysOut2, while CP.SysOut3 may have a soft deadline followed by a hard deadline. Also CP.SysOut1 has higher risk value than CP.SysOut2 and CP.SysOut3 do.

The deadlines for these system outputs are decided based on the consideration of physical constraints. For example, the physical constraints include the frequency and accuracy of the radar data sent to CP, the flying speeds of the interceptors and the missiles, etc.

Suppose the system failure threshold is set to be 1000. Derived from this, the risk value of CP.SysOut1 after its hard deadline is missed is set to 400, the maximum risk value of CP.SysOut2 is set to 50, and the risk value of CP.SysOut3 after its hard deadline is missed is set to 200. These risk incursion values are assigned according to the system engineers' understanding of the relative importance of each system output. Different system engineers might assign slightly different numbers.

After the RIFs are decided, the next step is to further delineate and decompose the CP to multiple TMO's and derive an RIPF for each new TMO. The CP TMO can be decomposed into three TMOs: Radar Data

Queue (RDQ), Flying Object Tracking (FOT), and Interception Plan Data Store (IPDS).

The derivation of RIPFs from an RIF is based on the worst-case execution time analysis and the way the output of each TMO is used by other TMOs or actuators. Determining RIPFs for TMOs is practically to determine RIPFs for methods of TMOs including both method completion actions and specific output actions of each method. TMO consists two types of methods, time-triggered or spontaneous method (SpMs), and service methods (SvMs). Please refer to [Kim97] for the detailed description of TMO structure scheme. After reaching this step, the procedure for deriving RIPFs is completed. The derived RIPF set can be used by resource allocators, such as the processor scheduler, the communication channel scheduler, and the I/O devices scheduler.

3. THE RIPF-DRIVEN SCHEDULERS AND EXPERIMENTAL RESULT

Since the derived RIPF set also incorporates deadline information for each SpM and SvM, the RIPF-driven resource schedulers can schedule various resources at least as efficiently as the deadline-driven resource schedulers do. In this section, we discuss two RIPF-driven algorithms:

Algorithm 1: RIPF-LLF

Step 1: Execute the least-laxity-first (LLF) Algorithm; If a zero total risk arrangement is found, schedule the task set using that arrangement and return; Otherwise, go to the next step.

Step 2: Compare the risk values of the RIPFs when N timeslices (called the vision-window) have elapsed without completing the associated computation unit. Schedule the task with the maximum value. If there are more than one RIPF which have the maximum value, compare the first derivatives of them and schedule the task with the maximum value of the first derivative. If there are more than one RIPF have the maximum value of the first derivative, choose one randomly.

Algorithm 2: RIPF/Laxity

Step 1: Execute the LLF Algorithm; If a zero total risk arrangement is found, schedule the task set using that arrangement and return; Otherwise, go to next step.

Step 2: Calculate the risk value of the RIPFs when N timeslices (called the vision-window) have elapsed, and divide it by its laxity. Schedule the task with the maximum value. If there are more than one RIPF which have the maximum value, compare the first derivatives of them and schedule the task with the maximum value of the first derivative. If there are more than one RIPF which have the maximum value of the first derivative, choose one randomly.

	Execution Period	Completion Deadline	Average Execution Time	Worst-case Execution Time	Deadline Violation under RIPF scheduler (within 60sec)	Deadline Violation Under EDF scheduler (within 60sec)
Radar->SpM1	100ms	60ms	9.3ms	10ms	141	0
Radar->SpM2	100ms	60ms	5.8ms	6ms	86	4
IPDS->SpM1	200ms	70ms	22.1ms	25ms	0	133
RDQ->SpM1	100ms	40ms	15.0ms	18ms	0	0
FOT->SpM1	500ms	80ms	25.3ms	27ms	5	50

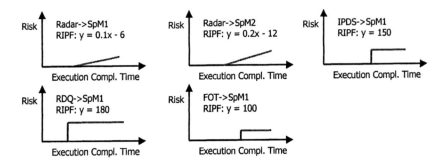

Figure 3. The experimental Data of the RIPF and EDF schedulers

Apparently, the complexities of both Algorithm 1 and Algorithm 2 are O(nlgn). Running Algorithm 1 should yield fairly good result in most application scenarios, while Algorithm 2 can yield a better result at the cost of slightly longer execution time. The selection of the size of the vision-window may affect the results of these two algorithms also.

Both Algorithm 1 and the EDF algorithm [Liu73] have been implemented in TMOSM, and the example application described in the previous section, CAMIN, has been run under the two scheduling algorithms in order to compare the performance.

Under normal circumstances, all TMOs in CAMIN can complete their tasks within the completion deadlines under both EDF and RIPF schedulers. To simulate the situation where the processor is under heavy demands, the deadlines of SpMs in Radar, FOT, IPDS, and RDQ TMOs were shortened by half. Figure 3 shows the measured data, the average and worst method completion times of SpMs, completion deadlines, and the RIPFs.

Figure 3 shows many deadline violations, and the nature of deadline violations under EDF is quite different from that under RIPF. Possible SpM execution orders under EDF and RIPF schedulers are shown in Figures 4 and 5, respectively.

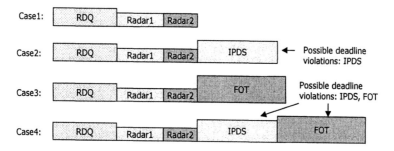

Figure 4. The possible SpM execution orders under the EDF

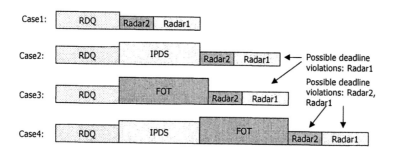

Figure 5. The possible SpM execution orders under the RIPF scheduler

Figure 4 shows that the EDF scheduler dispatches the RDQ SpM first because its deadline, 40ms, is the shortest. Then it dispatches Radar SpM1 (shown as Radar1 in the figure) and Radar SpM2 (shown as Radar2 in the figure), whose deadlines are 60ms each. The invocation intervals of these SpMs are 100ms, while IPDS SpM's invocation interval is 200ms and FOT SpM's invocation interval is 500ms, and thus in Case 1 there are no IPDS and FOT executions which need to be scheduled. When IPDS SpM and FOT SpM appear in Case 2 and Case 3, they are scheduled after the three SpMs mentioned above because their deadlines are 70ms and 80ms, respectively. When both of them appear in Case 4, FOT SpM is scheduled after IPDS SpM. According to the execution times and deadlines listed in Figure 3, there is a fairly good chance that IPDS and FOT miss their deadlines in Case 4.

Similarly, in Figure 5 the RIPF scheduler dispatches RDQ SpM first because the risk value to be incurred when the latter misses the deadline is 180. Then it dispatches IPDS SpM, FOT SpM, Radar SpM1 (shown as Radar1 in the figure), and Radar SpM2 (shown as Radar2 in the figure) according to their RIPFs. Considering the execution times and deadlines listed in Figure 3, there is a fairly good chance that Radar SpM1 and Radar SpM2 miss their deadlines in Case 4.

From these two figures, we can see that under tight resource condition, the EDF scheduler sacrifices the SpMs in IPDS and FOT first since their deadlines are the longest. In contrast, the RIPF scheduler sacrifices the SpMs in Radar first since their risk incursion values are the lowest. Considering the nature of CAMIN, occasional deadline violations of Radar SpMs may not cause serious result, but the deadline violations of FOT, IPDS or RDQ SpMs may cause the failure of missile interception, thus should be avoided if possible. Therefore, the CAMIN application shows better missile interception rates under the RIPF scheduler when the deadlines are set as in Figure 3, i.e., the processor availability is tight.

Our analysis and experiments have thus shown that: 1) If the deadlines of all tasks can be met, the EDF and RIPF schedulers perform equally well; 2) In the case where not all deadlines can be met under EDF, RIPF can do a better job by considering the potential risk values together with the deadline information in the RIPFs, which means less important tasks are sacrificed first.

4.   CONCLUSION

Deadline-driven scheduling, although a better alternative to the fix-priority scheduling, does not consider many important QoS requirements from the system designer, such as the impacts of deadline violations. A scheme for specification of not just timing and other QoS requirements associated with system output actions, but also the potential damages that failing to meet the requirements bring in, has been evolving in the authors' laboratory under the name of the risk incursion function (RIF) scheme. Two RIF-driven algorithms were proposed in this paper, and some experimental results on the comparison between RIPF-driven and deadline-driven scheduling algorithms were provided. The research on QoS-driven resource allocation in complex distributed RT systems is still in its early stage. In order to establish it as a widely practicable technology, further research on systematic derivation of RIPFs from the original RIF-based QoS requirements specification is desirable.

Acknowledgements: The research reported here was supported in part by NSF under Grant Numbers 99-75053 (NGS) and 00-86147 (ITR), and in part by US DARPA (NEST) under Contract F33615-01-C-1902 monitored by AFRL. No part of this paper represents the views and opinions of any of the sponsors mentioned above.

REFERENCES

[Fin67] Mark S. Fineberg and Omri Serlin, "Multiprogramming for hybrid computation", *Proc. AFIPS Conf.*, vol. 31, Anaheim, Nov. 1967, pp. 1–13.

[Kim97] Kim, K.H., "Object Structures for Real-Time Systems and Simulators", *IEEE Computer*, Vol. 30, No.8, August 1997, pp. 62-70.

[Kim99] Kim, K.H. Ishida, Masaki, Liu, Juqiang, "An Efficient Middleware Architecture Supporting Time-Triggered Message-Triggered Objects and an NT-based Implementation", *Proc. 2nd IEEE CS Int'l Symp. on Object-Oriented Real-time Distributed Computing (ISORC '99),* St. Malo, France, May, 1999, pp.54-63.

[Kim00] Kim, K.H., "APIs for Real-Time Distributed Object Programming", IEEE *Computer*, June 2000, pp.72-80.

[Kim01] Kim, K.H, Liu, Juqiang, "QoS-driven Resource Management in Real-Time Object Based Distributed Computing Systems", *proc. FTDCS'01 (The 8th IEEE Workshop on Future Trends of Distributed Computing Systems)*, Bologna, Italy, October 2001, pp. 222-230.

[Kim02] Kim, H.J., Park, S.H., Kim, J.G., and Kim , M.H., "TMO-Linux: A Linux-based Real-time Operating System Supporting Execution of TMOs", to appear in Proc. *ISORC 2002 (5th IEEE CS Int'l Symp. on OO Real-time distributed Computing)*, Washington DC, Apr. 2002.

[Kop97] Kopetz, H., 'Real-Time Systems: Design Principles for Distributed Embedded Applications', *Kluwer Pub.*, ISBN: 0-7923-9894-7, Boston, 1997.

[Liu73] C.L. Liu and J.W. Layland. "Scheduling algorithms for multiprogramming in a hard real-time environment", *J. ACM*, 20(1):46-61, Jan. 1973, pp.46-61.

[Pal00] Pal, P.P., et al, "Using QDL to Specify QoS Aware Distributed (QuO) Application Configuration", *Proc. ISORC 2000 (3rd IEEE Int'l Symp. on Object-Oriented Real-time Distributed Computing),* March 2000, Newport Beach, CA, pp. 310-319.

[Ser72] Serlin, O., "Scheduling of time critical process", proc. AFIPS conf., Vol. 40, Atlantic City, NJ, May 1972, pp.925-932.

IEEE-1394 A standard to interconnect distributed systems

Romualdo Santamaria
Mindready Solutions Inc.
2800 avenue Marie-Curie, Saint-Laurent QC, Canada H4S 2C2
Email: romualdo.santamaria@mindready.com

Abstract: With its high-speed deterministic communication, its low cost and its guaranteed bandwidth, the IEEE-1394 high-performance serial bus (also known as FireWire®) is ideal for interconnecting the components of modular distributed systems such as computers and I/Os. Mindready's paper will cover the following points: design of a typical industrial control system, heterogeneous computer systems and their limitations, isochronous data transmission, node synchronization, IEEE-1394 parameters and IEEE-1394 within the transport of digital data.

1. INTRODUCTION

Every so often, a new technology comes along that greatly simplifies the way to implement distributed systems. The IEEE-1394 high-performance serial bus (also known as FireWire®) is one of such technologies. Originally conceived by Apple Computer, IEEE-1394 has become the de facto serial bus for:

- Consumer electronics market

- PC peripherals

- Home automation systems

- Multimedia and entertainment systems

However, this new serial bus technology is also intended to revolutionize the way distributed system developers and system integrators design and build. With its high-speed deterministic communication, its low cost and its guaranteed bandwidth, IEEE-1394 is ideal for interconnecting the components of modular distributed systems such as computers and I/Os.

Today's modular systems - with their highly complex interconnection requirements - have challenged distributed systems developers with obstacles such as:

- Distributed shared memories and shared peripherals
- Synchronization between devices
- Controlled latency and jitter
- Topology restrictions
- ID switches and terminators
- Expensive cables and boards
- Connectors and bridges
- Bandwidth limitations
- Hot plugging and plug and play capabilities

2.   THE DESIGN OF A TYPICAL INDUSTRIAL CONTROL SYSTEM

To appreciate the impact of using IEEE-1394 in distributed computing, let's examine the design of a typical distributed industrial control system.

A typical industrial control system usually requires:
- A network of computers capable of performing real-time calculations, based on analog or digital I/O input provided by one or more lower-level industrial computers
- A control console that allows an operator to monitor and control the entire distributed system

Let's use a car manufacturer as an example. This manufacturer needs to implement multiple robotic arms – all working in tandem on an assembly line.

A network of industrial computers – the arm's nerve center, controls each arm. These systems typically include several processor boards and I/O boards and work as a distributed system. It repeatedly monitors the signals from the arm that encodes parameters such as:

- The current position of the arm
- The current speed of the arm
- Pressures being sensed by the arm
- Video images of the arm, and whatever it is handling

Based on the values of these parameters, it calculates corrections in real-time and periodically sends new values back to the arm, thus ensuring accurate execution of the command stream.

Needless to say, all the arms in this multiple-arm system must be perfectly synchronized, in real-time, to do their job. Data transfers and calculations must be performed within a specific time limit in order to guarantee the required system behavior. This can only be accomplished with a synchronized communication path — between all of the modules —that provides zero tolerance for error, as well as minimizes or controls latency and jitter. The slightest unpredicted "hiccup" in the communication system will adversely impact the behavior, with possibly catastrophic results.

3. HETEROGENEOUS COMPUTER SYSTEMS POSE SPECIAL PROBLEMS

Heterogeneous computer systems with different operating systems pose another challenge. An Ethernet connection can be used to provide a communication path between an industrial distributed computer system and the operator console – usually a Sun workstation (running on Solaris) or a PC (running on Windows NT)., This approach however, has several disadvantages. Ethernet is not deterministic and extensive development time might be required to ensure that the needs of the real-time system are satisfied.

Modular real-time systems often collect data from various types of computer hardware platforms. For example, the data entering in a system might be originating from any of the following subsystems:

- An IP (Industry pack) mezzanine board
- A PMC mezzanine board
- A VMEbus board
- A CompactPCI board
- A Personal Computer

- A SPARC workstation

If these subsystems are housed in multiple chassis, then bus-to-bus bridges are needed to interconnect them. While these bridges perform satisfactorily, they are expensive (typically $5,000 per bridge) and this cost is further increased by the need to create protocol software to support communication between the subsystems.

In addition to the hardware and software costs of interconnecting heterogeneous platforms, all activities undertaken jointly by two or more platforms must be synchronized. This makes the development of distributed real-time applications a difficult task, even for the most experienced developers.

4.   WHAT IEEE-1394 PROVIDES

IEEE-1394 provides a solution to these problems with:

- A scalable architecture
- A flexible peer-to-peer architecture
- A low cost implementation
- A high-speed deterministic mean of communication

The fact that IEEE-1394 is a bus that allows direct read/write access to memory in remote nodes is a major advantage allowing the systems to be a big pool of distributed memory and peripherals. However, it is the synchronized channel scheme of communication, added to the bus functionality that makes IEEE-1394 the perfect communication media for distributed real-time applications.

IEEE-1394 is a real bus with functionality similar to the PCI bus, which gives 1394 an advantage in comparison with communication links like Ethernet. 1394 does not have collisions and every asynchronous action is acknowledged signalling to the sender that the receiver has successfully accepted a message. Since there are typically several nodes on a IEEE-1394 bus, some arbitration method must be provided to determine which node has priority when multiple nodes are waiting to use the bus. This arbitration is provided by the Physical Layer, which is typically implemented in hardware.

The arbitration algorithm that is provided by the physical layer is called Fair Arbitration. This form of arbitration serves a very important function in real-time systems by ensuring that no single node is allowed to monopolize the bus.

The arbitration is controlled by idle periods on the wire. Depending on the length of idle periods, the nodes can determine the state of the bus.

The fairness protocol is based on the concept of fairness interval. A fairness interval consists of one or more periods of bus activity, separated by short idle periods called subaction gaps, and is followed by a longer idle period known as an arbitration reset gap. At the end of each subaction gap, bus arbitration is used to determine the next node to transmit.

When using fair arbitration, an active node can initiate sending a packet once in each fairness interval. Once a node sends in a fairness interval, an internal arbitration flag is cleared disabling the node from arbitrating again during the same interval. Once all the nodes who need the bus have successfully won arbitration and been disabled, an arbitration reset gap occurs. This ends the fairness interval. At that point, the internal arbitration flag of all the nodes is reset, a new fairness interval begins, and all nodes are enabled to arbitrate again.

5.   ISOCHRONOUS DATA TRANSMISSION

IEEE-1394 also provides a *synchronous* form of communication, called *isochronous* data transmission. Isochronous data transmissions are given priority over *asynchronous* data transmissions.

Isochronous data transmissions are initiated once every 125 µsecs by the cycle master, which transmits a special *cycle start packet* to trigger all the waiting isochronous data transmissions from other nodes. After transmitting this special packet, all nodes waiting to send isochronous packets start arbitrating for transmission until all nodes finish sending their pending isochronous packets.

All isochronous packets have to be transmitted within the 100 µsec in the 125 µsec period.

If the transmission of isochronous packets takes less than 100 µsec, then the cycle master accepts asynchronous packets for the remainder of the cycle.

Isochronous transmission was originally included in the IEEE-1394 standard to support multimedia applications - such as a live video feed - where uninterrupted transport of time-critical data and just-in-time delivery reduce the need for costly buffering. Fortunately, isochronous transmission is also ideal for interconnecting real-time computer systems because it provides automatic synchronization between the local clocks in the various nodes and guarantees a predetermined communication bandwidth without extra programming.

6.   NODE SYNCHRONIZATION

The cycle master (driven by its own internal 8 kHz clock) attempts to start a new cycle every 125 μsecs. However, the beginning of any particular cycle might be delayed slightly if an asynchronous packet is still being sent when the time for the new cycle arrives. Thus, there might be some "jitter". However, the *average* cycle time will still be 125 μsecs. All nodes supporting isochronous communications have a timer running at 24.576 MHz. Each time a cycle starts, the cycle master node writes the value of its internal timer into the timer of all other nodes. This provides synchronization between all nodes. The cycle start message provides the timing information if a particular cycle start is delayed, this way all nodes know by how long, and can therefore manage and control resulting jitter.

7.   IEEE-1394 PARAMETERS

There are parameter values that must be specified locally in each node before IEEE-1394 packets can be exchanged between nodes. These parameters include the IEEE-1394 node number, IEEE-1394 bus number, and IEEE-1394 response flag.

The IEEE-1394 node number
A node number is a unique number (between 0 and 63) that is associated with each node on the bus. This number is dynamically re-configurable, allowing the software in each node to change its node number at any time. Node number 63 is used to broadcast within a single 1394 bus.

The IEEE-1394 bus number
The IEEE-1394 bus number allows nodes on different IEEE-1394 buses to communicate with each other. Each IEEE-1394 bus is assigned a unique

number between 0 and 1023. Bus number 1023 is the local bus for each 1394 bus.

The IEEE-1394 response flag

The IEEE-1394 response flag tells each node in the system whether it must send a 'response packet' for every read request packet, or write request packet that it receives.

8.   IEEE-1394 REVOLUTIONIZES THE TRANSPORT OF DIGITAL DATA

In a distributed industrial control application (such as the robot controller mentioned earlier) the developer can use IEEE-1394's isochronous transmission to:

- Synchronize the timers of all nodes on the bus with the cycle start timer of the master node
- Guarantee data delivery
- Guarantee on-time delivery
- Guarantee data transmission at a pre-determined minimum rate

This is all accomplished without any extra programming. This way, isochronous transmission reduces latency and controls jitter, and the data exchange intervals are controlled natively on the bus, with no extra programming.

The developer can interconnect up to 63 devices on each IEEE-1394 bus in a peer-to-peer fashion, communicating digitally at up to 400 Mbps. This peer-to-peer communication allows each node's internal address to be mapped in the local address map of each other node on the same IEEE-1394 bus.

The result is a much simpler integration of multiple heterogeneous computer platforms, which is often necessary to provide enough processing power for today's demanding real-time applications.

In addition, no expensive bridges are required. All nodes can exchange data over the IEEE-1394 bus by simple read and write operations. For example, suppose an IP (Industry Pack) mezzanine board is plugged into a mezzanine site on the IEEE-1394-to-VMEbus adapter board. Its I/O registers would then be mapped to the local address space of each other node on the IEEE-1394 bus (such as a SUN workstation or another VMEbus rack) without any special software drivers or protocols, or any special interface hardware.

This eliminates the need for any dedicated bridges, and simplifies the integration of different devices in real-time systems. The design time, the project costs are significantly reduced, and the versatility of the resulting distributed real-time system is increased. Systems can also be upgraded and/or expanded very easily, reducing concern about what additional equipment might be needed at some future time.

The IEEE-1394 serial bus allows for all communications to be performed over thin, easy-to-handle 6 conductor cables. Cable length is limited to 4.5 meters by the arbitration mechanism and the signal propagation delay. However, high quality cabling and/or repeaters can be used to extend that distance.

IEEE-1394's flexible cabling topology allows for much easier installation than standards requiring rigid cabling topologies, such as point-to-point and hubbed architectures. Tree and daisy chain topologies are supported. As a practical matter, the topologies are limited only by the number of ports on the bus-switching chip, which can be up to 6 ports.

Finally, IEEE-1394 interfaces are designed to allow hot plug and play. For example, suppose one of the robotic arms in the distributed system is in need of service – possibly even removal and replacement. With IEEE-1394, the manufacturing process can continue uninterrupted while this is being done. There would be no need to shut down the entire production line just to add or remove that one node.

9.   SUMMARY

Without a doubt, IEEE-1394 is revolutionizing the way data is being transported in distributed real-time systems, and as such, is changing the way developers and systems integrators design, build and interconnect these systems.

The IEEE-1394 specification currently supports speed of up to of 400 Mbps, and is expected to reach speed of up to 3.2 Gbps with the recent advent of 1394b, an enhanced version of 1394. This provides an easy evolutionary path—without any changes in the application code—for users who are currently developing real-time applications with ever-increasing bandwidth requirements. Because IEEE-1394 is rooted in mass-market solutions, chips and cables are widely available at a low cost. These same low-cost components can be used in IEEE-1394-based real-time systems.

Currently deployed particle acceleration and flight simulation systems have demonstrated that IEEE-1394 provides:

- An easily scalable architecture

- A flexible peer-to-peer topology

- A low cost implementation

- High-speed, deterministic communication

Based on this demonstrated performance and relatively low cost, IEEE-1394 is poised to become the de facto standard for interconnecting heterogeneous real-time computer systems.

Deterministic and High-Performance Communication System for the Distributed Control of Mechatronic Systems Using the IEEE1394a

Mauro Zanella, Thomas Lehmann, Thorsten Hestermeyer, Andreas Pottharst
University of Paderborn, Germany
zane@mlap.de, torkin@upb.de, herster@mlap.de, pottharst@lea.upb.de

Abstract: The complexity of mechatronic elements has grown along with the customer requirements in automotive and public transportation. The mechatronic systems can not be designed as a stand-alone unit, but as a part of an interacting network. To attend safety and synchronisation between processing elements we present in this paper the use of IEEE1394a for a deterministic communication system. As a case study we use the Novel Railway System Paderborn, which will be implemented using the hardware platform RABBIT.

Key words: time-triggered communication, mechatronics, distributed real-time control, IEEE 1394a

1. INTRODUCTION

As almost no other technology, mechatronics is an essential element of many innovations in automotive engineering. New functions and improvements of already existing functions, as well as the compliance with traffic regulations and customer requirements, have only become possible by the increasing use of mechatronic systems, especially in the fields of driving, safety, reliability, and functionality. The car manufacturer has to meet demands regarding fuel consumption, emission, ride comfort, power, drive dynamics, and ergonomics. Along with the functionalities that increase in number and have to cooperate, the complexity of the entire system will increase.

Synergy effects resulting from distributed application functionalities via several micro-controllers and the use of sensor information through the network bring about more complex system architectures with many different sub-networks operating with different velocities and different protocol implementations. Networking may even reach a state of such complexity that a careful systematic design becomes necessary.

To manage the increasing complexity of these systems a deterministic behaviour of the communication network must be provided for, in particular when dealing with a distributed functionality or redundant realization of certain nodes. This can be achieved by applying the design philosophy of time-triggered operation [2] to the communication network (time-triggered protocol activities [3]) and on the application level (time-triggered task activation [4]). The optimum is reached when a globally synchronized time base (global time) is available to all nodes of the network at a measure of precision fulfilling the real-time requirements of the application.

Actually the TTTech company, Bosch and the joint venture of BMW and DaimlerChrysler offer solutions for networks regarding time-triggered operation, namely TTP/A [3], TTCan [1], and FlexRay [5].

Our contribution to this enterprise is the application of IEEE1394a for a deterministic, high- performance and fault-tolerant communication system in the field of distributed control systems. The IEEE1394a bus (also known as FireWire or iLink) is a high-speed serial bus for communication of up to 400 Mbit/s.

RABBIT, a modular rapid-prototyping platform for distributed mechatronic systems [6], will be used for implementation and evaluation purposes. The main features of RABBIT are its flexibility and extensibility, brought about by an open system interface and high modularity. An overview of the main features of the IEEE1394a bus, as well as the RABBIT system, will be given in Chapter 2.

This paper will also present the structuring and the development of the drive module of the Neue Bahntechnik Paderborn (Novel Railway System Paderborn) [7] as a case study. More details of the NBP and its mechatronic function-oriented structure are to be found in Chapter 3.

2.   DETERMINISTIC COMMUNICATION SYSTEM USING RABBIT AND IEEE1394A

2.1   RABBIT – a Modular Rapid-Prototyping Platform for Distributed Mechatronic

We employ the RABBIT platform [6] to demonstrate the possibility of its being implemented in the case-study due to its modularity and flexibility.

RABBIT offers the chance of checking up on novel approaches to the research on rapid-prototyping systems.

The hardware modules comprise three main components: microcontroller, FPGA (Field Programming Gate Array), IEEE 1394a (FireWire). Each module is a board of its own and can operate in stand-alone or combined mode. At the moment, two new modules have been developed on the basis of these main components, the first one for the control of stepper motors, and the second one for the communication between RABBIT (System bus) and dSPACE (PHS-bus).

One node of the RABBIT system consists of a rack which can contain the different modules, as shown in Figure 1, connected via a local system bus.

The CPU module of the node is provided by a PowerPC module. It consists of an MPC555 [8] with its on-chip peripheral devices and an extra bus interface to transmit the memory bus signals to the local system bus:

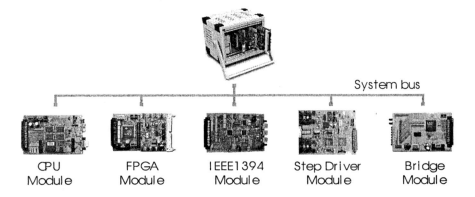

Figure 1: Implemented RABBIT modules

The main component of the DSP module is a Virtex-E FPGA [9]. In addition to the system-bus interface the Vertex-E also has an internal bus interface. Via this bus it is possible to connect I/O devices, e.g., ADCs, DACs, and encoders. These components are mounted on a piggyback board.

The IEEE1394 module provides three ports for communication. It has an MPC555 bus interface to communicate the link-layer chip to the local bus (asynchronous), and an exclusive bus interface to the DSP module for isochronous communications.

2.2   IEEE1394a: a High-Speed Serial Bus

The 1394 high-speed serial bus was conceived in 1986 by Apple Computers, who chose the trademark 'FireWire', and adopted as IEEE 1394 standard in 1995. At about the same time Sony introduced its trademarked iLink as a significant variation of the standard. A large number of IEEE 1394 products are now available including digital camcorders, integrated and stand-alone digital video editing systems, digital VCRs, digital still and video cameras, digital audio players, harddisks, and plenty of other infrastructure products, such as connectors, cables, test equipment, software toolkits, and emulation models.

Some features of the IEEE1394a are the following [10]:

- "Hot-pluggable": devices can be added and removed while the bus is active
- Scalability: the standard defines 100, 200, and 400 Mbps devices; the connection can thus support the different speeds on a single bus
- Flexibility: the standard supports free-form daisy chaining and branching for peer-to-peer implementations
- Support of two types of data transfer: asynchronous and isochronous
- Global timebase (125 us): for synchronizing events and data
- Multi-master capability

For conventional memory-mapped data access, asynchronous transfer is appropriate and adequate. The isochronous data transfer provides guaranteed data transport at a pre-determined rate, a feature that is especially important in control applications with time-critical data transfer.

The high data rates of FireWire, the ability to mix isochronous and asynchronous data on a single line, and the global timebase encouraged us to employ this bus for real-time communication in distributed mechatronic applications.

2.3   Time-Triggered Communication Using the IEEE1394a

Purely time-triggered operation of the communication system means that any activity is determined by the progression of a (globally synchronized) time. Sending, receiving or other activities depend on a predefined time schedule and the current state of the clock [1].

In the case of the IEEE1394a, a global clock rate of 8 kHz is implicitly included in the system, i.e., communication on the bus is basically made up of cycles (time-slot) of 125 us each. Figure 2 displays two communication cycles on the bus. After start of the cycle, including the timestamp, the time slot is divided into two parts: the first one is for isochrounous (channels) and the second for asynchronous communication (packet) [10].

In the case of distributed control applications, the cyclic and deterministic data transfer will be performed in the shape of isochrounous messages, and with administrative data (e.g., tracing, parameter changes) the asynchronous section will be used:

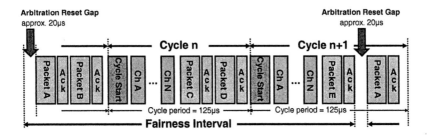

Figure 2: A series of transactions

A static scheduler with regard to the entire system has to be defined in order to determine which process and which processor will send and receive data in a pre-defined time slot, as defined in the time-triggered operation. Due the complexity of the entire system, it is nearly impossible to develop the control algorithms and to distribute them to several Electronic Control Units (ECUs) taking into account, for instance, system stability, partitioning, code generation, and deadlocks.

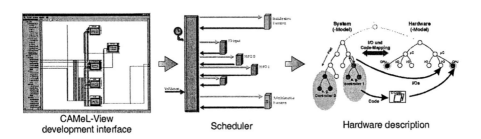

Figure 3: Code generation and mapping in CAMeL-View

Systematic development methodology, as presented in [11], is applied to the scope from modelling to analysis to synthesis and up to C-code generation for the real-time applications. High-level software tools, such as CAMeL-View[12] and Alaska [13], help the engineer during these stages.

In our case we use the software tool CAMeL-View which allows a modular and hierarchical model description of the system. The entire control algorithm is designed in dependence of the physical structure of the system, as described in Chapter 3 (CMS, AMS, MFM). From this structured model the C-code is generated according to the interdependence of variables and control strategies [14]; it runs on the ECUs.

The design of a static scheduler for one processor which takes into account the hard real-time (control algorithms and communications) and soft real-time (administrative tasks) conditions is described in [15].

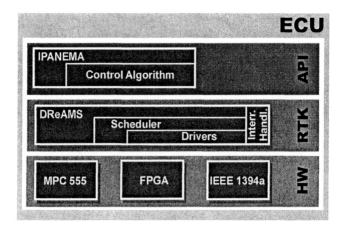

Figure 4: Software implementation of an ECU (RABBIT)

The next step is to map the abstract inputs and outputs of the model to the actual I/Os of the ECUs (microcontrollers). A further hardware description is comprised in the CAMeL-View modelling tool in parallel to the system model. In this description the inputs/outputs of the system model are linked to the respective hardware I/Os via a mapping description [16]. Communication and administration between processes will be implemented by means of the software platform IPANEMA (Integration Platform for Networked Mechatronic Applications) [17]. The objects defined in IPANEMA offer services on the application level. The re-configurable real-time operating system DReAMS (Distributed Extensible Application Management System) [18] can be used for the lower-level services. Complex micro-controllers, in our case the Motorola PowerPC MPC555, provide the engineer with many peripheral devices as a System-on-a-Chip. To configure the interrupt system of such complex microcontrollers a configuration software is in the works. It will include a synthesis of a interrupt request dispatcher [19].

3. **CASE-STUDY:** *NEUE BAHNTECHNIK*
    PADERBORN **(NOVEL RAILWAY SYSTEM**
    PADERBORN)

Two major drawbacks of conventional railway systems as compared to cars are the rigid timetables, which the customer has to submit to, and the necessity to change trains in order to reach one's destination. With its new logistical concept, the Neue Bahntechnik Paderborn (NBP - Novel Railway System Paderborn) presents a system that solves these problems. It features fully automated transport by small shuttles which make up convoys on their way if the occasion arises. These shuttles combine the common wheel/rail technology with the linear motors of the maglev trains. In order to prove the functionality of the shuttles and the basics of the logistical concept, a test track will be built up in Paderborn at a scale of 1:2.5.

Due to the complexity of the system the shuttle prototypes are structured in a modular/ hierarchical way. According to mechatronic design principles each physical aggregate disposes of its own information processing, thus forming a Mechatronic Function Module (MFM) [20] with sensors, actuators and information processing supporting the mechanical part of the module. The three major modules of an NBP shuttle are the guidance module, the linear drive module and the suspension/tilt/steering module. All these modules, linked by an additional mechanical structure, make up the Autonomous Mechatronic System (AMS), a shuttle which has its own sensors and information processing but modifies the system behaviour only by means of the MFMs. The information processing of the AMS makes up the highest hierarchical level in the control structure of the mechanically linked system. In order to control shuttles in a convoy an even higher control level is needed. These shuttles, cross-linked only by this higher-level control, form a Cross-linked Mechatronic System (CMS). A CMS can rely on its own sensors and information processing but cannot be allocated to a mechanical structure.

As regards the linear motors for railway vehicles, they fall into either one of two categories: long-stator or short-stator motors. A short-stator linear motor is designed either as an asynchronous motor with an electrified primary on the vehicle and a reaction plate between the rails (e.g., Linear-Metro Tokio, Kobe). When the primary is mounted between the rails with the secondary on board of the shuttle, we obtain a long-stator motor. In most cases the secondary is electrified. In synchronous operation DC is applied to the secondary. Thus, the vehicle moves at the speed of the migrating wave (e.g., the Transrapid). Supplying AC to the secondary leads to asynchronous operation (NBP). Hence relative motion between vehicles becomes possible on a primary that is not split into sections. Additionally it is possible to transfer energy from the track to the shuttle in order to spare catenary wires.

In practice the primary is divided into sections so that the primary need not be current-carrying along the whole of the track. In order to ensure a smooth and accurate motion of a shuttle it is extremely important that the migrating wave be continued in phase and at the correct amplitude and frequency from one primary section to the next (see Figure 5). Therefore data connections and information processing must be provided to control primary and secondary currents:

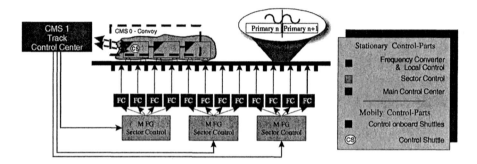

Figure5: Information structure of the NBP system with the focus on the linear motor

The information processing of the CMS Convoy is located on one "Control Shuttle" which is determined dynamically. This control shuttle communicates with the stationary track control center in two ways: for real-time data there is a serial radio transmission. As far as the stator control goes, the track-control center transfers the rotor information and information on the required wave phase and speed to the appropriate sector controls that control four frequency converters each. The frequency converters again have local control units of their own to compute the necessary currents. The track-control center and the sector controls will be implemented using the RABBIT platform. The basis of the frequency converters (also a micro-controlled unit) will be a commercial product with a peer-to-peer synchronized serial bus communication to the sector-control unit as an add-on. This means that 126 ECUs (26 RABBITs and 100 frequency converters) will be interlinked along the test track. Our focus in this work lies on the communication between the track-control center and the sector controls (26 ECUs).

4.   STATE OF AFFAIRS

The aim is a consistent design of all elements, from the system model to the automatically generated source code for all subsystems. With RABBIT it is possible to preserve the hierarchical structure of the control model and its subsystems. The aim is to show that our concept can be successfully applied to the driving module of the NBP.

Presently we are testing the IEEE1394a in the lab on other applications. A compact RABBIT hardware is also in the design stage and going to be implemented in the NBP application. The reason for developing it is the high-frequency electromagnetic noise generated by the servos and the small space available for an installation on the test track. Moreover, the missing code-generation modules for the CAMeL-View tool are being developed.

5.   REFERENCES

[1]   Müller, B.: Zeitgesteuerte Kommunikation mit CAN. Auto&Elektronik, Germany, February 2001.

[2]   Kopetz, H.: The Time-Triggered Approach to Real-Time System Design. Technical University of Vienna, 1997.

[3]   Kopetz, H.; Grünsteidl, G.: TTP – A Protocol for Fault-Tolerant Real-Time Systems. IEEE Computer, January 1994.

[4]   Krüger, A.; Domaratsky, Y.; Holzmann, B.; Schedl, A.; Ebner, Ch.; Belschner, R.; Hedenetz, B.; Fuchs, E.; Zahir, A.; Boutin, S.; Dilger, E.; Führer, T.; Nossal, R.; Pfaffeneder, B.; Poledna, S.; Glück, M.: OSEKtime: A Dependable Real-Time Fault-Tolerant Operating System and Communication Layer as an Enabling Technology for By-Wire Applications. SAE 2000 Congress, Detroit, MI, March 2000.

[5]   FlexRay für verteilte Anwendungen im Fahrzeug. Elektronik Automotive, Germany, May 2001.

[6]   Zanella, M.; Robrecht, M.; Lehmann, T.; Gielow, R.; de Freitas Francisco, A.; Horst, A.: RABBIT: A Modular Rapid Prototyping Platform for Distributed Mechatronic System. SBCCI 2001 - XIV Symposium on Integrated Circuits and Systems Design; Brasília, Brazil, 2001.

[7]   Lückel, J.; Grotstollen, H.; Jäker, K.; Henke, M.; Liu, X.:. Mechatronic Design of a Modular Railway Carriage. IEEE/ASME International Conference on Advanced Intelligence Mechatronics (AIM '99), Atlanta, GA, 1999.

[8]   Motorola, Inc.: MPC555 Evaluation Board Quick Reference, 1999.

[9]   Xilinx – The Programmable Logic. Data Book 2000. San José, CA, 2000.

[10]   IEEE Computer Society: IEEE Standard for a High Performance Serial Bus, New York, NY, March 2000.

[11]   Lückel, J.; Koch, T.; Schmitz, J.: Mechatronik als integrative Basis für innovative
         Produkte. Mechatronik - Mechanisch/Elektrische Antriebstechnik, VDI-Verlag,
         Düsseldorf, 2000.

[12]   Hahn, M.: OMD - Ein Objektmodell für den Mechatronikentwurf. VDI-
         Fortschrittberichte, Reihe 20, Nr. 299, VDI-Verlag, Düsseldorf, 1999.

[13]   Maißer, P.; Jungnickel, U.: Ljapunov-stable Position Control of Constrained
         Multibody Systems. Proc. 3rd International Heinz Nixdorf Symposium: Mechatronics
         and Advanced Motion Control, Paderborn, Germany, 1999.

[14]   Homburg, C.: Mechatronic Processing Objects. ASIM '98, Zurich, Switzerland,
         1998.

[15]   Zanella, M.; Stolpe, R.: Distributed HIL Simulation of Mechatronic Systems
         Applied to an Agricultural Machine. DIPES '98, Eringerfeld, Germany, 1998.

[16]   Zanella, M.; Koch, T.; Meier-Noe, U.; Scharfeld, F.; Warkentin, A.: Structuring and
         Distribution of Controller Software in Dependence of the System Structure. CBA2000,
         Florianópolis, Brazil, 2000.

[17]   Honekamp, U.: IPANEMA - Verteilte Echtzeit-Informationsverarbeitung in
         mechatronischen Systemen, VDI-Fortschrittberichte, Reihe 20, Nr. 267, VDI-Verlag,
         Düsseldorf, Germany, 1998.

[18]   Ditze, C.: Towards Operating System Synthesis. Diss., Universität Paderborn; HNI
         2000 (HNI-Verlagsschriftenreihe, Bd. 76), Paderborn, Germany, 2000.

[19]   Lehmann, T.; Zanella, M.: Modelling and software synthesis of interrupt systems.
         GI/ITG/GMM Workshop: Methoden und Beschreibungssprachen zur Modellierung und
         Verifikation von Schaltungen und Systemen,Tübingen, Germany, 2002.

[20]   Honekamp, U.; Stolpe, R.; Naumann, R.; Lückel, J.: Structuring Approach for
         Complex Mechatronic Systems. 30th International Symposium on Automotive
         Technology & Automation – Mechatronics/Automative Electronics, Florence, Italy,
         1997.

A Consistent Design Methodology for Configurable HW/SW-Interfaces in Embedded Systems
Embedded Systems Design

Stefan Ihmor, Markus Visarius, Wolfram Hardt
{ihmor | visi | hardt}@upb.de
University of Paderborn, Warburger Str.100, D-33098

Abstract: In the embedded systems domain predictability, fault tolerance and high-speed data transmission rates are key challenges for the interface design. Multiple tasks and channels communicate through different protocols with each other. In this paper we present a consistent design approach for configurable real-time interfaces. An interface design methodology therefore should regard the relationship between distributed tasks, channels and supported protocols within a HW/SW Codesign scenario. The model dependent parameters are important information for this process and are represented in a formal UML-based way. As result of the design process an interface-block (IFB) is generated which considers all these parameters. A complex embedded system in the context of a case study implements a collision avoidance algorithm for two interacting robots. It demonstrates the usability of this concept for an implementation of HW/SW-interfaces with respect to the real-time restrictions..

Key words: dynamic reconfigurable interface design and modeling, HW/SW Interfaces

1.   INTRODUCTION

In this paper we present a new modeling approach for configurable real-time interfaces. The interface design is driven by high needs in data transmission techniques and rising computing performance in terms of operations per second in the embedded system domain. Much effort has been spent in improving these aspects but the affected interfaces also have to be discussed to avoid weak points in system-architecture. Especially embedded systems (ES) include several kinds of interfaces, mostly in form of HW/HW-

or HW/SW-interfaces. In many cases modern ES are distributed systems, need to be fault tolerant, have to cope with several kinds of media and hard real-time restrictions of multiple tasks have to be met. As a result the large amount of different interfaces leads to the need for an automated design process for reconfigurable real-time interfaces. This process requires a consistent and integrated design methodology, from the specification to the implementation.

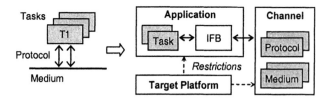

Figure 1. Overview of interface design relevant aspects

The main components of our interface design view can be structured into four parts: task, medium, protocol and target platform dependencies (see Figure 1). This is a refinement of the very general view symbolized on the left side of Figure 1. The traditional parts protocol and medium are merged to a logical block named "Channel". Functional or spatial dependent tasks are joined together with an interface-block (IFB) to the "Application". All relationships between the application, the channel and the target platform with respect to the design process can be modeled in UML. The structure and the dependencies between these items are represented by class diagrams. Timing aspects are modeled in form of sequence charts and activity diagrams. The charts and diagrams have to include sufficient information to specify the IFB that implements the reconfigurable thus dynamic interface. Tasks as well as the IFB may be implemented in hardware or software.

Every communication between two distributed tasks is processed by the dedicated IFB, which handles the medium access on the one hand and controls the task activation on the other hand. This means that the IFB is an active interface. To guarantee hard real-time restrictions the whole system uses a static pre-processed scheduling for medium access. The parameters which are needed to specify the IFB are separated from the UML models of the different tasks, the media and the target platform.

Reconfiguration of the IFB means to change the scheduling strategy implemented in the control unit. The executed IFB behavior from the task activation to the medium access and the internal IFB control may be varied. Our approach also supports the usage of full custom protocols. These are defined by the appropriate task specification and are only restricted by the data transfer rate of the used medium through its physical properties. As these full custom protocols need to be adaptable to the target platform the platform dependent parameters have to be considered in the design process as well. A design methodology from an abstract formal specification model (UML) to a dedicated hardware description language (HDL) or a programming language (SystemC) is considered to realize this approach.

2. APPLICATION RELEVANCE

Several techniques for interface design like SLIF or OCB have been presented in the past. But all these ideas are limited to a partial viewpoint on the design process. Using an IFB-model includes several advantages: Different channels, protocols and tasks are supported and all implementation relevant parameters can be extracted from one abstract modeling language. The requirements are modeled in the well-known and easy-to-understand UML [2, 3, 7] technique in form of class diagrams, sequence charts and statecharts. Therefore it is important to define an exact semantic meaning for the specification language in addition to a non-ambiguous syntax description. An automaton based approach in form of statecharts offers a compact methodology to specify the behavior of the IFB. Afterwards the transformation to the Timing Dependency Graph (TDG) [5] can be done to include timing constraints within the automaton representation. So the time constraints can be modeled high-level, here by UML sequence charts and then transferred to the TDG. The VHDL code which is generated by a transformation of the IFB is the input for the succeeding synthesis process. Special restrictions of the synthesis process have to be considered by the VHDL code generation as well. This can be done by modeling these parameters within the platform dependent diagram. Eventually the restrictions and properties of used synthesis tools can be counted to the platform parameters itself.

Full custom protocols which have been mentioned in the introduction are a further advantage of the IFB model and can be calculated automatically from the specification. Although SDL is one of the common ways for modeling protocols and interfaces [11, 13], this paper considers a UML conform approach to possess a consistent description formalism to specify all necessary information needed for the design process [3, 4, 12].

3. MODELING OF INTERFACE PARAMETERS

There are three possible fields of application for an IFB-model: For medium access of tasks, task adaptation and protocol conversion. The first case covers a consistent bus access of several tasks to multiple channels. If you want to include one task to an existing design the IFB works as an adapter (see Figure 2) and in case there are only channels the IFB acts as a protocol-gateway.

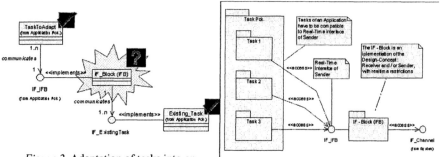

Figure 2. Adaptation of tasks into an existing context

Figure 3. Task-IFB-Level as packet diagram

A set of UML packet diagrams is used to describe the hierarchical content of the interface structure. An excerpt of the packet structure is shown in Figure 3. You can see the "Task-IFB-Level", where several tasks access the "IF_IFB" of the IFB. Also the connection from the IFB to the channel interface "IF_Channel" is symbolized in the lower right of the figure.

As UML was chosen as the modeling language a class diagram is the adequate form to represent structures and dependencies of the required IFB parameters. Figure 4 shows a task's diagram which can either be a HW-block or a SW-program. "Task" is a class that communicates with the abstract class "IF_IFB" which is implemented within the IFB and defines its interface. The parameters in the class model are extensible and have to be adjusted to the appropriate model.

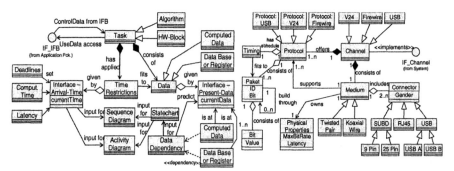

Figure 4. Task modeled as UML class diagram

Figure 5. Channel modeled as UML class diagram

Figure 5 represents a channel which includes the medium as well as the protocol aspect. The class "Channel" that implements the abstract class "IF_Channel" defines the access point for the IFB. Some specific realizations of denoted classes are modeled using inheritance for the class channel, protocol and medium with the connectors.

The third class diagram represents the target platform dependent parameters for SW or HW (see Figure 6). Main class of the diagram is "Target Platform". It is associated to classes "HW-Target" and "SW-Target". "Technical Requirements" and "Synthesis Process" are connected to the HW-development by compositions. Prohibited and recommended kind of source code can be modeled in the "Synthesis Process".

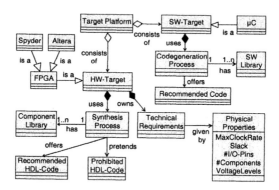

Figure 6. Target platform modeled as UML class diagram

Another important aspect for HW-target code generation is the used component library. A SW-target consists of a "Code Generation Process" that offers "Recommended Code" and uses a specific "SW Library".

The next step is to explain the IFB-model [6, 8] which is parameterized by the information given in the diagrams. The succeeding chapter deals with the representation of an IFB by statecharts and an overview of the functional concept. Statecharts are extended automata and seem to be good candidates for an automated code generation for FPGAs [5, 10]. Sequence charts are used to specify the timing aspect of the included statecharts and the control unit within the IFB.

4.   PROTOTYPING

An FPGA has been chosen for the hardware implementation of the IFB. A micro-controller can be taken for a software implementation as well. The medium, e.g. twisted pair cable is connected to the prototyping platform. Tasks can be implemented separated from the platform or integrated as well. The protocol as an abstract element is implemented within the IFB which consist of a control unit and a generator pipeline – the sequence- and the protocol generator. The job of the control unit is to activate tasks and handle the generator pipe. The sequence generator communicates with the tasks to fetch and collect their data and prepare it for the protocol unit. Further on predefined pieces of data can automatically be inserted here which allows complex features instantiated in sequence generation. That is very useful if a receiving task (actor) expects a dedicated data stream and the sending task, like simple sensor, only generates fragments of the data content available. In the protocol generator these sequences are adapted to the appropriate protocol. Another feature of the protocol generator is the medium access which is guarded by the control unit.

An automata based approach has been selected to implement the IFB-model because the synthesis process is supported very well for this design methodology [10]. Therefore Figure 7 represents the resulting structure of the communicating automata. On top the "Control Unit" controls the sequence generator (SG), the protocol generator (PG) and as here included the task (Task). The control unit requires feedback information in form of status signals. To realize dynamic interfaces different behavior is implemented by sub-automata of the SG, PG and where necessary of the task.

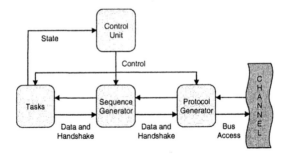

Figure 7. Automata based way to implement an IFB

The sub-automata of SG and PG realize the "generator modes". To execute different behavior the control unit activates dedicated sub-automata through the SG and PG and the task itself, respectively. The communication flow between task and channel is routed through the SG- and PG-FSM using data signals and handshake wires. Figure 8 represents the dependencies as a UML class diagram.

As the main class of the diagram, "Control Unit" implements the abstract interface-class "IFB_Control". On the left "IF_IFB", the interface to the tasks is implemented by the sequence generator and on the right the protocol generator accesses the interface of class "Channel". The "Protocol" defined in the "Channel" class diagram is a template for the possible instances of the generator pipe. To the sequence generator a "data template" is offered in this way, which is used for data preparation for the protocol generator. The requirements for the creation of the supported protocols within the PG are extracted from the "protocol template".

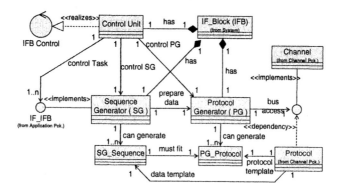

Figure 8. UML class diagram of an IFB

The illustrated kind of implementation is for the access of tasks to different media. In case of adaptation or protocol conversion the IFB fulfills nearly the same job which differs only in its meaning.

The design process, in combination with the IFB is a step towards an automated code generation, because it offers a unified and capable solution for the explained problems. It will be necessary to refine the demonstrated class models to accomplish an entire high-level and automated design process. For some constructs it's obvious how a transformation could look like, e.g. state charts to VHDL automata. But therefore it's necessary to define the syntax and semantic meaning for a unique mapping.

5. EXPERIMENTAL RESULTS

A scenario with two integrated interacting industry robots demonstrates that the concept can be realized for practice relevant application (see Figure 9). One of the robots (R1) is manually controlled by a joystick, whereas robot R2 executes a predefined job. In case of an potential collision R2 has to swerve to avoid any contact between R1 and R2.

To fulfill this task, a TTP/A communication between the controlling FPGAs, using a serial V24 connection, has been established [9] in form of an IFB. On this way the motor data of robot R1 is submitted from FPGA1 to FPGA2. The FPGAs are connected to the robots also using a serial V24 channel which is realized by an IFB as well. The serial V24 (RS232) interface is a common interface in the embedded systems domain and can be used to set up a real-time communication. The design methodology of an IFB (see Figure 10) is illustrated by the V24 interface as an example.

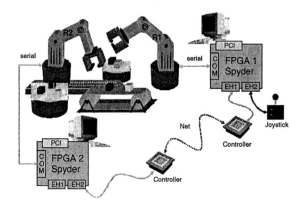

Figure 9. UML Scenario of the interacting robots and the different communication channels

Figure 10 and 11 show the specification of the used V24 serial interface for manual robot control. The aspects "Task, Control Unit, Sequence Generator and Protocol Generator" are represented as statecharts. The task differentiates between an active joystick control and a homing state.

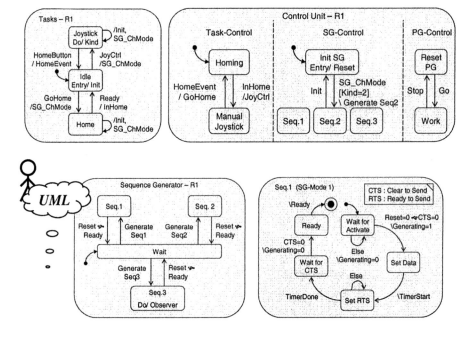

Figure 10. Specification of the Task, CU and SG as statechart

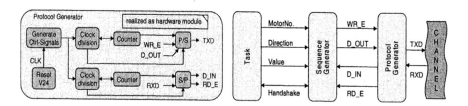

Figure 11. Specification of the PG and the communication flow

The resulting data stream is prepared in the SG and transmitted by the PG that implements a standard V24 UART HW block. A control unit is used to control the other units. The right side in Figure 11 characterizes the control- and data flow within the generator pipe. The submitted data is received by robot R1 which is directly connected to the channel. To get the joystick data to the "Task"-FSM another IFB is realized that serves as physical interface.

6. CONCLUSION AND FUTURE WORK

In this paper we have presented a new concept for reconfigurable real-time interfaces. It has been shown that the concept offers a consistent, level-comprehensive, easy-to-extend and well-defined approach for interface design. In this way interfaces with widespread properties can be consistently modeled and implemented by an IFB.

The demonstrator's serial interface has been used to illustrate that our approach covers all demanded requirements in the application domain, from modeling to the implementation of real-time interfaces. Furthermore our approach is dedicated to automatic code generation based on abstract modeling techniques.

Future work will concentrate on the aspect of code generation towards HW (VHDL or Verilog) and SW (C). This includes aspects of graph transformation from formal abstract modeling languages as well as the computation of full custom protocols. These can be deployed beside standard protocols to fit best to the demands of the comprised tasks.

In addition, validation of timing restrictions has to be considered. Therefore a schedule has to be computed from all the information derived from the task requirements. On this basis automatic evaluation can decide whether the required system performance meets the offered bandwidth or not. In case of success a schedule for the distributed IFB nodes has to be computed. This will be important input for the HW/SW repartitioning. The mentioned extensions will advance our approach to automatic design of HW/SW real-time interfaces.

REFERENCES

[1] A. Burns, *Real Time Systems and Programming Languages*, Addison-Wesley, Harlow [u.a.], third edition, Ada 95, real time Java and real time POSIX., 2001

[2] G. C. Buttazzo, *Hard Real Time Computing Systems: Predictable Scheduling Algorithms and Applications*, Kluwer, Boston [u.a.], third edition, 2000

[3] B. P. Douglas, *Doing Hard Time: Developing Real-Time Systems with UML, Objects, Frameworks and Patterns*, Addison-Wesley, Reading Massachusetts [u.a.], first edition, 2000

[4] B. P. Douglas, *Real-time: Developing Efficient Objects for Embedded Systems*, Addison-Wesley, Reading Massachusetts [u.a.], third edition, 1998

[5] W. Hardt, T. Lehmann, M. Visarius, *Towards a Design Methodology Capturing Interface Synthesis*, University Paderborn, Computer Science Department, 2000

[6] W. Hardt, M.Visarius, S. Ihmor, Rapid Prototyping of Real-Time Interfaces, FPL – Field Programmable Logic conference in Belfast, 2001

[7] G. Hassan, *Designing Concurrent, Distributed, and Real-Time Applications with UML*, Addison-Wesley, Boston [u.a.], 2000

[8] S. Ihmor, *Entwurf von Echtzeitschnittstellen am Beispiel interagierender Roboter*, Master Thesis, University of Paderborn, 2001

[9] H. Kopez, *Principles for Distributed Embedded Applications*, Kluwer Academic Publ., Boston [u.a.], fourth edition, 2001

[10] D. J. Smith, *HDL Chip Design, A Practical Guide For Designing, Synthesizing and Simulating ASICs and FPGAs using VHDL or Verilog*, Doone Publications, Madison, AL, USA, seventh edition, 2000

[11] J. Teich, *Digitale Hardware / Software-Systeme, Synthese und Optimierung*, Springer-Verlag, Berlin Heidelberg, 1997

[12] K. Tindell, *Analysis of Hard Real-Time Communications*, Real-Time Systems, pp. 147-171, 1995

[13] P. Verissimo, *Real-Time Communication*, Addison Wesley – ACM Press, Reading, Mass., 1993

Low Latency Color Segmentation on Embedded Real-Time Systems

Dirk Stichling, Bernd Kleinjohann
C-LAB, Fürstenallee 11, D-33102 Paderborn, Germany

Abstract: This paper presents a color segmentation algorithm for embedded real-time systems with a special focus on latencies. The algorithm is part of a Hardware-Software-System that realizes fast reactions on visual stimuli in highly dynamic environments. There is furthermore the constraint to use low-cost hardware to build the system. Our system is implemented on a RoboCup middle size league prototype robot.

Key words: computer vision, color segmentation, embedded systems, low latency, RoboCup

1.   INTRODUCTION

Today most low-cost robotic systems navigate very slowly, e.g if you watch a RoboCup game you will see a lot of slowly moving robots. There are two reasons for this: At first, mostly commercially available platforms are used. Because of their widespread usage they are built to be safe in a lot of different areas, thus they are comparatively slow. The second reason is the system architecture. Often PCs are used to control the robot. There are some major drawbacks on PCs because they are not designed to be used as an embedded real-time system. They lack special hardware to control all sensors and actors and the operating system often has no real-time capabilities. There often arise high latencies between an event and the reaction of the system.

We are building a robot which is capable of navigating safely through a RoboCup field with a speed of up to 20 km/h. But there is one major constraint: usage of low-cost hardware for building such the robot.

2.   APPROACH

Every robotic system consists of three major parts: The *perception*, the *processing* and the *manipulation*. For each of these parts we use microcontrollers which are specialized on their tasks. The only sensors we use are consumer electronic analog video cameras because of their low price. We developed a color image segmentation algorithm especially for embedded real-time systems. During the last years a lot of color image segmentation algorithms have been proposed [1], but only little attention has been paid to minimizing latency.

Thus we built a system with only vision-based perception and a behavior-based control system which is directly coupled with the perception and the actors. A good overview of behavior-based robotics is given in [4].

This paper presents a color segmentation algorithm as part of the vision-based perception of our system. The focus is on minimizing the latency of the vision part. The algorithm meets the following requirements which suffice for the RoboCup scenario:

> ➤ It has to be able to analyze 25 frames per second
> ➤ There are no predefined colors for the segmentation process.
> ➤ The shape of the objects is not relevant. The algorithm should only yield the position and size of the objects.
> ➤ It has to cope with the YUV color-space because most image hardware provide the data using this color space. Detailed information about this color space is given on [5].

3.   RELATED WORK

Somehow similar to our work is the Polly System built in 1993 at the MIT [6]. One design goal was to use off-the-shelf low-cost hardware. So the only sensor input was one analog camera. They realized a task-based vision system capable of analyzing a 64x48 grey-scale image at 15 hertz. The control system had different layers and the low-level navigation also used behavior-based programming techniques. Newer robots have been built at the MIT based on the Polly System using the Cheap Vision Hardware [7]. Our system uses 352x288 pixel color images as input which permits higher flexibility and also analyzes the images with 25 Hz.

At CMU in Pittsburgh a fast color segmentation algorithm and implementation for robots called CMVision has been developed in 2000 [8]. It can discriminate 32 different colors organized in color cubes which has to be defined statically. So the algorithm is very sensible to changing lightning conditions. Compared to CMVision and other fast color segmentation algorithms our color segmentation algorithm does not use any predefined colors.

An algorithm for fast and robust segmentation of natural color scenes has been proposed in [9]. The algorithm called CSC (Color Structure Code) is based on hierarchical region-growing on a special hexagonal topology. The system is applied in two reactive applications from the field of autonomous vehicle guidance.

Another very low-cost active vision system for embedded microcontrollers has been proposed in 1997 [10]. It uses a special frame grabber chip in conjuction with a 8-bit microcontroller.

4.   METHODOLOGY

Most computer vision algorithms are divided into different steps which are evaluated sequentially. This has two major drawbacks:

1. *High latency:* Because the second step of an algorithm does not start before completion of the first step (which implies that the full input image has already been transmitted to the main memory) the latency is at least the sum of one image's transmission time and the run-times of all steps (except the first one because the first step may run in parallel to the image transmission).
2. *High memory consumption:* Because each step is evaluated individually the complete data that each step produces has to be stored in memory.

Thus we propose a methodology that overcomes these drawbacks. The main idea is to perform the image analysis during the image transmission instead of doing it afterwards. To realize this we introduce two techniques:

1. *Linear Processing:* The camera's input image is transmitted to the main memory top-down line-by-line. Therefore each step of the computer vision algorithm has to work line-based only depending on data of lines already processed.
2. *Incremental Concurrency:* Instead of evaluating the steps of the algorithm sequentially for every *input image* the steps are evaluated for every *line* of the input image. That is possible because the Linear-Processing technique takes care of the right data dependencies.

Using these techniques the latency of the implementation may be lowered dramatically. If the processor is fast enough the latency is as low as one image's transmission time plus the run-times of all steps (except the first one) only for the last image line.

Because the individual steps are processed for every image line the data for only one line has to be turned over to the next step. In some cases a step only needs the data of the actual line, thus there is no need to store the data of other lines which minimizes the overall memory consumption.

Section 5 depicts a color segmentation algorithm which was designed using these techniques *Linear Processing* and *Incremental Concurrency*.

5.   COLOR SEGMENTATION ALGORITHM

Using the techniques described in section 4 we designed a color segmentation algorithm for embedded systems. The algorithm is divided into two individual steps:

1. *Line-based Region-Growing:* In every scan line of the image regions with similar color are grown from left to right.
2. *Region-Merging:* The regions created in the first step are merged if they are similar in color and spatial near to each other.

Region-growing and region-merging techniques are not new to computer based image segmentation [11,12]. What's new here is the usage of these techniques in combination with the techniques proposed in section 4.

5.1   Data Structures

On embedded devices you often don't have much computation power. Thus you need to use data structures which are easy to compute. We use moments up to second order as region descriptors because the operations for adding pixels to a region or merging two regions are computationally fast and they are sufficient to describe position and size of the regions. Moments are often used in computer vision algorithms to describe image objects [2,3]. The definition of the moment *M(p,q)* of a region is as follows:

$$M(p,q) = \sum_{(x,y)\in region} x^p y^q$$

We use the moments *M(0,0)*, *M(1,0)* and *M(1,1)*. They describe the number of pixels and the center of the region and are computational simple.

Additionally we need the central moments $C(p,q)$ of a region with (c_x, c_y) being the center of the region:

$$C(p,q) = \sum_{(x,y) \in region} (x - c_x)^p (y - c_y)^q$$

We use the central moments $C(1,1)$, $C(2,0)$ and $C(0,2)$. For easier reading we use the following notation:

$$a = (M0,0), c_x = \frac{M(1,0)}{M(0,0)}, c_y = \frac{M(0,1)}{M(0,0)}, v_x = C(2,0), v_y = C(0,2), v_{xy} = C(1,1)$$

Using these six moments every region is represented as an ellipse. The representation as an ellipse is only for visualization and is not used for the algorithm because ellipses are computationally difficult to handle.

The following computations show that two regions are merged very fastly. The data of the two regions to be merged are notated with ^ and ~.

$$a = \hat{a} + \tilde{a}, c_x = \frac{\hat{a}\hat{c}_x + \tilde{a}\tilde{c}_x}{a}, c_y = \frac{\hat{a}\hat{c}_y + \tilde{a}\tilde{c}_y}{a},$$

$$v_x = \hat{v}_x + \hat{a}(c_x - \hat{c}_x)^2 + \tilde{v}_x + \tilde{a}(c_x - \tilde{c}_x)^2,$$

$$v_y = \hat{v}_y + \hat{a}(c_y - \hat{c}_y)^2 + \tilde{v}_y + \tilde{a}(c_y - \tilde{c}_y)^2,$$

$$v_{xy} = \hat{v}_{xy} + \hat{a}(c_x - \hat{c}_x)(c_y - \hat{c}_y) + \tilde{v}_{xy} + \tilde{a}(c_x - \tilde{c}_x)(c_y - \tilde{c}_y),$$

The computations for the merging process take constant time and do not depend on the number of pixels of the two regions. The same holds for adding one pixel to a region ($\hat{a}=1$). This is important for the WCET of this algorithm as described in section 5.4.

Beside these six moments the average color value using the YUV color space of all pixels of the region completes the data structure of a region. The regions are managed using a connected list. Inside the list the regions are sorted by the y-coordinate of the uppermost pixel of the region. The major advantage of this kind of sorting is that during the region-growing step the regions are automatically created in that order und during the region-merging step this ordering speeds up the search process dramatically as explained in section 5.3.

5.2 Region-Growing

As describe before the region growing step is executed individually for every line and from left to right. Vision hardware often provides pixels using the YUV color space. Therefore the region-growing step only uses this color space to avoid time consuming color space conversion of all pixels.

All achromatic pixels are skipped because only colored regions are relevant for our scenarios (It is simple to extend the algorithm to detect non-colored regions as well). We discriminate chromatic and achromatic pixels in a way similar as proposed in [13]. Achromatic pixels are those which are too dark, too light or are nearly grey.

When finding the first colored pixel a new region is created. Then the next pixel to the right is visited and a decision is made whether the color is similar to the color of the actual region. If it is similar the pixel will be added to the region otherwise the region is finished and the algorithm skips to the next pixel.

To have a computational simple decision whether two colors are similar we simply use the euclidian distance of the two colors inside the YUV color space and define a threshold for similarity.

All lines are processed this way which results in a representation as shown in figure 1. All regions created during this step have height one because the y-coordinate of the pixels is always the same. This implies that v_y and v_{xy} is 0 and v_x only depends on a and is calculated using a lookup-table. Thus all moments are calculated very fastly. The number of pixels is needed to get a. The sum of all x-coordinates of the pixels and one division has to be done to calculate c_x. c_y is equal to the actual line number.

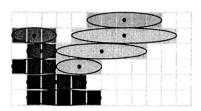

Figure 1. Representation after the region-growing step

This region-growing step handles each input line individually without any data dependability to other input lines. Therefore the requirements of the techniques introduces in section 4 are fulfilled. Because there is no data dependability to other input lines there is no need to store the whole input image in memory if the algorithm is in sync with the image input hardware.

5.3   Region-Merging

After the region growing step we need to merge the created regions. We have to compare each region with every other region whether they are spatial near to each other and similar in color.

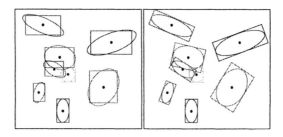

Figure 2. Possible approximations of an ellipse

How can we define *spatial near* using our data structure. The moments can be visualized using ellipses, thus *spatial near* could mean overlapping ellipses. Those calculations are computationally expensive because you need a lot of trigonometrical operations and thus you can't do it on low-cost embedded devices. Figure 2 shows two possible approximations of an ellipse. On the left figure you see an approximation using axis-parallel rectangles and on the right figure rectangles which are parallel to the main axis of the ellipses. The former is the easiest one in respect to computation time but also the most inaccurate one. The approximation can be provided using a lookup-table.

We also had to compare the colors of two regions. During the region growing step we use the YUV color space to decide whether pixels are similar in color or not. The YUV color space is not very suitable for comparing the colors of the regions because here higher euclidian distances in the color space are treated as similar. That's why a color space like HSI is more suitable. So when comparing two regions we calculate the euclidian distance of the colors and use a threshold to decide whether to merge or not.

A problem is the time of the search process because in the simplest case every newly created region has to be compared with every other region. So with n regions you'll get a time cost of $O(n^2)$. That's why we sort the regions spatially using a connected list.

For every region in the list the algorithm follows the list backwards until the first region which lowermost pixel is higher than the uppermost pixel of the actually processed region. Using this technique the processing time of the region-merging part is shorten dramatically.

This region-merging step only needs the data of the line-based region-growing step of the actual image line and the previously created regions. Therefore this step complies to the requirements introduced in 4. Figure 3 shows an example image with the segmentation result.

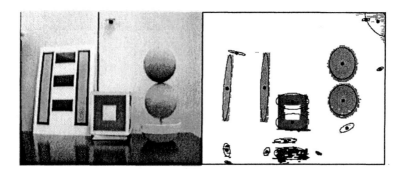

Figure 3. Example image and color segmentation

5.4   WCET-Analysis

For a lot of applications real-time capabilities are needed (e.g. to hold the image analysis in sync with the input image hardware). Therefore the Worst-Case-Execution-Times (WCET) must be known *a priori*.

A WCET-analysis is possible for the line-based region-growing step because all of the following computations take constant time and the number of pixels per line is constant and known a priori:

1. Decision whether a pixel's color is similar to the color of a region (Euclidian distance)
2. Adding a pixel to a region's data structure (shown in 5.1)
3. Creation of a new region (Initialization of data instance); the maximum number of regions in one line is known a priori and can be shorten introducing a minimum length of newly created regions.

The WCET-analysis of the region-merging step is more difficult. As shown in section 5.1 the computation of merging two regions is independent of the regions' data and thus the computation time is constant. The time to compare two regions whether they are spatial near and similar in color is constant and known a priori as well. But the number of comparisons is not known a priori because it depends on the number of regions as already shown in section 5.3. A maximum number of regions can be given because a maximum number of regions for every line is known and the number of images lines is also known. But this estimation is a lot higher than the number of comparisons normally needed in average input images. Therefore the region-merging step has to be optimized in the future (e.g. by using different data structures) to yield a better WCET.

6. IMPLEMENTATION

We implemented the algorithm using a Philips TriMedia 1100 based microcontroller board running at 100MHz. While the image hardware is sending the input image to the main memory the CPU already does the image analysis of the first lines. For the merging step we use the axis-parallel approximations of the ellipses because the operations for the comparisons are fast and tests have shown that the approximation is sufficient for most applications. The implementation needs about 500kByte RAM at run-time. During several tests we showed that in most cases the system was capable of processing 25 frames per second and the delay time between start of the analog transmission of an image and the segmentation results was less than 40ms. Table 1 shows a comparison of our algorithm with the CMVision [8] and the CSC [9]. Latencies were not given in those papers.

Table1: Comparison with other color segmentation implementations

	Image Size	Framerate	System
CMVision [8]	320x240	30 fps	30% of 350MHz Pentium II
CSC [9]	256x256	5 fps	100% of 167MHz SPARC CPU
Our Implementation	352x288	25 fps	100MHz TM1100

7. CONCLUSION

We have shown that it is possible to build a low-cost embedded vision system which is capable of doing low latency color segmentation. Low latency vision systems are important to build very fast acting and reacting robots e.g. in the RoboCup scenario.

Color segmentation is one important part of a vision system but normally that is not sufficient. So we plan to integrate edge-detection to our system in the near future.

The color segmentation algorithm will be connected to a special behavior-based system which is also designed be have low-latencies. Crucial is the overall response time of a system therefore the perception, the processing and the manipulation have to have low latencies. Only pure computing power is not enough to build fast reacting systems.

8.   REFERENCES

[1] W. Skarbek and A. Koschan, "Colour image segmentation - a survey" Tech. Rep. 94-32, Technical University Berlin, 1994.

[2] C.-H. Teh and R. T. Chin, "On image analysis by the methods of moments" *IEEE Transactions on Pattern Analysis and Machine Intelligence*, vol. PAMI-10, pp. 496-513, July 1988.

[3] R. J. Prokop and A. P. Reeves, "A survey of moment-based techniques for unoccluded object representation and recognition" *Computer Vision, Graphics, and Image Processing. Graphical Models and Image Processing*, vol. 54, pp. 438-460, Sept. 1992.

[4] R. C. Arkin, *Behavior-Based Robotics*. Cambridge: MIT Press, 1998.

[5] C. Poyton, "Frequently asked questions about color." Website: http://www.inforamp.net/~poynton.

[6] I. Horswill, "Polly: A vision-based artificial agent" in *Proceedings of the 11th National Conference on Artificial Intelligence*, (Menlo Park, CA, USA), pp. 824-829, AAAI Press, 1993.

[7] L. Lorigo, R. Brooks, and W. Grimson, "Visually guided obstacle avoidance in unstructured environments" in *Proc. IROS97*, pp. 373-379, 1997.

[8] J. Bruce, T. Balch, and M. Veloso, "Fast and inexpensive color image segmentation for interactive robots" in *IEEE/RSJ International Conf. on Intelligent Robots and Systems*, IEEE, 2000.

[9] V. Rehrmann and L. Priese, "Fast and robust segmentation of natural color scenes" in *Computer Vision - ACCV 98* (R. Chin and T.-C. Pong, eds.), vol. I, (Hong Kong, China), pp. 598-606, jan 1998.

[10] G. Wyeth, "Implementing active vision in embedded systems" in *Proc. of Mechatronics and Machine Vision in Practice 4*, pp. 240-245, IEEE Computer Society Press, 1997.

[11] A. Tremeau and N. Borel, "A region growing and merging algorithm to color segmentation", *Pattern Recognition*, vol. 30, no. 7, pp. 1191-1203, 1987.

[12] F. Moscheni and F. Dufaux, "Region merging based on robust statistical testing" in *SPIE Proc. VCIP'96*, (Orlando, Florida), March 1996.

[13] N. Ikonomakis, K. Plataniotis, and A. Venetsanopoulos, "A region-based color image segmentation scheme" in *Proceedings of Electrical Imaging '99, vol. 3653 of SPIE*, (San Jose, California), pp. 1202-1209, Jan 1999.

Soft IP Design Framework Using Metaprogramming Techniques

Vytautas Štuikys, Robertas Damaševičius, Giedrius Ziberkas, and Giedrius Majauskas
Kaunas University of Technology, Software Engineering Department
Studentu 50, 3031-Kaunas, Lithuania
{stuik,damarobe,ziber,giedmaja}@soften.ktu.lt

Abstract: We discuss the application of the metaprogramming techniques for soft IP design. Two metaprogramming paradigms are considered: the internal (using capabilities of the single language) and external (based on the usage of the target language and external metalanguage simultaneously) ones. The novelty of our approach is that we apply the concept of the multi-dimensional separation of concerns implemented via metaprogramming for the design of parameterized soft IPs for embedded systems in order to achieve higher flexibility, reusability and customizability.

Key words: soft IP, multi-dimensional separation of concerns, metaprogramming

1.   INTRODUCTION

In recent years there has been a considerable progress in developing methods for automating design and co-design of embedded systems (ES) in both technological and methodological aspects [1,2]. However, the ever-growing complexity of ES combined with the requirement to decrease time-to-market is forcing hardware (HW) designers to apply concepts and methods previously used primarily in software (SW) design. The concept of soft IPs (aka virtual components - VCs) in HW design is a good example. The soft IPs are highly customizable components described either in HDLs such as VHDL and Verilog, or in programming languages like C/C++.

The design of soft IPs for ES is a complex task due to the following reasons. Having in mind the requirements for flexibility, scalability and customizability, a critical issue in the design of ES is their architecture. One way to reduce the architectural design time and costs is to reuse the pre-existing soft IPs. However, smart products require various combinations of high performance, low cost and low power. The customization of IPs to fit application, if not pre-programmed, may require extensive design efforts.

Developers usually design general-purpose ES for reuse in numerous applications. Because the context of their usage is usually unknown, these designs often focus on the functionality issues only. On the other hand, the extreme specialization results in highly efficient design yet usable only in a single application. The design of highly reusable IP blocks doesn't solve the problem of adaptation for a particular context. The designer has to find the balance between the generalization of functionality and the specialization of performance characteristics.

The aim of this paper is (1) to formulate the role of the multi-dimensional separation of concerns [3,4] in soft IP design. (2) To introduce the metaprogramming techniques and address their usage for designing customizable soft IPs. Our contribution and novelty is the analysis and application of the *internal* and *external* metaprogramming techniques based on the *multi-dimensional separation of concerns* (MDSoC).

The structure of the paper is as follows. We consider related works in Section 2. We explain the multi-dimensional separation of concerns and its role in Section 3. We consider the internal and external metaprogramming paradigms and their usage in soft IP design in Section 4. We present experiments, evaluation and conclusions in Sections 5, 6 and 7, respectively.

2.   RELATED WORK

In recent years there has been a great interest in dealing with the IP problems, as well as organized initiatives, such as VSIA. Lennard *et al.* [5] explicitly demonstrate the power of the separation of concerns in handling complex problems in system-level design. Seepold [6] focuses on the extension of the existing methodologies and generalisation to drive the development of IP reuse and VCs. Vermeulen *et al.* [7] propose a system-level IP reuse methodology intended for soft and firm IP blocks. Designs are described in three layers of operations, which in combination allow structural and behavioural reuse.

The need for the customisation has been reported in [8]. The paper claims that even the most frequently reused components, although they implement a well-established standard, require a tiny customization to fit in the application. Chou *et al.* [9] use higher-level design abstractions that allow raising the level of abstraction of specifications above the low-level target-specific implementation thus allowing the designers to focus on global architectural and functionality decisions.

Faraboschi *et al.* [10] emphasize the role of scalability and customizability for ES. Rau *et al.* [2] distinguish most important features of ES architecture as follows. Specialization involves tailoring of reusable-but-not-efficient general-purpose ES to the application domain. Customization refers to a specialization of a similar available IP. Automation allows speeding up design using parameterized IP libraries and design frameworks.

Haase [11] proposes to use large libraries of highly parametric *DesignObjects*^{TM} tailored in terms of customer requirements to support IP reuse. Givargis *et al.* [12] consider the parameterization of the entire HW architectures in terms of area, power, performance and functional requirements. Koegst *et al.* [13] focus on the specification of reuse-based designs targeting correct embedding and functional flexibility, and describe reuse-focused parameterization techniques.

New innovative paradigms of the MDSoC, multi-language specifications and multi-paradigm design are discussed in a number of papers. Jerraya *et al.* [14] discuss the usage of multi-language specifications for system design. The design of a complex ES may require the combination of several specification languages for different aspects of implementation.

Ossher and Tarr [3,4] introduce the concept of the MDSoC. Authors claim that major difficulties associated with SW reuse, component integration, system composition & decomposition, and modifications of SW systems are due to a lack of the separation of concerns. They consider the separation of overlapping concerns, various dimensions (kinds) of concerns, and deal with interaction and integration of concerns. Although this field is still in the initial stage, there are reports of the benefits of the MDSoC. Murphy *et al.* [15] study the separation of concerns in OO systems. Kande and Strohmeier [16] apply the MDSoC in software architecture description, which allows considering systems from multiple perspectives.

3. SEPARATION OF CONCERNS AND DESIGN

3.1 Motivation and role of the multi-dimensional separation of concerns

The MDSoC has far-reaching and challenging objectives [3,4]: (1) to reduce SW complexity. (2) Improve comprehensibility. (3) Promote traceability throughout SW lifecycle. (4) Limit the impact of change, facilitating evolution and non-invasive adaptation and customization. (5)

Facilitate reuse. (6) Simplify component integration.

There may be a variety of concerns used for describing and implementing a complex system. A particular concern may have multiple *dimensions* to be considered at different stages of the design process. The separation of concerns, however, is not enough for dealing with a complex system. Finally, concerns must be integrated. The environments and tools are actually *integrated and specifically represented concerns*, which address the prescribed objectives and requirements.

Concerns and their dimensions can be *orthogonal* (independent) and *overlapping* (dependable). It is comparatively easy to identify and integrate concepts for the orthogonal separation, e.g., the multi-language approach in SW/HW co-design [1,14]. The orthogonal separation can be introduced intuitively, presented implicitly and does not require the usage of an explicit model. In case of the overlapping concepts, we usually need to build a model in order to extract the benefits of the relationship as follows.

1. The concern "view" applied to an IP model has two dimensions: pure *behavioral* and pure *structural*. The functionality of the model can be revealed through the concern "process" which also has two dimensions: *sequential* and *concurrent*. For dealing with overlapping concerns, one need to have the relationship model like that proposed in [17] for transforming sequential VHDL models into concurrent ones for higher performance.

2. After analyzing VHDL and introducing the concern "role" of the VHDL constructs and their dimensions (*lower-*, *higher-level construct*), we can conceive metaprogramming in VHDL as will be explained in Section 4.

3.2　　　Explicit MDSoC in design space

The concept of the MDSoC is especially useful in the domain of ES design where a variety of requirements exist at different levels of abstraction. These requirements restrict the design space of soft IPs. We conceive the design space as a set of all feasible implementations of the domain model. The reuse library is an implementation of the design sub-space [18]. The design space and concerns are the result of domain analysis.

The design space is multi-dimensional with multiple aspects of concern: data structure, behavior, performance, etc. Commonalties and variability of each aspect must be captured by suitable abstractions. These abstractions help to organize the multi-dimensionally related IPs into IP families, which in turn are composed of families of lower level IPs. Commonalties reflect the shared context that is invariant across the IP family, whereas the variations, which capture the distinguishing properties of IPs, have to be specified at a higher level of abstraction and represented via parameters.

We represent the concerns explicitly via the generic parameter names, and the design space implicitly by the generic IPs. The design space is sliced by the generic parameters to meet the specific requirements (Figure 1, a).

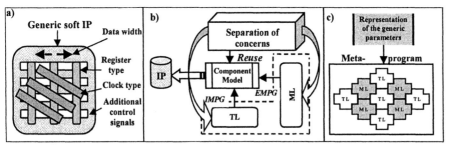

Figure 1. Our approach explained: (a) slices of concern in a generic register model; (b) the framework of IP design at the higher-level; and (c) composition of a metaprogram in EMPG

A component may be parameterized in terms of its functionality (specific functionality is selected from a family of the related one), size (data path width, RAM size, etc.), control (e.g. pipelining), performance characteristics (power, area, delay), synthesis tools and target technology. Slices do not exist in isolation; they can be interrelated differently. A metaprogram integrates slices into a single IP. The designer can instantiate a detailed component design, which is a specialization of a generic soft IP with respect to specified parameter values. We implement the concept of the MDSoC using the metaprogramming techniques as follows.

4. METAPROGRAMMING AND SOFT IP DESIGN

4.1 Internal and external metaprogramming paradigms

Metaprogramming (MPG) is the programming technique that enables a manipulation with other program structures. The higher-level metaprogram uses lower level constructs as data. The basis of MPG is a separation of the domain artifacts from the knowledge of how to customize and glue them together. This allows achieving program generalization and customization.

MPG can be implemented in several ways. At the abstraction level, we need to analyze the capabilities of the given target language (TL) and separate the concerns, which relate to implementing the basic functionality, from those, which allow expressing generic solutions and customized specifications. This separation may be accomplished, for example, *implicitly* using only the internal capabilities of the TL, or *explicitly* either introducing some extensions to the TL or using an external metalanguage (ML).

At the implementation level, we need to build the architecture of the IP, to evaluate the properties of the soft IP model, and specify the required matching between properties using the appropriate abstractions. To achieve this, we separate the concerns at both the abstraction and IP model levels (Figure 1,b). We categorize two kinds of metaprogramming: the *internal* (IMPG) and *external* (EMPG) ones. The first one uses the internal capabilities of the TL, while the second uses TL and ML simultaneously.

The key features of IMPG are as follows. A designer: (1) works in one environment only (e.g., VHDL). (2) Implicitly separates the concerns within the environment. (3) Allocates a specific role for particular TL constructs: higher-level (e.g., **if**-*generate,* **for**-*generate*) for expressing the generalized functionality, and lower-level ones for expressing the domain functionality. (4) Manipulates with lower-level constructs using the higher-level ones.

The essence of the EMPG is as follows. A designer: (1) works in two environments. (2) Implements the separation of concerns explicitly, where TL is for basic domain functionality, and external ML is for customization, adaptation and generalization only. (3) Manipulates with TL using ML.

As the EMPG is still not matured enough, we explain the basic principles by analyzing the concrete languages (*VHDL* as a TL, and *Open PROMOL* [19] as a ML) as a case study for the EMPG for further discussion.

The concept of external functions is at the core of Open PROMOL, which has the following properties: (1) ML is an open set of external functions; it is TL-independent. (2) A function describes the manipulation with its arguments (parameters, TL code, or other functions). A variety of manipulations are supported in terms of structural programming. (3) External modules and nesting across the hierarchy of the external modules enhances flexibility of the hierarchical parameterization. (4) ML supports the conditional parameterization, i.e. the usage of a particular parameter dependent upon the pre-specified condition. (5) ML specification has a unified interface for customization of a given specification and interfacing with other specifications. (6) The result of processing of the PROMOL specification is an instance (in a TL) customized to the particular requirements of a designer.

We present some of these properties by a generic specification describing the majority vote function in VHDL with the introduced ML (Figure 2, a), and its instance (Figure 2, b). Note that the interface of a PROMOL specification is between a pair of '$'. A generic specification is a composition of the HDL code, which describes features common for the entire IP family, and ML code, which specifies the slices of concerns represented by the generic parameters (Figure 1, c).

```
$                                              process (X0, X1, X2)
"Enter the order of the majority function"       variable count: arrtype;
                {3,5,7}   order:=3;             begin
"Enter data width" {1..32}   width:=8;           count(0) := 0;
$                                                count(1) := 0;
process (@gen[order,{, },{X},0])                 if (X0 = X1) then
  variable count: arrtype;                         count(0) := count(0)+1;
  begin                                          end if;
@for[i,0,order/2,{                               if (X0 = X2) then
    count(@sub[i]) := 0; }]                        count(0) := count(0)+1;
@for[i,0,order/2,{                               end if;
@for[j,i+1,order-1,{                             if (X1 = X2) then
    if (X@sub[i] = X@sub[j]) then                  count(1) := count(1)+1;
      count(@sub[i]):=count(@sub[i])+1;          end if;
    end if; }]                                   if (count(0) >= 1) then
}]                                                 MAJ_OUT <= X0;
@for[i,0,order/2,{                                 IS_MAJ <= '1';
    if (count(@sub[i])>=@sub[order/2]) then      else
      MAJ_OUT <= X@sub[i];                         if (count(1) >= 1) then
      IS_MAJ <= '1';                                 MAJ_OUT <= X1;
    else }]                                          IS_MAJ <= '1';
      IS_MAJ <= '0';                             else
@for[i,0,order/2,{                                 IS_MAJ <= '0';
    end if;                                       end if;
}]                                               end if;
end process;                        a)          end process;                  b)
```

Figure 2. A metaprogram (fragment) implemented in Open PROMOL (a) and its instance (b)

4.2   Comparison of IMPG and EMPG paradigms

At the core of MPG are parameterization, customization and interfacing mechanisms. Although there are many similarities between the MPG techniques, both of them have some strengths and weaknesses (see Table 1).

Table 1. Comparison of parameterization and interfacing in MPG paradigms

MPG characteristics	Internal MPG in VHDL	External MPG in ML
Main mechanism	Generics, generate statements	External functions
Parameterization model	Hierarchical	Hierarchical & conditional
Level of separation	Implicit (intuitive)	Explicit (external)
Customization interface	Package, generic map	Unified user-oriented
Instance naming	Automatic	Pre-programmed (manual)

The main strength of IMPG is the integration with existing tools and design methodologies. Only one design environment is required. When the number of parameters is small enough the method suits well for black-box reuse. However, this technique has some drawbacks. The method depends upon TL. Furthermore, components cannot be easily adapted for synthesis using different tools. Users often encounter the overgeneralization problem when they try to adapt the component manually.

The weaknesses of IMPG are often the strengths of EMPG (and vice versa). The usage of a TL-independent ML allows automatic (pre-programmed) adaptation to limitations of a particular synthesizer, and automatic documentation generation. The end-user has access to customized instances. An instance is much more readable than the generic component. This technique has some problems too. Firstly, it requires two design environments, thus the validation process is more complex. Secondly, the component name clashing must be prevented (manually or automatically).

5.   EXPERIMENTAL RESULTS

We consider the following cases in our experiments: (1) Soft IP design from scratch for fine-grained and middle-grained components using IMPG. (2) The same as in the previous case, but using EMPG. (3) Customizations of the middle- and coarse-grained components using EMPG. (4) Wrapping third party IPs with tiny modifications using EMPG.

By tiny modifications we mean changing either the parameter value or library component in the retrieved IP in order to adapt it to the restrictions of our synthesis tools[1]. By wrapping we mean a family of the related instances, which differ in functional or/and technological characteristics, and are represented with EMPG technique as a single IP. Those characteristics and generic parameters for a wrapped generic multiplier IP are given in Table 2.

Table 2. Generic multiplier synthesis results

Generic parameter values				Synthesis results	
Multiplier type	Synthesis tool	Width, bits	No. of cells	Delay, ns	Power
Serial	Cadence	16	441	27.84	-
		32	849	53.27	-
		64	1663	98.94	-
	Synopsys	16	324	7.32	3.7817 uW
		32	599	8.20	6.6184 uW
		64	1131	8.14	12.7298 uW
Mont-gomery	Cadence	16	277	19.45	-
		32	540	29.91	-
		64	991	47.83	-
	Synopsys	16	355	2.80	9.5598 uW
		32	660	2.80	17.184 uW
		64	1237	2.80	32.4107 uW
Booth	Synopsys	16	8	198.16	2.5410 mW
		32	16	410.43	10.4788 mW

[1] We use *Cadence* (**0.7 um**) and *Synopsys* (**1999.10**) synthesis tools

6.   EVALUATION AND DISCUSSION

We have presented the framework for soft IP design methodology. The main focus has been given to the MDSoC and MPG techniques. The MDSoC can be considered as a pre-design analysis paradigm aiming at the identification, decomposition, encapsulation and integration of dimensions of concerns in order to improve the design characteristics. The MDSoC allows dealing with complex systems and raising the abstraction level of the design.

We demonstrate the usage of the MPG techniques, which are useful for customization, modification, wrapping, and generalization of IPs. Furthermore, the techniques allow generating soft IPs automatically and building more efficient and productive systems. We have also suggested the external MPG technique based on the usage of the external metalanguage (ML). The strength of the external MPG is its applicability to the different dimensions of TL models. Furthermore, by introducing an external ML we can extend the capabilities of MPG in soft IP design significantly.

On the other hand, the MDSoC and MPG techniques are still not matured enough, and a great deal of research must be done in the field of soft IP design. The suggested framework gives only preliminary results, but we believe in strength of the introduced techniques. The belief is also based on works of other authors who recognize and apply (at least implicitly) the concepts described explicitly in this paper.

7.   CONCLUSIONS AND FUTURE WORK

The multi-dimensional separation of concerns is at the core in design of complex systems in general and soft IPs in particular. When introducing the separation of concerns we can understand better the design process and capture the essential domain artifacts to improve it. The internal and external metaprogramming techniques are only two cases at the abstraction level, which demonstrate the power of the separation of concerns. The external metaprogramming yields additional capabilities for customization and wrapping of soft IPs. The future work aims at extending dimensions at the soft IP model from customized IPs to the distributed customized soft IPs.

8.   REFERENCES

[1]   R. Ernst. Codesign of Embedded Systems: Status and Trends. *IEEE Design and Test of Computers*, April-June 1998, pages 45-54.

[2] B.R. Rau, and M.S. Schlansker. Embedded Computer Architecture and Automation. *IEEE Computer*, April 2001, pages 75-83.

[3] H. Ossher, P. Tarr, W. Harrison, and S.M. Sutton, Jr. N Degrees of Separation: Multi-Dimensional Separation of Concerns. In *Proceedings of the ICSE'99*, 16-22 May 1999 Los Angeles, pages 107-119.

[4] H. Ossher, and P. Tarr. Multi-Dimensional Separation of Concerns and The Hyperspace Approach. In *Software Architectures and Component Technology: The State of the Art in Software Development*, ed. M. Aksit. Kluwer Academic Publishers, 2000.

[5] C. K. Lennard, P. Schaumont, and G. de Jong. Standards for System-Level Design: Practical Reality or Solution in Search of a Question? In *Proceedings of the DATE 2000*, 27-30 March 2000 Paris, pages 576-583.

[6] R. Seepold. Reuse of IP and Virtual Components. In *Proceedings of the DATE'1999*, 9-12 March 1999 Munich.

[7] A. Vermeulen, F. Catthoor, D. Verkest, and H. De Man. Formalized Three-Layer System-Level Reuse Model and Methodology for Embedded Data-Dominated Applications. In *Proceedings of the DATE'2000*, 27-30 March 2000 Paris, pages 92-98.

[8] J.F. Agaësse, and B. Laurent. Virtual Components Application and Customization. In *Proceedings of the DATE'1999*, 9-12 March 1999 Munich, pages 726-727.

[9] P. Chou, R. Ortega, K. Hines, K. Partridge, and G. Borriello. IPChinook: An Integrated IP-based Design Framework for Distributed Embedded Systems. In *Proceedings of the 36th ACM/IEEE on DAC*, 21-25 June 1999 New Orleans, pages 44-49.

[10] P. Faraboschi, G. Brown, J.A. Fisher, G. Desoli, and F. Homewood. Lx: A Technology Platform for Customizable VLIW Embedded Processing. In *Proceedings of the ISCA'00*, 12-14 June 2000 Vancouver, pages 203-213.

[11] J. Haase. Design Methodology for IP Providers. In *Proceedings of the DATE'1999*, 9-12 March 1999 Munich, pages 728-732.

[12] T. Givargis, and F. Vahid. Parameterized System Design. In *Proceedings of the CODES'2000*, 3-5 May 2000 San Diego, pages 98-102.

[13] M. Koegst, P. Conradi, D. Garte, and M. Wahl. A Systematic Analysis of Reuse Strategies for Design of Electronic Circuits. In *Proceedings of the DATE'98*, 23-26 February 1998 Paris, pages 292-296.

[14] A.A. Jerraya, M. Romdhani, Ph. Le Marrec, F. Hessel, P. Coste, C. Valderrama, G.F. Marchioro, J.M. Daveau, and N.-E. Zergainoh. Multilanguage Specification for System Design and Codesign. In *System Level Synthesis*, NATO ASI 1998, eds. A.A. Jerraya, J. Mermet. Boston: Kluwer Academic Publishers, 1999.

[15] G.C. Murphy, A. Lai, R.J. Walker, and M.P. Robillard. Separating Features in Source Code: An Exploratory Study. In *Proceedings of the 23rd International Conference on Software Engineering*, 12-19 May 2001 Toronto, pages 275-284.

[16] M. M. Kandé, and A. Strohmeier. On The Role of Multi-Dimensional Separation of Concerns in Software Architecture. In *OPSLA'2000 Workshop on Advanced Separation of Concerns in Object-Oriented Systems*, 15-19 October 2000 Minneapolis.

[17] A. Prihozhy, and M. Solomennik. Generating Concurrent Net Schedules from Sequential VHDL Models. In *FDL'2001*, 3-7 September 2001 Lyon.

[18] H.P. Peixoto, M.J. Jacome, A. Royo, and J.C. Lopez. The Design Space Layer: Supporting Early Design Space Exploration for Core-Based Designs. In *Proceedings of the DATE'1999*, 9-12 March 1999 Munich, pages 676-683.

[19] V. Štuikys, R. Damaševičius, and G. Ziberkas. Open PROMOL: An Experimental Language for Target Program Modification. In *System-on-Chip Design Languages*, eds. A. Mignotte, E. Villar, L.S. Spruiell. Kluwer Academic Publishers, 2002.

How to integrate Webservices in Embedded System Design?

Achim Rettberg, Wolfgang Thronicke
University of Paderborn & Siemens Business Services / C-LAB,
Fuerstenallee 11, D-33102 Paderborn,Germany
Tel:. +49 5251 606110, Fax: + 49 5251 606065,
Email: achim.rettberg@c-lab.de, wolfgang.thronicke@c-lab.de

Abstract: The structure of Internet applications and scenarios is evolving rapidly. New software architectures and formats for transfer of data and site-spanning interoperability are emerging and reshaping the realm of web-centered computing . These changes are having repercussions that will change the established methodologies of design processes and business-to-business applications. Therefore, these effects on the domain of the electronic design automation (EDA) have to be considered and their validity shown.. In this paper we present an approach to exploit webservices technology in the field of embedded system design.

Key words: webservices, embedded system design, collaborative design

1.   INTRODUCTION

In general the structure of Internet applications is changing rapidly. New information technologies and standards are emerging and - together with new infrastructures (high speed internet, wireless applications, UMTS) - design processes and business-to-business transactions are reshaping.

In addition to Internet technology that has been a true enabler for distributed technologies and applications the development in this area is shifting towards service-oriented structures. This falls into line with the evolution of programming paradigms: Object-orientation denotes the view of a program during design and execution as a collection of objects that send messages to each other invoking certain qualified operations. Deliberate design of software-systems seemed to become feasible and several methodologies have proven their value in this field, like UML-based techniques [12], [13]. However, the notation had to be augmented to cope with describing distributed systems effectively. Using *distributed objects* complex networked applications with high interoperability could be specified. On the one side, definition and implementation on object level is still the adequate design style for tightly coupled components, on the other side with respect to Internet scenarios the concept of interacting *services* is now the state-of-the-art specification method. This *service-based* programming paradigm is backed by new Internet protocols and languages like SOAP [14] and WSDL [15] which serve exactly the purpose of defining and describing services and their intercommunications. New applications or services can rely on services from other service-providers. Since the client of a service is not defined at the time the service is provided the deployment and publication are a most important part during its life cycle. With UDDI [16] a "dictionary" with a standardized access mechanism has been defined to alleviate this problem.

Since issues like time-to-market and distributed development and design are common factors in the affected processes, this progress affects the traditional tool-centered engineering domains as well. Moreover the sophistication of tools reaches a new level as the design technology for new products evolves rapidly. So they present valuable assets for a company by forming an important part of their intellectual property (IP).

Using the *service-centered* approach such companies have the chance to offer their knowledge without the need to transfer programs or algorithms. For the user of such services one important question is how to integrate such a service into their work environment. Usually integration focuses on the principle of coupling existing applications or components tightly together to ensure smooth and reliable operation. The resulting (and available) integration environments use therefore proprietary integration mechanisms on top of existing base-technologies like CORBA [18], JAVA [19], and JAVABEANS [20] or similar middleware components. In fact, CORBA-Services for instance realize conceptually the same idea as webservices with WSDL. They define a common interface that can be accessed from different applications. The important difference of this approach is that webservices are build on top of a foundation that is centered on the Internet platform. Which means the common denominator for running such services is a standard webserver technology (or any kind of server implementation supporting Internet protocols), TCP/IP networks and the HTTP protocol accompanied by the flexible XML metaformat. Thus integration technology will change and hopefully become as the usual way of accessing content in the Internet [17]. The usage of this technology for embedded system design is of high interest, because on the one side it offers more freedom for the user and on the other side new business concepts or licensing models for the tool vendor.

This paper is organized as follows. First we describe the web-based integration scenario. Then, we present a collaborative design environment for embedded system design, called PARADISE [2]. After that, we describe the combination of the web-based integration scenario with the existing PARADISE environment. We conclude with a discussion of the presented approach.

2. THE WEB-BASED INTEGRATION SCENARIO

For integration aspects, webservices can provide a suitable solution to overcome certain critical issues in exploiting remote facilities: Description and protocols. With XML-based formats like WSDL and SOAP, that additionally defines the messages which are used to access and control remote services, a common infrastructure is provided.

Popular pre-web integration methodologies have been focusing on combining tools and software components by using enabling technologies. These have supplied the inter-tool "glue" which allowed assembling a new solution from these parts and supports reuse in different scenarios. The new scenario using a web-service is shown in Figure 1: The main difference concerning the integration method is that there is no tight coupling of the integrated service in the client's process. The integration efforts are usually taken at the site of the provider of the webservice. The provider registers his service at a webservice directory where it can be queried using a standardized format. As a result the client retrieves the description and address of the service and can locally integrate the webservice interface. Using this two-step approach of dynamically integration has different advantages:

- The provider can move the implementation of the webservice to another server, which will be reflected in the directory. So the client process adjusts automatically to the new location (address).
- For reliable services the provider can supply different instances of the webservice at different sites, so that the others will compensate the failure of one server.
- Different providers may offer the same service at different costs. So the client can select dynamically the most cost-effective one.

There are certain advantages that appear during the design phase of an application: The designer of a new client process can search for needed services conveniently in the directory and create highly distributed scenarios without configuring network structures or determining concrete hosts. Since WSDL is standardized, effective user-friendly integration assistants will simplify the whole integration process on the implementation side so that more weight can be laid on conceptual issues. The XML-based webservice technology is well supported from major IT-providers with sets of tools, so it can be assumed that this standard will have a lasting life cycle in the fast changing world of applications and technology trends.

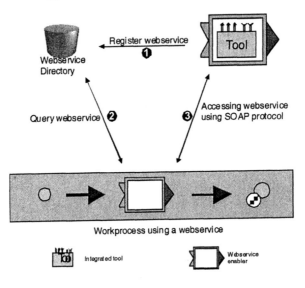

Figure 1. Integrating a webservice

However, ordinary integration technologies still have their merits. Because webservices represent a weak coupling and require a more dynamic processing for the protocols a certain overhead is generated which slows down the interaction. Especially "popular" webservices may have long latencies that reflect the same behavior as visiting a heavy-loaded webservers. In the intranet the common integration techniques are to be preferred because the location of tools and applications under direct administration. Additionally this technique of integration allows an efficient adaptation to the clients requirements, whereas changing a webservice depends on the cooperation of the service provider. Usually there are different clients with contradicting requirements which are not easy to meet by the provider.

3. THE PARADISE APPROACH

The PARADISE design environment is implemented with the ASTAI(R) tool [11] that has been developed at C-LAB [2], [3], [4]. This design environment focuses on the design of embedded hardware/software systems. The design complexity of embedded systems combined with a very tight time-to-market window has revolutionized today's embedded system design process. Several interacting design dimensions to implement parallelism, distribution over different locations, hard real-time requirements [1] and the collaboration have to be addressed by a design environment. Furthermore the usage of IP components is important for embedded system designs [10].

Consequently, the modern, structured design process has to deal with heterogeneous requirements and restrictions. Therefore, the collaborative work is very important for efficient embedded system design. That mean, hardware and software designers and system architects must synchronize their work progress to optimize and debug a system in joint effort. The PARADISE environment distinguishes between these different design domains (see Figure 2). Each design domain reflects a core competency in the design of an embedded system. Each design domain is structured by levels and views. For example the HW-Synthesis design domain corresponds to the structuring of Gajski Y-Chart [7], [8]. PARADISE integrates this databased design methodology with a variety of tools that are suitable for certain design steps. For the first time, the distribution of tools, data and developers over different network domains is possible. This means that any developer at any location can launch a tool from another location. The ASTAI(R) software ensures consistency and the protection of private data. All design steps can be monitored and controlled by means of a design flow. Developers with access to local or remote locations can incorporate existing design data in the design flow. Therefore, system designs can then be carried out with the aid of the bottom-up or top-down method. Besides the integration of tools in a workflow, ASTAI(R) supports the distribution and generation of a design data. Also the update of design data is well supported. Tools within a workflow for which input data does not exists or is invalid yet are automatically blocked until the data is available and valid. Newly generated data is initially classified as local data until developers release it explicitly. Releasing the data effects all levels within the hierarchical design flow to be notified without delay. Developers on these other levels can then accept or reject this data. This protocol is managed by ASTAI(R) by using the Internet. Therefore, the location at which a design data, tool or design flow is stored or installed is irrelevant. A complete overview of the installed tools within PARADISE can be found in [2], [5] and [6].

To show the practicability of the PARADISE design environment two design scenarios are shortly described. The first example is the design of a traffic light controller and the second one is the extension of mobile robot.

The traffic light controller is specified on a very high level of abstraction using Predicate/Transition-Nets (Pr/T-Nets). This formalism is supported within the PARADISE design environment by the 'System Engineering and Animation' tool SEA. The tool provides a homogeneous model based on Pr/T-Nets. To analyze the worst-case execution time (WCET) of a single task, we use the C-LAB Hard Real-Time System (CHaRy) [1]. This is a software synthesis system for distributed (parallel) periodic hard real-time applications. The application is described on a high level (e.g. using SEA), whereas the implementation is left to CHaRy. CHaRy analyzed the WCET for each task of the task-graph. The annotated task-graph is read into the tool SSEA which was developed jointly at the ETH Zurich and the University of Paderborn for the purpose of solving the generalized hardware/software-partitioning problem. This includes also the design space exploration of multi-objective cost functions for the system-level synthesis of embedded systems. For a detailed description of the traffic light controller design see [3]. This design scenario shows the modeling of an embedded system on a high-abstraction level by using PrT/Nets and how to analyze the model with the respect of mapping model tasks to functional units of a given target architecture.

The second design scenario is the extension of a small mobile robot called Pathfinder. This mobile robot is an experimental platform and is as simple as possible in order to keep the focus on the methodological issues and not on the vehicle itself. The *Pathfinder* until now is fully operational, see [21]. The software has been manually coded and implemented on the *Pathfinder*. The architecture is component aware, i.e. is prepared to integrate new modules that add functionality. For demonstration of our IP-based design approach we extend our example in order to establish an advanced interaction facility of the vehicle with it's environment, especially persons being around there. Thus we would like to communicate with people around the *Pathfinder*, i.e. the robot is equipped with a microphone and speakers. Any solution that will fit the needs has to be aware of the existing system architecture and it's real-time characteristics. The time-critical parts of this new functionality are speech compression and decompression tasks. Therefore, the tools of the PARADISE design environment are used to develop or integrate existing solutions in the *Pathfinder* architecture. For the extension of the architecture we use the modeling tool SEA. CHaRy analyzed the WCET for the different software tasks. Within PARADISE we use a generalized approach to HW/SW-partitioning problem which has been implemented by the previously mentioned tool SSEA. The tool TEReCS decides which of the developed or existing solutions really can be combined, i.e. whether their interfaces are compatible. For a detailed description of the scenario see [10].

At this time four partners participate in the PARADISE design environment. These are namely the C-LAB, the University of Paderborn with two different departments and the University of California at Irvine. The main server is located in the C-LAB. All other partners run clients and small servers to distribute the appropriated tool in the environment over the Internet.

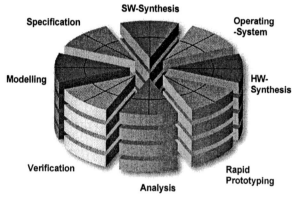

*Figure 2.*PARADISE design domains

4. SYSTEM DESIGN WITH WEBSERVICES

Surely, the presented realization of the PARADISE design environment is a good structuring of today's embedded system design but it lacks by using new approaches like webservices. Therefore, the extension of PARADISE with webservices is a solution to integrate this new trend in the electronic system design area. Clearly, it is not necessary to use webservices for in-house realization of a design environment, because ASTAIR(R) offers all necessary services for integration and workflow implementation for in-house solutions. Additionally ASTAI(R) takes full advantage of the Intranet infrastructure leading to a very efficient integration of tools. Webservices are only necessary for collaborative work between different departments on different locations.

In our approach we interpreted a tool as a webservice. Consequently in the area of embedded system design, especially for our PARADISE scenario, each tool from an EDA vendor could be registered in the webservice directory (see Figure 1). Through this directory any client can transparently select and access the tools required for a certain design-task.

Furthermore, the designs or workflows can also be interpreted as webservices and be registered in the webservice directory. This mechanism has the following advantages for the user of such a system:

- Webservices are in fact a standardized integration approach. They are not limited to one environment, but can be integrated into every software-system that is webservice-aware.
- Webservices can be built from other webservices. This means the integration of tools as webservices into complex design flows which can be republished as a new high-level webservice. Through this approach a client could easily access a complete design methodology.
- The directory can act like a marketplace enabling a client to choose from different solutions the most suitable one for his design problems.

Consequently, the combination of PARADISE by the webservice scenario, described in section 2 offers a really new design method for embedded systems.

Currently ASTAI(R) is expanded by a webservice integration module. This module will provide the following functionality:

- Any "regular" tool can be encapsulated by the server-side module and thus becomes accessible as a webservice. Therefore a standard set of tool-control functions is provided by the tool-webservice module. Using this part conceptually any web service-aware program or tool could use the integrated tool. On the tool site, there is not necessary to install any ASTAI(R) specific software components.
- The integration module on the ASTAI(R) side is embedded into ASTAI(R)´s tool encapsulation specification and therefore virtually undistinguishable from other tools from the ASTAI(R) point of view.
- The actual configuration for a tool is stored in a tool description file using XML. This definition serves two purposes: First it is used by the tool-webservice module to configure the actual calling parameters of the webservice. Additionally a query of these tool properties is possible through the webservice. Second the tool description is used to create an appropriate webservice stub for ASTAI(R) in order to make the tools properties visible in workflows, especially in the workflow editor.

On the client side within the PARADISE environment it is not necessary to deploy ASTAI(R) itself. Only the integration module for ASTAI(R) has to be installed which can be interpreted as a webservice adapter.

5. CONCLUSION AND FUTURE WORK

The notion of "webservices" has introduced a very promising new integration approach, fully based on open Internet standards. This alliance including structured portable data formats addresses both data and service integration issues. In combination with already proven environments, this technology can leverage the power of distributed scenarios in combination with a standardized integration approach. More important "providing a service" may offer a greater market-potential than "supplying a tool" in highly cooperative design environments.

This paper introduces webservices as means to integrate remote tools in a workflow-driven design process for embedded systems. Thus alleviating certain aspects of tool access and extending the area of integration beyond a single environment.

However, the implementation and toolkit support of webservices is yet under development and is estimated to become commercially usable in 2002. Our solutions will provide us with basic components start using this technology in the design domain.

REFERENCES

[1]   Peter Altenbernd: "Timing Analysis, Scheduling, and Allocation of Periodic Hard Real-Time Tasks" Dissertation, Paderborn, 1996

[2]   W. Hardt, A. Rettberg, B. Kleinjohann. *"The PARADISE design environment"*, 1st Embedded System Conference, Auckland (New Zealand), 1999

[3]   A. Rettberg, W. Hardt, J. Teich, M. Bednara. *"Automated Design Space Exploration on System Level for Embedded Systems"*, Ninth Annual International HDL Conference and Exhibition, San Jose (USA), March 2000

[4]   A. Rettberg, F. Rammig, A. Gerstlauer, D.D. Gajski, W. Hardt, B. Kleinjohann. *"The Specification Language SpecC within the PARADISE Design Environment"*, in Proceedings of the Distributed and Parallel Embedded Systems Workshop (DIPES 2000), Paderborn, October 2000

[5]   A. Rettberg, W. Thronicke. " "Collaborative Design for Embedded Hardware/Software Components with the Distributed PARADISE Environment", Proceedings of the 5th World Multi-Conference on Systemics, Cybernetics and Informatics (SCI 2001), Orlando, FL (USA), July 2001

[6]   A. Rettberg, W. Thronicke, "The Distributed PARADISE Environment for
        Collaborative Design of Embedded Hardware Components", Proceedings of the
        8th European Concurrent Engineering Conference (ECEC 2001), Valencia
        (Spain), April 2001
[7]   Franz J. Rammig. *"Systematischer Entwurf digitaler Systeme"*. B. G. Teubner,
        Stuttgart, 1989
[8]   D.D. Gajski, *"Silicon Compilation"*, Addison Wesley Publishing Company,
        1988
[9]   R. Ernst, *"Codesign of Embedded Systems: Status and Trends"*, Journal of IEEE
        Design & Test of Computers, pp. 45-54, April-June 1998
[10]   W. Hardt, F. J. Rammig, C. Böke, C. Ditze, J. Stroop, B. Kleinjohann, A.
        Rettberg, and J. Teich, *"IP-based System Design with the PARADISE Design
        Environment"*, accepted for Journal of Systems Architecture, The Euromicro
        Journal
[11]   http://www.c-lab.de/astair
[12]   Ivar Jacobson, Grady Booch, James Rumbaugh. *The Unified Software
        Development Process*. Addison Wesley. 1998. ISBN 0-201-57169-2
[13]   Sinan Si Alhir. *UML in a Nutshell*. O'Reilly. 1998. ISBN 1-56592-448-7
[14]   Technical Report: *SOAP Version 1.2 Working Draft*.
        http://www.w3.org/TR/soap12
[15]   Technical Report: Web Services Description Language (WSDL) 1.1.
        http://www.w3.org/TR/wsdl
[16]   Universal Description, Discovery and Integration. http://www.uddi.org
[17]   Heinz-Josef Eikerling, Wolfgang Thronicke, Siegfried Bublitz. *Provision and
        Integration of EDA Web-Services using WSDL-based Markup*. FDL 2001.
        Lyon.
[18]   Robert Orfali, Dan Harkey, Jeri Edwards, Robert Crfali. *Instant CORBA*. John
        Wiley & Sons. 1997. ISBN 0471183334.
[19]   Java 2 Platform Enterprise Edition. http://java.sun.com/j2ee
[20]   Mark Wutka. *Special Edition Using Java 2: Enterprise Edition (J2EE)*. Que.
        May 2001. ISBN 0789725037.
[21]   http://www.c-lab.de/~pathfinder

This work has been partially funded under grant number 01 M 3048 E
(German BMBF project "IP-Qualifikation für effizientes Systemdesign
(IPQ)").

Design and Realization of Distributed Real-Time Controllers for Mechatronic Systems

M. Deppe and M. Zanella
Mechatronics Laboratory Paderborn (MLaP), University of Paderborn, Germany

Abstract: Developing distributed embedded control systems increases the need for a consistent design approach. Our example is taken from the mechatronic design in the automotive industry and illustrates our structuring concept for a modular realization of real-time-critical controllers. In our consistent design approach we employ the structured modelling of mechatronic systems, a modular integration platform for real-time software implementation and a modular hardware platform based on FPGAs and microcontrollers.

Key words: Mechatronics, hardware-in-the-loop simulation, distributed real-time control, FPGA, IEEE 1394

1.   INTRODUCTION

Demands on the information-processing unit in mechatronic systems are steadily increasing. This is particularly evident in the automotive industry. Ever more aggregates with mechatronic functions are integrated and linked. The result is a complex network of control units in the car. For the essential control of the car dynamics, for instance ESP (Electronic Stability Program), ABS (Anti-lock Braking System) and ASR (Anti-Spin Regulation) are linked to real-time control units. Designing and testing interlinked control units entails various problems. There is no standardized approach to the design of distributed mechatronic systems from specification to realization. Major problems are the stability and safety of distributed control algorithms and the data transfer between the different ECUs (Electronic Control Unit).

Our work is concerned with the transition, maintaining the structure, from the model representation of a mechatronic system to the implementation of the control algorithms on the prototypical application.

The appropriate modular real-time hardware is based on common platforms, such as FPGAs (Field Programmable Gate Arrays) and microcontrollers. Results of the work presented will be illustrated by an exemplary application called the X-mobile. The X-mobile [1] is an autonomous vehicle at the scale of 1:8. The real challenge in the design of the X-mobile is due to the modularity and flexibility of the system:

Figure 1. X-mobile

The vehicle has four fully independent wheel drives, steering and active suspension. Figure 1 displays the mechanical construction. The development of the vehicle offers a chance of checking up on novel approaches to the research on mechatronic systems. Different strategies and control laws can be tested with the X-mobile, e.g., speed or/and torque drive control, drive and suspension independent or coupled. Moreover, due to its complexity, the X-mobile serves for testing real-time soft- and hardware.

2.   STRUCTURED DESIGN OF MECHATRONIC SYSTEMS

For a general design approach one needs first of all a structuring concept for mechatronic systems. At the lowest level of mechatronic systems, we define Mechatronic Function Modules (MFM). An MFM consists of a passive mechanical frame, sensors, actuators, and discrete-continuous information processing. The MFM concept combines the idea of information encapsulation, developed in software engineering, with that of the aggregate which is a well-established term in engineering. An MFM is assigned a certain task within a mechatronic system, usually the task to control its dynamic behavior. It disposes of physical and informational interfaces for interconnection.

The next hierarchical level is that of the Autonomous Mechatronic System (AMS). An AMS consists of a passive mechanical frame, sensors, and information processing. It has no actuators of its own but uses the mechanically coupled MFMs for actuation. Information processing at the AMS level, such as a human-machine interface, has the task to manage the autonomy of the system.

When more than one AMS are to be employed in a co-operating system, the necessary co-ordination has to be realized on the information-processing level. Those AMSs that operate in an co-operating system are called Cross-linked Mechatronic Systems (CMS) [2].

To design hierarchical control systems according to this structuring concept the MLaP proposes a generalization of the cascade pinciple [2] which was originally widely used for single-input single-output (SISO) systems in control engineering.

Nevertheless, the development of a mechatronic product requires interdisciplinary proceeding using an integrative software environment that makes possible co-operative design, simulation and optimization functionalities. As a result, the MLaP has developed CAMeL (Computer-Aided Mechatronics Laboratory) [3]. Its modelling tool allows to build up models at the topological and mathematical levels with the help of object orientation. CAMeL offers different derivation formalisms for mechanical multibody systems, analysis, visualization, and optimization tools. The software system allows to build up models from different mechatronic domains (mechanics, hydraulics, information processing). In the development of mechatronic systems hardware-in-the-loop simulation (HILS) for a system test in the lab is used. In the HILS the stepwise transition from the structured modular model representation of the mechatronic system to actually mounted mechanical, hydraulic and electrical aggregates takes place. The modular-hierarchical structuring concept for mechatronic systems supports this stepwise transition from the structured model to the informationally distributed HILS.

3. INTEGRATION PLATFORM FOR NETWORKED MECHATRONIC SYSTEMS

IPANEMA (Integration Platform for Networked Mechatronic Systems) [4] is a platform concept used for distributed real-time simulation, a basic requirement of HILS. It allows a hierarchical and modular processing of control tasks according to the principles of the structuring concept. Although IPANEMA was mainly used for software realization of controllers [5] the structure is even suitable for our new hardware realization using FPGAs.

IPANEMA structures each partial control task in distributed simulation in an object-oriented way. Objects of the calculator class implement the simulation kernels treating the individual partial models. They do not comprise any functionality as to administration and data management. These tasks will fall to objects of the assistant class to relieve the calculator objects. To every calculator object an assistant is assigned. By their services, assistants provide a neat distinction between those parts of the simulation environment that have to operate under hard real-time conditions (calculator objects) and those that may run under soft ones.

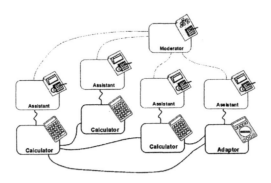

Figure 2. IPANEMA

Assistant objects encapsulate the corresponding calculator object against an object of the moderator class that serves as a sort of interface to the user and the control panel. Moderator objects coordinate the actions of the assistant/calculator team whenever this becomes necessary (e.g., to start or stop a simulation run). In order to couple a technical process (the physical part of a mechatronic system) with digital information processing (in this case, simulation) another class, the adaptors, is available. Adaptor objects transform the physical values relevant for simulation into their numerical equivalents (including scaling and offset).

4.   MODULAR RAPID-PROTOTYPING PLATFORM

The aim of RABBIT [6], our modular rapid-prototyping platform for distributed mechatronic systems, is to help the designer in the development of mechatronic systems at the simulation and implementation stages. The hardware comprises three main components: IEEE 1394, MPC555 microcontroller, and FPGAs. The most important features of RABBIT are its flexibility and extensibility, brought about by an open system interface and high modularity. The platform allows a distributed implementation of control algorithms.

One node of the RABBIT system consists of a rack which can contain the different modules, as shown in Figure 3, connected via a local system bus.

The driver module consists of power drivers, galvanic isolators for inputs and the on-board intelligence, a Xilinx Spartan-II FPGA. The FPGA is employed with control algorithms which require high sample rates. Thus the board can also work in stand-alone mode.

The main component of the DSP (Digital Signal Processing) module is a Xilinx Virtex-E FPGA. In addition to the system-bus interface, the Virtex-E also has another, local system bus interface. Via this bus, it is possible to connect I/O devices, e.g., ADCs, DACs, and encoders. These components are mounted on a piggyback board. Each DSP module can be equipped with two of these piggyback boards. The piggyback I/O configuration can be adapted to the specific demands of the application. The DSP module is designed for fast/parallel discrete controllers (e.g., current controllers and ultrasonic motors) as well as for digital filter algorithms. Sample rates of up to 100 kHz and higher are possible.

The microcontroller module of the node is provided by the Motorola PowerPC [7]. It consists of an MPC555 (52.7 MIPS, 40 MHz) with its on-chip peripheral devices and an extra bus interface to transmit the memory bus signals to the local system bus. The on-chip peripherals are the serial communication (RS232), CAN interface, 32 ADC (10 bit / 10 µs) and PWM (in/out) interfaces, and 50 timers. Hence the PowerPC module can also work in stand-alone mode. Its core has a 32-bit integer ALU and a 64-bit floating-point unit combined in the PowerPC RISC architecture. Thus the complex control algorithms, e.g., linear / nonlinear or continuous / discrete, can be mapped to this unit of the RABBIT system.

The fourth element is the IEEE 1394 module [8]. The bus is a multi-master bus (tree topology) which configures itself at the system start or on hot-plugging of a further network device. Each module has three communication ports. IEEE 1394 allows isochronous communication at a cycle frequency of 8 kHz with a bandwidth of 400 Mbit/s. This allows real-time communication of distributed control systems and high-speed field bus systems.

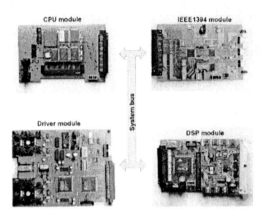

Figure 3. Implemented RABBIT modules

5. PREPARING CONTROL LAWS FOR HARDWARE REALIZATION

Modern control design methods allow to create complex multi-variable control laws. The need for a transparent and consistent design process often leads to the software implementation of controllers, i.e., to the programming of microprocessor devices in a high-level language using floating-point variables. This approach is inappropriate for applications with high sample rates ($f_s > 20$ kHz) as well as for highly modular applications consisting of cheap processing nodes. With high-level design tools, such as VHDL, and logic-synthesis CAD tools designed for large low-cost reprogrammable FPGAs, a rapid prototyping of complex modular control laws has become possible [9].

The state-space approach is a unified method for modelling and analyzing linear and time-invariant control laws. The mathematical equations are divided into two parts: a set of equations (1) relating the state variables to the input signal and a second set of equations (2) relating the state variables and the current input to the output signal. The general form of the state-space equations into which even complex control systems including observers etc. can be converted is:

$$\dot{\underline{x}} = \underline{\underline{A}} \cdot \underline{x} + \underline{\underline{B}} \cdot \underline{u} \tag{1}$$

$$\underline{y} = \underline{\underline{C}} \cdot \underline{x} + \underline{\underline{D}} \cdot \underline{u} \tag{2}$$

The controllers are automatically laid out for a hardware realization. For this task we use our own software tool called *ZSCAL*. The differential equations must be transformed into difference equations and scaled from the floating-point to the fixed-point or integer ranges of numbers. The final result of the software-supported controller transformations described above is a controller specification that can be automatically converted into VHDL and C code.

For hardware implementation the description in the shape of a differential equation (1, 2) is transformed into a more efficient, reduced algebraic shape, usually a recursive difference state equation:

$$\underline{x}_{k+1} = \underline{\underline{A}}_d \cdot \underline{x}_k + \underline{\underline{B}}_d \cdot \underline{u}_k \tag{3}$$

$$\underline{y}_k = \underline{\underline{C}}_d \cdot \underline{x}_k + \underline{\underline{D}}_d \cdot \underline{u}_k \tag{4}$$

Now every signal is represented by a sequence $\{f_k\}$. Numerical transformations like those with an implicit rectangular or trapezoidal integration are widely used to transform controllers from continuous to discrete time.

Our approach uses simulations with worst-case controller excitations to determine the minimum and maximum values of the controller state vector $\underline{x}$. The minimum and maximum values of the controller in- and outputs can be determined quite easily because they are always defined by controller output limitations (for outputs) and sensor signal ranges (for inputs). With these scaling factors the new discrete and scaled ABCD matrices are computed.

Nevertheless the coefficients of the ABCD matrices might still be out of range. To avoid this effect the matrices have to be prepared by factoring out a value which is a power of two. This means a shift-operation during runtime before assigning the result to the left hand sides of (3) and (4). Shifting causes a loss of precision with the controller evaluation.

The choice of the word length is a compromise between the numerical precision of the controller and the hardware resources required for an implementation. It is useful to provide different word lengths for states, inputs, outputs, and internal multiplication/addition registers. Our approach provides a simulation-based possibility to select the number of bits for the controller variables before starting the target-specific synthesis of the controller. We designed a software component for the modelling and emulation of scaled state-space controllers with a word length that can be varied at runtime. The simulation can either be performed before or at the hardware-in-the-loop stages.

6.   APPLICATION EXAMPLE

The controller realization of the X-mobile is based on the use of RABBIT nodes. According to the principle of modularity all four wheel suspensions are made up in essentially the same way. The steering angle of the wheel module is regulated by means of a DC motor and a gear. The steering-angle setpoint of the global steering controller located at the AMS level of the system and the measured steering angle are the inputs of the local steering controller. A *PID-T$_l$* control law computes the controller output; the latter serves as an input for the power electronics which controls the DC motor current. This controller operates at a sample rate of 330 Hz.

The suspension of the X-mobile consists of a trailing link with a passive spring-damper unit. Additionally, in the revolute joint of the trailing link a torsion spring is set whose base displacement is regulated by means of a DC motor and a gear. To evaluate this displacement the relative torsion of the spring and the displacement of the trailing link are measured. The suspension force from the global suspension controller at the AMS level serves as a setpoint for the local *PID-T$_l$* suspension-force controller also operating at a sample rate of 330 Hz.

The four drives of the vehicle are mounted in the wheel hubs. The rotating speeds of the motors are determined by means of rotational encoders. The wheel drive (DC motor) is controlled by a *PID* current controller to achieve a drive torque according to the setpoint. Due to the low inductivity of the DC motors the current alteration is very fast. So the current controller operates at a sample rate of 20 kHz.

In addition to the so-called local controllers of the wheel modules at the MFM level, a global vehicle controller is needed. This controller determines the setpoints for the local controllers at a frequency of 330 Hz.

The upper part of Figure 4 displays the modular-hierarchical control structure of the X-mobile. Consideration of the different sample rates of the controllers yields the corresponding logical structure. The logical structure reflects the encapsulation of control parts by IPANEMA calculator objects. Here it is necessary to use 5 calculators to separate the fast current controllers from the other controllers which are operating at a sample rate about 60 times lower.

To obtain the physical structure of the control application, one has to bear in mind the aspects of saving space, weight and power which are of vital importance because the X-mobile is built up at the scale of 1:8. Hence for this second version of the X-mobile we use a customized single-board solution, combining an MPC555- and a FPGA module of the RABBIT system. The power electronics is made up of 4 boards located at the wheel modules. The current controllers are transformed to fixed-point arithmetic and mapped to the FPGA module, every one of them encapsulated and running in parallel with timers of their own. The slower controller parts are based on floating-point arithmetics and mapped to the MPC555 module.

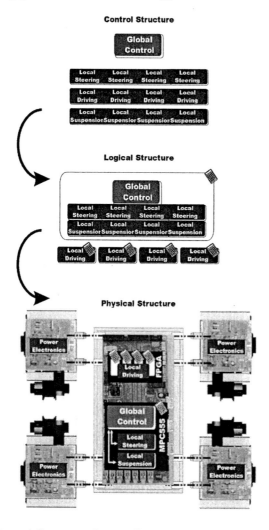

Figure 4. Steps towards controller realization for the X-mobile

7. STATE OF AFFAIRS

The paper presented the realization of modular controllers. In our consistent design approach we employ a structured concept for modelling mechatronic systems, a modular integration platform for real-time implementation, and a modular hardware platform based on FPGAs and microcontrollers. The example of the X-mobile served to demonstrate our modular-hierarchical realization concept for controllers.

The modular-hierarchical realization concept results in modular systems with distributed information processing. It allows to maintain the control structure from the initial modelling phase to a distributed prototyping of the system. Thus a coherent approach to the prototyping of distributed controllers is available.

REFERENCES

[1] Zanella, M.; Koch, T.; Scharfeld, F. (2001). *Development and Structuring of Mechatronic Systems, Exemplified by the Modular Vehicle X-mobile.* IEEE/ASME International Conference on Advanced Intelligent Mechatronics (AIM 2001), Como, Italy.

[2] Lückel, J.; Hestermeyer, T.; Liu-Henke, X. (2001). *Generalization of the Cascade Principle in View of a Structured Form of Mechatronic Systems.* IEEE/ASME International Conference on Advanced Intelligent Mechatronics (AIM 2001), Como, Italy.

[3] Meier-Noe, U.; Hahn, M. (1999). *Entwicklung mechatronischer Systeme mit CAMeL.* 3. Workshop Transmechatronik: Entwicklung und Transfer von Entwicklungssystemen der Mechatronik, Krefeld, Germany.

[4] Honekamp, U. (1998). *IPANEMA – Verteilte Echtzeit-Informationsverarbeitung in mechatronischen Systemen.* Fortschr.-Ber. VDI, Reihe 20, Nr. 267, VDI-Verlag, Düsseldorf, Germany.

[5] Stolpe, R.; Deppe, M.; Zanella, M. C. (2000). *Rapid Prototyping von verteilten, hierarchischen Regelungen am Beispiel eines Fahrzeugs mit hybridem Antriebsstrang.* Zeitschrift it & ti, 42. Jg., Heft 2, pp. 54-58.

[6] Zanella, M.; Robrecht, M.; Lehmann, T.; Gielow, R.; de Freitas Francisco,A.; Horst, A. (2001). *RABBIT: A Modular Rapid Prototyping Platform for Distributed Mechatronic Systems.* SBCCI 2001 - XIV Symposium on Integrated Circuits and Systems Design; Brasília, Brazil.

[7] Motorola, Inc. (1999). *MPC555 Evaluation Board Quick Reference.*

[8] Anderson, D. (1999). *FireWire systems architecture: IEEE 1394a.* 2nd ed., MindShare, Inc., Addison-Wesley, Reading, MA, Menlo Park, CA.

[9] Cumplido-Parra, R. A.; Jones, S. R.; Goodall, R. M.; Mitchell, F.; Bateman, S. (2000). *High Performance Control System Processor.* 3rd Workshop on System Design Automation (SDA 2000), Rathen, Germany, pp. 60-67.